MANAGERIAL ECONOMICS

Also by Stephen Hill

FUNDAMENTALS OF MANAGERIAL ECONOMICS
(*with Julian Gough*)

TIME, WORK AND ORGANISATION
(*with Paul Blyton, John Hassard and Ken Starkey*)

MANAGERIAL ECONOMICS

THE ANALYSIS OF
BUSINESS DECISIONS

Stephen Hill

MACMILLAN

First published 1989 by
THE MACMILLAN PRESS LTD
Houndmills, Basingstoke, Hampshire RG21 2XS
and London
Companies and representatives
throughout the world

ISBN 0–333–39863–7 (hardcover)
ISBN 0–333–39864–5 (paperback)

A catalogue record for this book is available
from the British Library

Printed in Hong Kong

Reprinted 1990, 1991, 1992

To Julian
Teacher, critic and friend

Contents

Preface

An unspecified number of years ago, as a newly appointed lecturer, I was summoned to see my then Head of Department.

'I want you to teach Managerial Economics', he said.

'Fine,' I replied, and realising my interview was over, made to leave. As I reached the door I turned, and asked:

'Just what *is* Managerial Economics?'

'Anything you want it to be!' was the reply.

It has taken years for the wisdom of that remark to sink home. Go to the library and count the number of managerial economics texts. Without too much difficulty I can think of at least forty, with an enormous variety of shapes, sizes and contents, including one I wrote with Julian Gough. Under these circumstances the introduction of yet another requires some justification.

A closer examination of the library of previous texts will reveal that they fall neatly into two camps. The largest group consists of the American texts, generally long and extremely comprehensive, including all those bits of economics that could possibly be relevant to business. Included in this 'kitchen sink' approach are introductions to mathematics and statistics, as well as economics.

The other group is made up of the British texts, generally still introductory but much shorter, reflecting a less unified approach to the subject.

This book is a departure from either of these approaches, spending relatively little time on basic economic analysis and providing a thorough theoretical and applications approach within the central theme of business decision-making. Each chapter is followed by a specific application, drawing on the experiences of myself and others to illustrate some aspect of that chapter. Applications range from the marketing of computers to bidding for a consignment of contraband butter.

However, it would be a mistake for the reader of this (or any other) book to consider that the information within puts them in the

ix

position of being able to confidently manage a business. This is a book of ideas that can profitably be applied to business. However, the information within it needs to be tempered by the experience of reality before it can become more than just an academic exercise. Besides, if the author of this (or any other) book knew the secrets of business success he'd hardly be spending his time writing books!

The central theme is that business decisions can be improved by the adoption of a logical and consistent decision process. The first four chapters identify such a process, and build in the decision concepts of optimisation and marginal analysis, tempered by the constraints of objectives, measurement and uncertainty. Chapters 5 to 8 define the decision environment within which decisions must be made, by examining the informational requirements of a logical business decision process, as well as assembling the building blocks that make up an economic theory of the business firm. Chapters 9 to 13 examine particular decision areas, using the previously acquired framework and ideas. Finally, Chapter 14 lists some neglected decision areas and provides a critique of the methodology used throughout, as well as some suggestions for further study.

The book ends by listing some examination questions for practice and contemplation. Questions are at the end of the book, rather than the end of each chapter, since one of the major problems for students facing examinations is the identification of what parts of economics go with each question. Good luck!

STEPHEN HILL

Acknowledgements

Any book of this sort, despite having one author on the title page, is actually the product of considerable cooperation between a wide variety of people. Prior thanks must go to the many students who have reasoned with, argued against and often corrected the author.

The author would like to thank the many people who agreed the use of material for applications, and in particular the editors of *Managerial and Decision Economics*.

Thanks also to Chris Patrick and Nigel Piercy for writing Applications 5 and 10 respectively, and to Brian Moores and Mark Goode for ideas and programming advice. Howard Griffiths and Jennifer Pegg of Macmillan provided encouragement and flexible deadlines.

Finally, thanks to Judy for the domestic tranquillity(!) conducive to writing and to Christine Long for her cheerful, rapid and efficient typing. By the end of this book, Chris was almost able to read my writing.

S.H.

CHAPTER 1

A framework for decisions

Contents

Introduction

The basis of successful management is the effective practice of decision-making. Effective decision-making occurs by accident rarely enough to make these decision-makers legendary – the exceptions that prove the rule. In the majority of successful organisations (and the organisations most likely to be durable), effective decision-making must build upon the firm foundations of training and experience.

Effective decision-making is characterised by the adoption of structured decision processes. This means no more than using a logical, sequential and ordered approach to solving problems. Managerial economics is the application of what may be called scientific method to business problems, utilising the products (and more importantly the methodology) of economic science to make better decisions. Better decisions are those that more effectively (and consistently) achieve the given objectives of the decision-maker. As the chapters of this book unfold, powerful and sophisticated techniques for decision-making will be outlined. The point needs emphasising, however, that effective decision-making requires more than the adoption of given techniques. It is the contention (and central theme) of this book that decision-making can be made *more* effective simply by approaching problems in a logical and systematic way. Sometimes this will involve the use of mathematical or schematic models. More often, this approach means no more than the application of a little common sense.

The purpose of this chapter is to outline what may be called the decision analytic method, which is completely general, and can be applied to all sorts of problems. An understanding of this method is the key to logical decision-making that separates the effective manager from the merely competent.

There are many managers who claim to make important decisions based on flair and intuition, and with considerable success. Often, however, this flair and intuition is no more than the decision analytic method in an unrecognised form.[1] Few of us can consistently make successful consecutive decisions by a 'seat of the pants' approach. The growth of managerial economics is entirely due to the benefits that structured decision-making brings to the efficient utilisation of resources.

The decision analytic approach

A decision is the act of conscious choice amongst alternatives. The decision analytic approach is no more than a structured method for making this choice, and can be represented diagrammatically as a five stage process (Figure 1.1).[2]

The importance of each stage depends upon the particular decision to be made. Many decisions are repetitive and of little consequence so that it is hardly worth the trouble of spelling out each stage (although even then it is probably worthwhile formalising the decision approach every now and then). The main point is that this framework can be applied to all decisions, however large or small, and, if fully understood and carefully applied, should lead to decisions that are superior in the long run to any intuitive approach.

Before discussing each stage in detail it is useful to define some terms. An *act* is the implementation of a particular decision. Even doing nothing may be an act if a decision has been made that this is the most appropriate behaviour. An *event* is an occurrence beyond

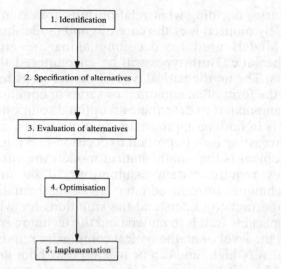

Figure 1.1 A simple decision framework

the control of the decision-maker. The choice of a judicious policy may influence events, but it is the nature of events that they can never be completely controlled in advance. An *outcome* is then the consequence of a particular combination of act and event. An optimal decision is the choice of that action which is expected to lead to the most preferred outcome.

Identification

A decision is necessary whenever there is a divergence between the *expected* outcome and the *desired* outcome. This involves identifying both what is likely to happen and what one would like to happen. For the business organisation, the usual objective is to increase profit, either by increasing revenue or by decreasing costs, or some combination of both. But the decision analytic method is applicable to any enterprise, whatever its objectives. For whatever the objectives, these can be best accomplished by using resources more efficiently, i.e. by making better decisions.

Identification is more than just recognising the need for a decision. It involves defining the problem explicitly, taking account of all of the factors that influence the problem. One common method of doing this is to construct a *decision-model*. As the name implies, this is just a simplified representation of the actual problem, designed to illustrate the essential relationships that influence the problem and omit those details which only obscure that problem. Of course, deciding what relationships are essential and which can be safely omitted is at the core of good model-building.

Models used for decision-making are either mathematical or schematic. Both types will be encountered throughout later chapters. The mathematical type of model seeks to express relationships in the form of an equation, or series of equations, which can then be manipulated to determine an optimal solution. The obvious difficulty is in finding appropriate equation forms, and is one reason why forecasting is so important to decision-making. A more fundamental problem is that mathematical models are often restrictive because they require certain assumptions to be fulfilled. Many of the techniques introduced later are of mathematical form, and it is as important to understand the situations for which these models are applicable as it is to understand the techniques themselves. Generally, the level of mathematical complexity required to find solutions is not very high, and can be mastered without great difficulty.

The schematic model is just a way of expressing relationships in diagrammatic form, and is usually descriptive in purpose. Rarely will diagrams be drawn with the precision required to find explicit solutions. More often diagrams are used to express relationships as an aid to understanding the decision-situation, and are particularly useful when a series of interrelated decisions are to be made.

The basic purpose of either sort of model is to *simulate* the decision situation, so that various options can be considered on paper without the expense or impracticality of actual experimentation. Clearly the effectiveness of the model depends critically on its representation of the actual situation. Many disagreements about courses of action stem from the different models (which may be implicit as well as explicit) on which decisions are based. One effective way of resolving disagreement is to clarify the different models on which views are based.

Specification of alternatives

To choose between alternatives, it is first necessary to determine the *range* of alternatives. The generation of alternatives usually involves reference back to previous decisions, research into possibilities and the exercise of imagination. At any moment the range of choice open to the decision-maker may be infinite, or at least very wide. However, many of the alternatives may not be feasible so that they may be easily (but carefully) dismissed, reducing the set of possible alternatives to manageable proportions.

To decide which alternatives are feasible involves categorising the variables that influence the problem into those the decision-makers can affect (control variables) and those beyond their influence (uncontrolled variables). The distinction is similar to that between actions and events. A particular choice of action is feasible if it can subsequently be implemented.

In many situations the search for alternatives is expensive in terms of the decision-makers' resources. Then, of course, a decision must be made about the amount of resources to spend on generating alternatives, by comparing the costs of search to the likely benefits that search would buy. Routine operating decisions are likely to be made with reference to some 'rule of thumb' that has proved adequate in the past. In this case, search activity is undertaken only if the performance associated with the routine decision begins to deteriorate. It is important that the performance of the routine decision rule is reviewed periodically, so that the actual outcome does not diverge substantially from the desired outcome.

Evaluation of alternatives

To make the decision it is necessary to be able to arrange the alternatives into some kind of order corresponding to how well they are expected to achieve the desired objectives. To do this normally involves quantifying the alternatives so that a value or range of values can be attached to each one.

The basic problem is one of information. For each alternative action the decision-maker must examine the possible events and estimate the corresponding potential outcomes. To attach a value to each outcome the relationships between the variables that determine the outcome and the outcome itself must be specified. Once this is achieved the value of future variables must be estimated. The accuracy of these estimates plays an important role in determining the success of the decision, so considerable attention will be given to different methods of preparing forecasts. Once again collecting information consumes resources, so that a decision must be made about the allocation of resources to forecasting, which will in turn depend upon the importance of the initial decision.

A related problem is that of uncertainty. All decisions concern the future and are therefore uncertain. The nature of uncertainty, and various possible ways around this problem, will be considered in more detail later. At this stage it is necessary to recognise that as well as estimating future variables we must also estimate how likely these future values are. This is a difficult question, but one that must be faced. It is better to make imperfect estimates in the face of uncertainty than to ignore uncertainty altogether.

Optimisation

Various techniques are applied to the decision model to determine the solution that best satisfies the chosen objective. Information collected in the specification and evaluation of alternatives is applied to the model to examine the consequence of different actions. If the model is sophisticated enough, solutions can be tested for sensitivity by allowing the variables of the model to change slightly and then by re-examining the consequences of each action. In this way, a solution can be chosen by reference not only to its most likely outcome but also to the full range of possible consequences.

The process of finding the best possible solution from a range of alternatives is called optimisation. Logic is applied to the model to generate solutions which can then be arranged in order of attraction. This order of attraction depends upon the prespecified criteria used to judge solutions.

The basic point is that optimisation is more a method of approach than a particular technique. It consists of considering all possible solutions, determining which are feasible, evaluating these and arranging them in order. Choosing the best solution should then be a relatively simple matter, guided by objectives.

Implementation

The problem for the managerial economist normally ends with optimisation. Not so the business manager. It is up to the manager to ensure that the solution is implemented, and to monitor the process of implementation. The success of the decision exercise does not depend on its sophistication or elegance, but on its impact on performance. The work of the decision analyst is more likely to be viewed sympathetically, and the proposed solution most likely to be successfully implemented, if the cooperation and coordination of others concerned has been sought throughout the decision process. It is essential to recognise that in complex organisations change does not occur instantaneously. Rather the organisation moves slowly (and often grudgingly) from one situation to another. As well as offering solutions it is necessary to plan for the transitional period from the current situation to the future envisaged situation. At the same time the rest of the world does not stand still. The decision environment needs close monitoring so that responses can be made to external changes as the decision is being implemented. The same reasoning obviously applies to the decision process. It is all too easy to find optimal solutions to a situation that no longer exists.

Conclusion

You should now be aware of the coherence of the decision analytic approach, together with some indication of its potential usefulness. In many ways, although the shortest, this is the most important chapter of this book. The decision system outlined is completely general and applicable to all decisions that can be made. Case 1 illustrates the framework outlined in this chapter, with an example that is hopefully not too close to home.

Application 1

Decision analysis – the overdraft

You receive the following letter:

> Dear Student,
>
> *Current Account – overdrawn £x*

Your account has become overdrawn to the above figure, although I can find no trace of the Bank's agreement to overdraft facilities. Would you kindly give your earliest attention to adjustment.

Yours sincerely,

Manager,
Big Bank Corporation.

You now have a problem, since the desired outcome (surplus) differs from the actual outcome (overdraft), so a decision must be made.

The first stage is to identify the problem. The initial step is to check that the problem exists by examining your account and ensuring the bank computer has not made a mistake (rare but not impossible). Having confirmed that the problem is real, you then seek time to find a solution by writing a suitably grovelling reply, pointing out all the unforeseen expenses you have recently incurred and all the hard work you have recently been doing, forcing you to overlook the problem, and promising to give 'your earliest attention to adjustment'.

The next step is to build a decision model. One simple model you could adopt is:

Surplus = Revenue − Expenditure

Given the model, alternatives are easily generated. You must increase revenue, or reduce expenditure, or some combination of the two.

A schedule of alternatives may look like the following:

Increase Revenue	*Decrease Expenditure*
Part-time job	Less entertainment
Borrow from family	Buy less books
Sell motorcycle	Sell motorcycle

Note that some entries occur twice – selling your motorcycle may both increase revenue and decrease expenditure. Alternatively, if it means more public transport use it could increase revenue *and* expenditure.

Having decided the alternatives, they must now be evaluated. This involves estimating variables such as the wage-rate for part-time jobs, the money you could save on books, etc. Given reliable estimates of the variables, the outcome corresponding to each action can be estimated. As well as monetary values, you would need to take account of the satisfaction or utility associated with each outcome (for example, your motorcycle may be your most treasured object, giving psychic income well in excess of its monetary value). It should then be possible to determine the optimal choice from alternatives, remembering to consider whether some combination of actions may be preferable to reliance on any single one. It may be necessary to define the best choice of action as that which is least painful!

Having made a choice, it only remains to implement it with sufficient vigour to satisfy the objective. As well as maintaining performance you should be alert to possible changes in the decision environment (such as wage increases, telephone bills, etc.).

CHAPTER 2

Optimisation – reasoning at the margin

Contents

Introduction

Economists have at their disposal a set of techniques that can be applied to particular decision problems. Whilst these techniques are powerful, they may also be restrictive in the sense of only being applicable in clearly defined specific circumstances. Much more fundamental are a range of concepts which can be called decision-tools. The purpose of this chapter is to introduce these general concepts which provide the basic foundation on which economic decision-making is built. In a sense this chapter, together with Chapter 1, are the most important in the book since an understanding of these concepts taken with the basic framework of decision-making should enable decision-making to be transformed to a scientific level.

Marginal analysis

Every decision involves the consideration of the costs and benefits associated with different actions. The basic principle of decision-making is that a particular action is worthwhile if it adds more to benefits than to costs. Note that it is the *addition* to costs and benefits that is important. The only variables to be taken into account in any decision are those affected by the decision. Thus what costs and benefits were is not only unimportant – it is irrelevant:

Consider the following situations:

— a cinema manager who must decide whether to introduce a late night show of the week's main feature
— the decision whether to drive down to the seaside this weekend
— the airline offering cheap standby flight tickets.

Each of these involves the balancing of costs and benefits. The factors the cinema manager should consider are the *extra* costs and revenues associated with the later showing. Variables such as the cinema rental and the cost of hiring the film are irrelevant, since they are incurred whether the late showing occurs or not. The only costs to consider will be those actually affected by the late show, such as staff overtime payments and extra heating costs. These extra costs need to be compared to the estimated extra revenue (allowing for any switching by customers from normal to late showing) to decide if the late showing is likely to be profitable.

Similarly, if you decide to drive down to the seaside this weekend the only travel costs will be the extra petrol and other running costs. Your monthly payment to buy the car must be made anyway.

The logic of standby air tickets should now be obvious.

All these are examples of *incremental* reasoning. At the heart of incremental reasoning is the concept of the margin. The marginal value is the change in one variable associated with a unit change in another variable. Thus, for example, the marginal cost of output is the change in total production costs associated with an extra unit of output. In the same way, the marginal revenue of output is the change in total revenue due to the sale of an extra unit of output. The importance of the concept of the margin is such that the claim can be made that *it is always in the best interests of the decision-maker when considering any action to take account of the marginal yield from that action*. The logic of marginal analysis can be defined in the form of two rules which form the basis of optimisation.

Optimisation

Rule 1

To maximise the return from any activity, that activity should be continued until the marginal return is zero. If the marginal return is positive, extra return can be gained by expanding that activity. For example, if the decision is how much to advertise to maximise profit, then the optimum is achieved when the marginal profit from the last advertisement is zero.

Profit can be defined as the difference between revenue and cost. Therefore the marginal profit equals marginal revenue minus marginal cost. If the marginal profit from any activity equals zero then marginal revenue must equal marginal cost. Thus expanding an activity until the marginal profit is zero is exactly equivalent to increasing it until marginal revenue equals marginal cost.[1]

Rule 2

Where there are a number of possible activities, the maximum overall return is achieved where each activity is undertaken until each yields the same marginal return. If this rule is not satisfied then overall return can be increased by switching resources from those with low marginal returns to those with high marginal returns. For example, suppose that the organisation has a given marketing budget which can be distributed between extra advertising expenditure and employing extra sales staff, both of which would increase sales revenue. The overall sales revenue from the budget will be maximised when the last £1 spent on advertising yields the same marginal revenue as the last £1 spent on sales staff, all the money being spent. If the last £1 spent on advertising had a higher return than that spent on sales staff, overall return could be increased by spending more on advertising and less on sales staff.

Marginal analysis – two rules for optimisation
1. To maximise the return on an activity, continue that activity until the marginal return equals zero.
2. To maximise overall return from a number of activities, continue each activity until the marginal returns from each are equal.

It is clear that in many situations, for example with a large number of sales staff and a large volume of advertising, the marginal information necessary for the application of the rules for optimisation is likely to be absent. However, this does not detract from their logical validity. *If* the overall profit is maximised, *then* the marginal cost must equal the marginal revenue. Moreover, it is often possible to estimate marginal values on the basis of more easily calculated averages. This is because marginal and average values have a logical relationship to each other that can be summarised as follows:

1. If the marginal is less than the average, then the average must be falling.
2. If the marginal is greater than the average, then the average must be rising. Therefore,
3. If the average is constant, the marginal must equal the average.

For example, suppose that as output increases from zero, the average (or unit) cost of output first of all falls, up to a given output, stays constant over the next range of output and then starts to increase. From the logical relationship between averages and marginals, over the output range in which average cost is falling, the marginal cost must be less than the average cost. When average cost is constant as output increases then marginal cost is equal to average cost. Finally, when average cost is increasing then marginal cost must be greater than average cost. Moreover, the rate of change of average cost indicates the *size* of the difference between marginal and average cost. If average cost falls slowly, then marginal cost must be slightly less than average cost, whereas if average cost fell quickly, the marginal cost must be substantially below average cost.[2]

Averages and marginals
1. If the marginal is less than the average, the average must be falling.
2. If the marginal is greater than the average, the average must be rising.
3. If the average is constant, the marginal must equal the average.

Because of accounting conventions, average data is usually more readily available than marginal data. The relationships outlined above suggest how this average data can be adapted for decision-making purposes. As always the degree of approximation necessarily depends on the importance of the decision being made. Certainly care must be taken to ensure that the cost of gathering information does not exceed the value of that information.

Mathematical optimisation

A word of caution!

In this and later chapters, mathematical approaches to optimisation will be introduced and applied. These techniques are relatively simple, and extremely powerful *in the right circumstances*. It is not uncommon to get carried away with the notion that decision-making is just the relatively simple matter of specifying a few functions and then optimising according to well-defined rules. This notion is not only wrong – it is extremely dangerous and has done considerable harm to the scientific decision approach. *All* mathematical approaches to decision-making need to be treated with considerable care and scepticism when contemplating actual decision-problems, since the realities of the decision situation are unlikely to be expressed in terms of a few simple formulae. Rather these mathematical tools can act as a useful guide and pointer towards the sort of solution that may be appropriate to a particular situation. Like all powerful tools (such as the bulldozer), it is not the tools themselves that create havoc but their ill-considered use.

The logic of marginal analysis often finds its most useful expression in the techniques of classical optimisation. Appendix 2A reviews the concepts and calculations of differentiation, and is essential reading for those who have yet to meet (or have forgotten) the notions of elementary calculus.

Appendix 2A goes on to examine the use of calculus to optimise (i.e. find the maximum or minimum) functions of one or more variables. This information will be of considerable use in later chapters when, for example, the order quantity to minimise total stock cost will be found. However, the practical value of calculus as a tool of optimisation is restricted by the severity of assumptions that must first be satisfied. To be differentiable, functions must be both smooth and continuous. Similarly, the substitution or Lagrangean methods of constrained optimisation (introduced in Appendix 2A) require constraints that can be expressed as equalities (for example the budget constraint that exactly £3000 must be spent). In many situations optimisation will be subject to inequality constraints (for example not more than £3000 can be spent, or not less than a particular amount must be produced). In these circumstances a programming method of optimisation must be used. The simplest of programming approaches is the method of linear programming.

Linear programming

The programming method of problem solving is the adoption of a particular approach which involves finding an initial solution and then examining whether movement from that solution would lead to improved performance. It is then no more than a method of searching amongst available alternatives, and using some test of performance to see if a particular solution can be improved upon. If a particular solution can be improved, the change is made and the next solution tested for possible improvement. Programming is then a logical sequential progression around potential solutions until improvement is no longer possible which is, by definition, the optimal solution. The linear programming method is the adoption of a particular programming approach when the objective function and constraints can be described by linear equations.[3]

Consider the following problem. An engineering firm produces two types of metric bolt. Bolt x is first machined and then polished, whilst bolt y requires more machining but less polishing, and is then anodised. The firm has limited capacity each week for each of these processes. The decision for the firm is how many of each bolt to make each week to maximise overall profit. Clearly, the more of bolt x the firm produces, the less machining and polishing time is available for bolt y. The following table shows the processing time per thousand of each bolt together with the process availabilities each week.

	Hours of machining	Hours of polishing	Hours of anodising
Bolt x	4	6	0
Bolt y	8	3	10
Available each week	60	54	60

Each thousand of bolt x results in a profit contribution of £60, whilst each thousand of bolt y gives a profit of £50.

The problem is then to maximise profit from x and y subject to the capacity constraints.

The first constraint (machining time) is that 4 times the number of x bolts plus 8 times the number of y bolts cannot exceed 60. This can be written as:

$$4x + 8y \leqslant 60$$

or $x + 2y \leqslant 15$ (dividing by 4)

Similarly for polishing

$6x + 3y \leqslant 54$

or $2x + y \leqslant 18$

and for anodising $0x + 10y \leqslant 60$

$$y \leqslant 6$$

The objective is to maximise profit, which is 60 times x plus 50 times y.

The problem can then be written in the *general form*, as:

Maximise $60x + 50y$

Subject to $x + 2y \leqslant 15$
                     $2x + y \leqslant 18$
                     $0x + y \leqslant 6$
                     $x, y \geqslant 0$

The final constraint is that neither x nor y can be negative. Note that this problem cannot be solved by substitution since the constraints are inequalities. Note also that both objective function and constraints are linear.

Because there are only two variables, this problem can be represented graphically. Consider the first constraint:

$x + 2y \leqslant 15$

This is represented by the line $C1$ in Figure 2.1. The solutions for x and y must lie on or inside this line. Repeating for the polishing and anodising constraints gives lines $C2$ and $C3$. Areas outside any of these constraints cannot be reached, given the production capacities. The solution must lie inside the area *0abcd* known as the feasible region. However, there are an infinite number of possible locations inside this area.

This is where the programming approach proves useful. Since the production of either bolt increases profit, the firm will always want to produce more bolts rather than less. This implies that the optimal solution cannot lie in the interior of the feasible region, but must be somewhere on the edge. Moreover, the optimal solution must lie at a corner of the feasible region.[4] With three constraints there are four corners to the feasible region (ignoring the origin, which must by definition be unprofitable). The problem has then been narrowed down from considering an infinite number of solutions, to considering just four. The programming approach works by starting off at the origin and then examining whether a move to the next corner would increase profit (as clearly it must). The process is then

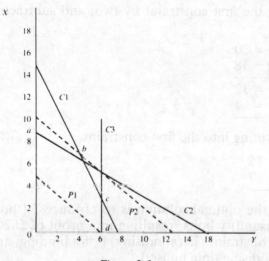

Figure 2.1

repeated, moving between corners of the feasible region until an improvement is no longer possible. By definition, when the answer is no the optimal solution has been found.

Returning to the example, to find the optimal solution involves taking account of the objective function. This is located in the diagram by choosing an arbitrary amount of profit.

The objective function is:

$$60x + 50y$$

Suppose profit was £300. This locates the objective function as $P1$ in Figure 2.1. This is well inside the feasible region and more profit can be earned. Larger amounts of profit would result in a line further away from the origin, but with the same slope as $P1$. The line $P1$ is then moved outwards parallel to itself, thereby increasing profit until it has moved out as far as possible and still represents attainable output. This occurs with line $P2$, passing through corner b. Further outward movement would represent output levels which do not satisfy the constraints. Hence the profit maximising output combination is at b, or the intersection of $C1$ and $C2$.

At that point, both constraints are binding, so that:

$$x + 2y = 15$$
$$2x + y = 18$$

Multiplying the first constraint by two, and subtracting the second constraint:

$$2x + 4y = 30$$
$$2x + y = 18$$
$$\overline{ 3y = 12}$$
$$y = 4$$

Now substituting into the first constraint,

$$x + 8 = 15$$
$$x = 7$$

Therefore, the optimal solution is to produce 7 (thousand) x bolts and 4 (thousand) y bolts, resulting in a profit of £620. Note that at this point, constraint $C3$ (anodising) is not binding, and there are 20 hours of anodising time unused.

The mathematical procedure for solving linear programming problems is called the Simplex method, and is only slightly more complicated. It basically involves working around the corners, following defined rules for each iteration, until improvement is no longer possible. Because the Simplex procedures are logical and repetitive, linear programming problems involving more than two variables are best handled by computer programs.[5] Application 2 includes a demonstration run of one such program for a more complex problem.

Appendix 2A

Elementary calculus

To examine the techniques of classical optimisation it is necessary first of all to consider the concept of a *derivative*.

Recall that the marginal value was defined as the change in one variable corresponding to a unit change in another variable. Suppose we have the unspecified relationship

$$y = f(x)$$

Then the marginal value of y is just the change in y corresponding to a unit change in x, written as

$$My = \frac{\Delta y}{\Delta x},$$

where Δ (capital Greek delta) refers to a change in one variable, and Δx equals one unit. Then, for example, marginal cost is the change in total cost corresponding to a unit change in output, and can be written as:

$$MC = \frac{\Delta TC}{\Delta Q}, \text{ where } Q = \text{output}$$

Now a derivative is just a precise specification of this general marginal relationship $\Delta y/\Delta x$. Suppose that when output increases by 500 units, total costs increase by £1200. We could then estimate marginal cost to be £2.4 (the change in total cost divided by the change in output). However, suppose that marginal cost itself changes throughout these 500 units of output. Then the estimate of marginal cost = £2.4 may not be too valuable for decision-making purposes. If we had the information that the first extra 20 units of output cost an extra £42, we would have the more accurate estimate of marginal cost as £2.1. The smaller the change in output, the more reliable the marginal cost estimate. Now the derivative of y with respect to x (written as dy/dx), is just the precise value of this marginal relationship for extremely small changes in x.

The concept of a derivative

If $y = f(x)$

Then the *marginal* value of y with respect to x is:

$$My = \frac{\Delta y}{\Delta x}, \Delta x = 1 \text{ unit}$$

The *derivative* of y with respect to x is:

$$\frac{dy}{dx} = \frac{\Delta y}{\Delta x}, \Delta x \to 0$$

The derivative gives the precise value of the tangent slope of a curve at a particular point.

The point can perhaps best be made graphically. Figure 2A.1 plots the relationship between x and y. We seek the marginal value of y at point h (where $x = a$). Suppose x changes from a to b. Then $\Delta y/\Delta x$ equals de/he, which is the slope of the line hd. Now suppose that x changes from a to c. Then $\Delta y/\Delta x$ is the slope of line hf

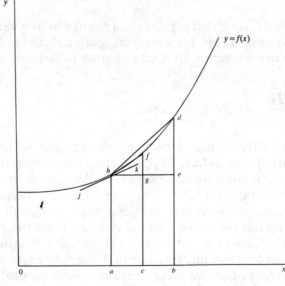

Figure 2A.1

($= fg/hg$). As the change in x becomes smaller and smaller, the marginal value of y gets closer and closer to the slope of the tangent at h. The value of the derivative is the slope of the tangent at h (slope jk). The derivative is just the precise value of the marginal relationship.

Derivatives are a useful decision-making concept because the rules of marginal analysis can be translated into simple conditions for finding the maximum or minimum of any differentiable function. For a function to be differentiable it must first be continuous (since if y is not a continuous function of x then $\Delta y/\Delta x$ clearly makes little sense for some values of x). Before these conditions are considered it is necessary to examine briefly how derivatives can be found.

Rules for differentiation

	Function	Derivative
1.	Constant $y = c$	$\dfrac{dy}{dx} = 0$
2.	First degree $y = ax$	$\dfrac{dy}{dx} = a$
3.	Power functions $y = ax^b$	$\dfrac{dy}{dx} = bax^{b-1}$
4.	Sums and differences $y = u + v$	$\dfrac{dy}{dx} = \dfrac{du}{dx} + \dfrac{dv}{dx}$
5.	Products $y = uv$	$\dfrac{dy}{dx} = \dfrac{udv}{dx} + \dfrac{vdu}{dx}$
6.	Quotients $y = \dfrac{u}{v}$	$\dfrac{dy}{dx} = \dfrac{v \cdot \dfrac{du}{dx} - u \cdot \dfrac{dv}{dx}}{v^2}$
7.	Function of a function $y = f(u)$ $u = g(x)$	$\dfrac{dy}{dx} = \dfrac{dy}{du} \cdot \dfrac{du}{dx}$

Suppose the decision-maker's problem is to determine the optimal price for a particular good. One of the factors to be taken into account is the relationship between demand (D) and price (P). The rules for differentiation can be examined by considering different forms this relationship may take.

1.   Constant functions

Suppose $D = 100$ (i.e. demand is a constant unaffected by price). Clearly a change in price has no effect on demand, and

$$\frac{dD}{dP} = 0$$

2.   First degree functions

If $D = 100 - 2P$, then every unit increase in price will reduce demand by 2 units. Therefore $dD/dP = -2$

If $y = ax$, then $\dfrac{dy}{dx} = a$

3.   Power functions

Suppose that $D = 4P^2$. Recall that dD/dP is defined as $\Delta D/\Delta P$ for very small changes in P. Consider what happens if price increases by a very small amount (ΔP). Then demand will change to:

$$D + \Delta D = 4(P + \Delta P)^2$$
$$= 4(P^2 + 2\Delta P . P + (\Delta P)^2)$$
$$= 4P^2 + 8\Delta P . P + 4(\Delta P)^2$$

To find ΔD we subtract $D = 4P^2$ from this expression

$$\Delta D = D + \Delta D - D$$
$$= 4P^2 + 8\Delta P . P + 4(\Delta P)^2 - 4P^2$$

Therefore $\Delta D = 8\Delta P . P + 4(\Delta P)^2$

Now divide both sides by ΔP

$$\frac{\Delta D}{\Delta P} = 8P + 4\Delta P$$

The derivative was defined as $\Delta D/\Delta P$ as ΔP gets very small. As ΔP approaches zero, $4\Delta P$ approaches zero and

$$\frac{dD}{dP} = 8P$$

More generally, if [6]

$$y = ax^b$$

$$\frac{dy}{dx} = bax^{b-1}$$

The remaining rules of differentiation can be illustrated by considering two unspecified functions of x, where

$$u = g(x)$$

$$v = h(x)$$

The following cases refer to situations where y is a function of both u and v.

4. Sums and differences

The derivative of a sum equals the sum of the derivatives.

if $y = u + v$

Then $\dfrac{dy}{dx} = \dfrac{du}{dx} + \dfrac{dv}{dx}$

for example, if $u = 3x^2$

$$v = -2x^3$$

$$\text{and } y = 3x^2 - 2x^3$$

Then $\dfrac{du}{dx} - 6x, \quad \dfrac{dv}{dx} - -6x^2$

and $\dfrac{dy}{dx} = 6x - 6x^2$

5. Products

The derivative of a product is the sum of the first term times the derivative of the second plus the second times the derivative of the first.

i.e. if $y = u \cdot v$

$$\frac{dy}{dx} = u \cdot \frac{dv}{dx} + v \cdot \frac{du}{dx}$$

for example, if $u = 4x^2$ and $v = x^2 - 1$

$$y = u \cdot v$$

then $\dfrac{du}{dx} = 8x$ $\dfrac{dv}{dx} = 2x$

and $\dfrac{dy}{dx} = 2x(4x^2) + 8x(x^2 - 1)$

$$= 8x^3 + 8x^3 - 8x$$

$$= 8x(2x^2 - 1)$$

6. Quotients

The derivative of a quotient is the denominator times the derivative of the numerator minus the numerator times the derivative of the denominator, all divided by the square of the denominator, i.e.

if $y = \dfrac{u}{v}$

then $\dfrac{dy}{dx} = v \cdot \dfrac{du}{dx} - u \cdot \dfrac{dv}{dx}$

e.g. if $y = \dfrac{2}{x^2}$ $(u = 2, v = x^2)$

$$\frac{dy}{dx} = x^2 \frac{(0) - 2(2x)}{x^4}$$

$$= \frac{-4x}{x^4} = \frac{-4}{x^3}$$

The quotient rule is strictly correct but complex and unexciting. Quotients are often easier to handle by using the laws of indices.

In the above example,

$$y = \frac{2}{x^2}$$

can be written $y = 2(x)^{-2}$

Applying the power rule, $\frac{dy}{dx} = -2.2(x)^{-3} = 4$

7. Function of a function

If $y = f(u)$ and $u = g(x)$

then $\frac{dy}{dx} = \frac{dy}{du} \cdot \frac{du}{dx}$

e.g. if $y = u^2 + 3u$

$\quad u = 2x^2 - 3x$

then $\frac{dy}{du} - 2u + 3$

$\quad \frac{du}{dx} = 4x - 3$

and $\quad \frac{dy}{dx} = (2u + 3)(4x - 3)$

Substituting, $= (2(2x^2 - 3x) + 3)(4x - 3)$

$\quad = (4x^2 - 6x + 3)(4x - 3)$

$\quad = 16x^3 - 12x^2 - 24x^2 + 18x + 12x - 9$

$\quad = 16x^3 - 36x^2 + 30x - 9$

The application of differentiation – maximising a function one variable

We have seen that a derivative gives the tangent slope of a curve at a particular point. Figure 2A.2 illustrates a curve with a minimum

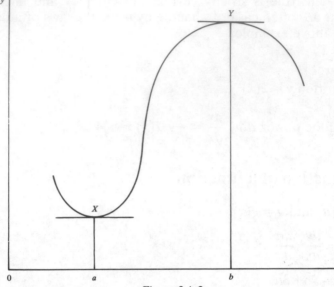

Figure 2A.2

value at point X and a maximum value at point Y. From Figure 2A.2 it is clear that at both X and Y, the tangent slope of the curve equals zero. If the slope is not zero, then the function must be either increasing or decreasing. Since the derivative is the tangent slope, when the function is at a maximum or minimum the derivative must equal zero. The converse gives an operational rule for finding the optimum:

— To find the maximum or minimum of a function, find the derivative of the function, set equal to zero and solve for the particular variable. This is known as the *first-order condition*.

EXAMPLE 1

Suppose that sales revenue (S) depends upon the quantity of advertising (A), in a relationship estimated as:

$$S = 14 + 16A - 2A^2$$

We seek the value of A to maximise S. First differentiate S with respect to A;

$$\frac{dS}{dA} = 16 - 4A$$

Then set to zero and solve;

if $16 - 4A = 0$

$A = 4$.

When advertising equals 4, sales revenue is at a maximum or a minimum. In order to distinguish between them, we need to consider the *second order* condition, which can be developed intuitively from Figure 2A.2.

Clearly, X is a minimum and Y is a maximum. Examining more closely, if X is just less than a the tangent slope is negative, and if X is just greater than a the tangent slope is positive. A general feature of minima is that as we approach the minimum point the tangent slope changes from negative to zero (and on to positive as the zero slope is passed). In the same way, at the maximum (point Y) the tangent slope changes from positive to zero to negative.

From Figure 2A.2 changes in the derivative as X increases could be plotted, to get the curve shown in Figure 2A.3. At both a and b the derivative is zero. Around a the derivative changes from negative to positive, whilst around b it changes from positive to negative.

To examine how the derivative changes, consider the tangent slope of the curve in Figure 2A.3. At point a the tangent slope is positive whilst at b it is negative. Recall that Figure 2A.3 plots the derivative, of the original function plotted in Figure 2A.2. The tangent slope of the derivative in Figure 2A.3 is just the derivative of the derivative, referred to as the *second-derivative* and denoted by

$$\frac{d^2y}{dx^2}$$

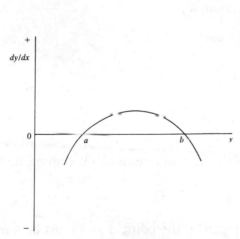

Figure 2A.3

In Figure 2A.3, the second derivative at *a* is positive, whilst at *b* the second derivative is negative. This is another property of minima and maxima respectively, and enables the *second-order* condition to be specified:

When the first derivative is zero, the second derivative distinguishes between a maximum and a minimum.

— if the second derivative is positive, this point is a minimum
— if the second derivative is negative, this point is a maximum

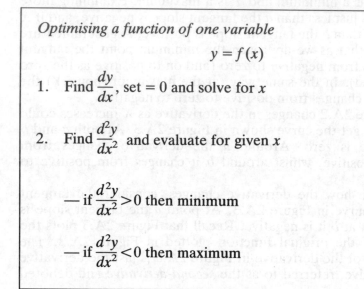

Optimising a function of one variable

$$y = f(x)$$

1. Find $\dfrac{dy}{dx}$, set $= 0$ and solve for x

2. Find $\dfrac{d^2y}{dx^2}$ and evaluate for given x

    — if $\dfrac{d^2y}{dx^2} > 0$ then minimum

    — if $\dfrac{d^2y}{dx^2} < 0$ then maximum

Returning to the example,

$$S = 14 + 16A - 2A^2$$

$$\frac{dS}{dA} = 16 - 4A$$

$$\text{if } \frac{dS}{dA} = 0, \quad A = 4$$

To check whether this is a minimum or maximum, find

$$\frac{d^2S}{dA^2} = -4$$

Since d^2S/dA^2 is negative, the point $A = 4$ must be a maximum. To maximise sales revenue, four advertisements must be undertaken.

EXAMPLE 2

Suppose the decision problem is to determine the number of maintenance engineers (E) to minimise the average cost per engineer, when total cost is related to the number of engineers by the equation:

$$TC = 3E^3 - 18E^2 + 4E$$

First find the average cost per engineer, which is simply total cost divided by the number of engineers:

$$AC = \frac{TC}{E} = 3E^2 - 18E + 4$$

To minimise, find the derivative, set equal to zero and solve for E;

$$\frac{dAC}{dE} = 6E - 18$$

if $\frac{dAC}{dE} = 0$, $\quad 6E - 18 = 0$

$$E = 3$$

Now $\frac{d^2AC}{dE^2} = 6 > 0$,

so to minimise average cost per engineer, six engineers must be employed.[7]

Functions of more than one variable – the partial derivative

Suppose that Demand (D) was affected by both Price (P) and Advertising (A), i.e.

$$D = f(P,A)$$

In order to measure the marginal effect of a change in one of the independent variables (Price or Advertising) on the dependent variable (Demand) then the other independent variable must be held constant, i.e.

The marginal effect of price on demand $= \dfrac{\Delta D}{\Delta P}$, A constant, and The marginal effect of advertising on demand $= \dfrac{\Delta D}{\Delta A}$,

P constant

The *partial derivative* of demand with respect to price is just the precise value of this marginal effect of price on demand, keeping advertising constant, and is written as

$\dfrac{\delta D}{\delta P}$ (where δ is the lower case Greek delta, in order to distinguish the partial from the total derivative).

More generally, consider the *multivariate* function,

$y = f(x, z)$

Then both x and z determine y, and the partial derivatives with respect to each can be found by differentiating y with respect to the relevant variable, treating the other variable as a constant.

For example, suppose that:

$$D = 100 - 2P^2 + 4A$$

Then $\dfrac{\delta D}{\delta P} = -4P, \quad \dfrac{\delta D}{\delta A} = 4$

The principles of optimising a function of two or more variables are identical to the single variable case. In practice, the second order conditions in particular are a little more complex and consequently are confined to Appendix 2B. The first order condition is analogous to the single variable case, and involves differentiating the function with respect to each of the independent variables, setting each equal to zero and solving. For each independent variable we find the corresponding partial derivative, set equal to zero and solve the resulting simultaneous equations.

For example, suppose that output (Q) is determined by the quantity of labour hours used (L, measured in thousands of man hours), and the quantity of machine hours (K, again measured in thousands of hours). Suppose further that the exact relationship between the output (Q) and the inputs (L and K) is given by the equation:

$$Q = 2L + K - L^2 - K^2 + KL$$

We seek the quantities of K and L to maximise output. To do this find the partial derivatives of Q with respect to K and L, set each equal to zero and then solve.

If $Q = 2L + K - L^2 - K^2 + KL$

$$\frac{\delta Q}{\delta L} = 2 - 2L + K$$

$$\frac{\delta Q}{\delta K} = 1 - 2K + L$$

Now set each of these partial derivatives to zero and then solve. Note that we get two simultaneous equations in K and L, which can be solved by manipulation.

$$2 - 2L + K = 0$$

$$1 - 2K + L = 0$$

multiplying the second equation by 2, and then adding to the first gives:

$$\begin{array}{r} 2 + 2L - 4K = 0 \\ 2 - 2L + \ \ K = 0 \\ \hline 4 \ \ \ \ \ \ -3K = 0 \end{array} +$$

therefore $K = 4/3$

To find L we substitute this value of K back into the first equation:

$$2 - 2L + 4/3 = 0$$

$$10/3 = 2L$$

$$L = 5/3$$

Therefore to maximise output we use $4/3 \times 100 = 1333$ machine hours, and $5/3 \times 1000 = 1667$ man hours. Substituting the values for K and L back into the equation for output gives an output level of $Q = 7/3$, or 2.33 units of output.[8]

Constrained optimisation – the Lagrangean method

To calculate the quantities of the inputs to produce the maximum output we have assumed that there are no restrictions on the possible values of K and L. In practice, of course, optimisation problems are subject to a variety of limitations – for example, neither K nor L could be negative, since negative machine or man hours makes no economic sense. Moreover, there may well be more precise limitations on the values of the independent variables. For instance, there could be practical limitations on the supply of machine or man hours available. These limitations on the values of the independent variables are the *constraints* within which the given *objective function* is to be optimised. If these constraints can be written in the form of *equalities* (for example some combination of K and L must equal a particular value), then the classical optimisation method can be extended to deal with the constraints either by substitution, or by the method of *Lagrangean Multipliers*. Substitution is a simpler procedure but is only possible if the constraints are of a simple kind. The Lagrangean method is more general, and can be used in a variety of circumstances beyond the scope of simple substitution. Methods of constrained optimisation where the constraints take the form of inequalities are rather different, and will be considered later.

Return to the problem of deciding the quantities of inputs (thousands of machine and man hours) to maximise output, when:

$$Q = 2L + K - L^2 - K^2 + KL$$

Now suppose that each man hour costs the organisation £1, whilst each machine hour costs £2, and suppose that the budget for buying machine and man hours runs to £3000. It seems reasonable to assume, since the objective is to maximise output, that all of the £3000 will be spent.[9]

Since K and L are measured in thousands of hours, the budget for output can be written as:

$$L + 2K = 3$$

The problem is now to maximise output subject to the budget constraint, i.e.

Max. $Q = 2L + K - L^2 - K^2 + KL$

s.t. $L + 2K = 3$

Note that the overall maximum was when $L = 5/3$, $K = 4/3$, which is now no longer possible since at these values:

$$L + 2K = 4.33$$

The substitution method

Since K and L are now related (via the constraint) we can express one in terms of the other and *substitute* into the objective function to obtain a function in just one variable which can be maximised in the usual way, i.e.

Since $L + 2K = 3$

$$L = 3 - 2K$$

Now $Q = 2L + K - L^2 - K^2 + KL$

Substituting for L,

$$Q = 2(3 - 2K) + K - (3 - 2K)^2 - K^2 + K(3 - 2K)$$

$$= 6 - 4K + K - (9 - 12K + 4K^2) - K^2 + 3K - 2K^2$$

Simplifying: $Q = -3 + 12K - 7K^2$

This function in one variable is maximised by finding the derivative, setting equal to zero and solving checking for a maximum via the second order condition, i.e.

$$\frac{dQ}{dK} = 12 - 14K$$

if $\dfrac{dQ}{dK} = 0, \quad 12 - 14K = 0$

$$K = 6/7$$

Now $\dfrac{d^2Q}{dK^2} = -14$, so $K = 6/7$ is a maximum for Q

Since $L + 2K = 3$

If $K = 6/7, \quad L = 9/7$

Unfortunately, the substitution method breaks down if the constraint is of more complex form (for example, if the constraint was $L^2 + 2K^2 = 3$, there would be two solutions expressing L in terms of K). The more general method is that of Lagrangean Multipliers, which can also handle optimisation with two or more constraints.

The Lagrangean method

To use the Lagrangean method the constraint must first be written in its *implicit* form. This means rearranging the constraint so that it must equal zero, i.e. if the constraint is

$$L + 2K = 3$$

the implicit form is

$$3 - L - 2K = 0$$

Now for each constraint we create an *artificial variable* denoted by λ (Greek lambda). If the constraint in its implicit form is multiplied by lambda and added to the objective function this in turn is transformed into the Lagrangean function (G). The Lagrangean function can now be optimised by taking the partial derivatives with respect to the independent variables (including lambda), setting each equal to zero and solving.

The problem was

$$\text{Max.} \quad Q = 2L + K - L^2 - K^2 + KL$$

$$\text{s.t.} \quad L + 2K = 3$$

Writing the constraint in its implicit form, multiplying by lambda and adding to the objective function gives the Lagrangean function:

$$G = 2L + K - L^2 - K^2 + KL + \lambda(3 - L - 2K)$$

Finding the partial derivatives with respect to L, K and λ, setting equal to zero, we get:

(i) $\dfrac{dG}{dL} = 2 - 2L + K - \lambda = 0$

(ii) $\dfrac{dG}{dK} = 1 - 2K + L - 2\lambda = 0$

(iii) $\dfrac{dG}{d\lambda} = 3 - L - 2K = 0$

We now have three equations in three unknowns, which can be solved simultaneously by manipulation. Note that differentiating the Lagrangean with respect to the artificial variable always results in the constraint in its implicit form, ensuring that the solution for independent variables must satisfy the constraint.

Multiplying the first equation by 2, and subtracting the second:

$$\begin{array}{r} 4 - 4L + 2K - 2\lambda = 0 \\ 1 + L - 2K - 2\lambda = 0 \end{array} -$$

(iv) $\quad 3 - 5L + 4K \quad\quad = 0$

Now multiply equation (iii) by two and add to equation (iv).

(iii)   ×2 $6 - 2L - 4K = 0$
             $3 - 5L + 4K = 0$ $+$
             _____
             $9 - 7L \qquad = 0$
             $\qquad 7L = 9$
             $\qquad L = 9/7$

Substituting $L = 9/7$ into the constraint

$9/7 + 2K = 3$

$K = 6/7$

These are, of course, the same results as by substitution. Note that when $L = 9/7$, $K = 6/7$, output is reduced to $Q = 15/7$, so that the introduction of the constraint reduces the maximum possible output.

An interpretation of the Lagrangean Multiplier

So far we have used the artificial variable (λ) merely as an instrument to obtain the optimal solution to the constrained problem. In fact, the artificial variable has a valuable economic interpretation in the sense that it conveys information that is useful for decision-making.

Consider the general constrained optimisation problem of maximising some function of two variables subject to the constraint that some other function of these variables equals a particular value.

i.e. Max. $m = f(x,y)$

s.t. $g(x,y) = a$

Where m is the objective function and a is the size of the constraint.
The Lagrangean form (L) is then:

$L = f(x,y) + \lambda(a - g(x,y))$

Differentiating with respect to a gives

$$\frac{dL}{da} = \lambda$$

The artificial variable then gives the marginal impact of a change in the size of the constraint on the objective function. If the constraint is increased by one unit, the maximum value of the objective function will increase by λ.

Returning to our example of maximising output subject to budget constraint, equation (i) was:

$2 - 2L + K - \lambda = 0$

Since, at the optimum, $L = 9/7$ and $K = 6/7$, we can find the value of λ.

$2 - 18/7 + 6/7 - \lambda = 0$

$$\lambda = 2/7$$

Hence increasing the constraint from

$L + 2K = 3$

to $L + 2K = 4$

would increase the maximum output by 2/7 units. Thus increasing the budget by £1000 would result in another 2/7 units of output. Whether this was profitable or not would depend on how the extra benefit of another 2/7 units of output compared to the extra cost of £1000.

Appendix 2B

Table 2B.1   Optimising a function of 2 variables

$$y = f(x_1, x_2)$$

1. Find the partial derivatives, set equal to zero and solve simultaneously

$$\frac{\delta y}{\delta x_1}, \frac{\delta y}{\delta x_2} = 0$$

2. *Maximum* if

$$\frac{\delta^2 y}{\delta x_1^2} < 0, \frac{\delta^2 y}{\delta x_2^2} < 0$$

$$and \left(\frac{\delta^2 y}{\delta x_1^2}\right)\left(\frac{\delta^2 y}{\delta x_2^2}\right) > \left(\frac{\delta' y}{\delta x_1, \delta x_2}\right)^2$$

3. *Minimum* if

$$\frac{\delta^2 y}{\delta x_1^2} > 0, \frac{\delta^2 y}{\delta x_2^2} > 0$$

$$and \left(\frac{\delta^2 y}{\delta x_1^2}\right)\left(\frac{\delta^2 y}{\delta x_2^2}\right) > \left(\frac{\delta^2 y}{\delta x_1, \delta x_2}\right)^2$$

Appendix 2C

Functions of more than one variable – second order conditions

Recall the problem from Chapter 2,

Maximise $Q = 2L + K - L^2 - K^2 + KL$

The first order conditions for a maximum was to set the partial derivatives to zero, i.e.

$$\frac{\delta Q}{\delta L} = 2 - 2L + K = 0$$

$$\frac{\delta Q}{\delta K} = 1 - 2K + L = 0$$

Solving simultaneously gave the solution that $K = 4/3$, $L = 5/3$. To check this is indeed a maximum involves the use of the second order conditions, set out in Appendix 2B.

Now $\dfrac{\delta^2 Q}{\delta L^2} = -2$, $\dfrac{\delta^2 Q}{\delta K^2} = -2$

so the first of the second order conditions is satisfied.

$$\frac{\delta^2 Q}{\delta L \delta K} = 1$$
(found by differentiating $\delta Q/\delta L$ with respect to K, or equivalently by differentiating $\delta Q/\delta K$ with respect to L)

So $\left(\dfrac{\delta^2 Q}{\delta L^2}\right)\left(\dfrac{\delta^2 Q}{\delta K^2}\right) = -2 \times -2 = 4 > \left(\dfrac{\delta^2 Q}{\delta^2 L \delta K}\right)^2 = 1^2$

So $K = 4/3$, $L = 5/3$ is indeed a maximum.

Application 2

A computer based approach to linear programming

Recall the engineering firm's problem in Chapter 2, producing bolts of type x and y to maximise profit subject to capacity constraints.

The form of the problem was:

Maximise $60x + 50y$

Subject to $4x + 8y \leq 60$ (machine time)

$6x + 3y \leq 54$ (polishing time)

$0x + 10y \leq 60$ (anodising time)

$x, y \geq 0$

The solution to this problem, found in Chapter 2 by the graphical method, was that $x = 7$, $y = 4$ and profit = £620. Recall that this left 20 hours of anodising time unused each week.

In an attempt to make use of this spare capacity, and to capture a market opportunity, the firm decides to introduce a third bolt (z). Bolt z is a de-luxe version for the custom-car market, with each thousand of bolt z produced requiring 4 hours of machine time, 2 hours of polishing but 20 hours of anodising. Each thousand of bolt z produced adds £80 to profits.

We now have a problem in three variables, with the form:

Maximise $60x + 50y + 80z$

Subject to $4x + 8y + 4z \leq 60$

$6x + 3y + 2z \leq 54$

$0x + 10y + 20z \leq 60$

$x, y, z \geq 0$

Solving this problem graphically would involve the use of three dimensions (x, y and z), and would quickly become complex. However, such a problem is easily handled by a range of software packages commercially available. In Application 2 there is a computer run of a BASIC language program called LINPRO, developed by Brian Moores and available for the Amstrad PCW8256 machine from Goode Software.

The program proceeds by asking a series of questions defining the problem and then awaiting a response through the keyboard. In the print-out that follows, questions have been answered to solve the three bolt production problem.

The answers show that profit is maximised at £720 by producing 8 units of bolt x and 3 units of bolt z. This leaves 16 hours of the first capacity constraint unused. The dual variable values are the *shadow prices* of the three inputs, and show that an extra hour of polishing time would add £10 to profits, whilst an extra hour of machine time adds nothing since the optimal solution leaves some machine time unused.

QUASAR – LINEAR PROGRAMMING
Release 1.0
*** COPYRIGHT GOODE SOFTWARE 1986 ***

You will now be prompted for the necessary information required to solve this linear programming problem, if you are in doubt to the structure of this routine press key E to exit from this programme otherwise press the RETURN key to continue. ?■

Drive is A:

!!!   Remember to order your constraints so that
less than or equal to constraints come first
equalities next
and finally greater than or equal to ones

TYPE : –1 FOR MAXIMUM OR 1 FOR MINIMUM ? –1
TYPE NUMBER OF VARIABLES ? 3
TYPE THE NUMBER OF CONSTRAINTS ? 3
TYPE THE NUMBER OF LESS THAN OR EQUAL TO CONSTRAINTS ? 3
TYPE THE NUMBER OF EQUALITY CONSTRAINTS IS ? 0
TYPE THE NUMBER OF GREATER THAN OR EQUAL TO CONSTRAINTS ?
0■

Drive is A:

? 4	CONSTRAINT LINE 1	:	ENTER COEFFICIENTS FOR : X 1
? 8	CONSTRAINT LINE 1	:	ENTER COEFFICIENTS FOR : X 2
? 4	CONSTRAINT LINE 1	:	ENTER COEFFICIENTS FOR : X 3
? 6	CONSTRAINT LINE 2	:	ENTER COEFFICIENTS FOR : X 1
? 3	CONSTRAINT LINE 2	:	ENTER COEFFICIENTS FOR : X 2
? 2	CONSTRAINT LINE 2	:	ENTER COEFFICIENTS FOR : X 3
? 0	CONSTRAINT LINE 3	:	ENTER COEFFICIENTS FOR : X 1
? 10	CONSTRAINT LINE 3	:	ENTER COEFFICIENTS FOR : X 2
? 20	CONSTRAINT LINE 3	:	ENTER COEFFICIENTS FOR : X 3

? 60	NOW INPUT THE VALUE OF THE RIGHT HAND SIDE FOR CONSTRAINT 1
? 54	NOW INPUT THE VALUE OF THE RIGHT HAND SIDE FOR CONSTRAINT 2
? 60	NOW INPUT THE VALUE OF THE RIGHT HAND SIDE FOR CONSTRAINT 3

? 60	ENTER OBJECTIVE FUNCTION COEFFICIENT FOR : X 1
? 50	ENTER OBJECTIVE FUNCTION COEFFICIENT FOR : X 2
? 80■	ENTER OBJECTIVE FUNCTION COEFFICIENT FOR : X 3

Drive is A:

ANSWERS:

VARIABLE	,	VALUE
X4		16
X1		8
X3		3

DUAL VARIABLES .

COLUMN	,	VALUE
V4		0
V5		10
V6		3

OBJECTIVE FUNCTION VALUE = 720

CHAPTER 3

Profits and objectives

Contents

Introduction

'A business firm is an organisation designed to make profits, and profits are the primary measures of its success. Social criteria of business performance usually relate to quality of products, rate of progress and behaviour of prices. But these are tests of the desirability of the whole profit system. Within that system, profits are the acid test of the individual firm's performance.'[1]

This is the opening paragraph of the first chapter of a book that can fairly be said to be the origin of Managerial Economics. Such was the centrality of profits, not only as an objective but as the very reason for the existence of the business organisation. Few modern authors, or indeed business managers, would be as forthright or as forthcoming in their views.

Chapter 1 of this book sees decision as an act of conscious choice amongst alternatives based on some predetermined criteria or objective. Chapter 2 developed the analytical tools necessary to optimise performance in a variety of modelled business situations. The purpose of this chapter is to examine objectives in more detail, and to define this decision criteria in a manner designed to have operational or practical value. The natural starting point for such an analysis in a market economy is an examination of profits, in terms of both the meaning of profits and the reasons why profit may or may not be the object of pursuit that motivates behaviour.

The nature of profit

All rational decisions involve the comparison of costs and benefits for alternative actions. By definition, the choice of a particular action precludes the adoption of other alternatives. It is the preclusion of other alternatives that gives a real economic cost to any action. Thus an hour spent studying managerial economics has an economic cost in terms of the things that we didn't do but could have done, instead of studying. The *opportunity cost* of any action is the benefit that we forgo by not taking the next best alternative. The opportunity cost of the hour spent studying economics may be the benefit we forgo by not studying something else, or the pleasure we miss by not spending the hour watching television, and so on, depending on our circumstances, needs and performances. Therefore, opportunity cost is both subjective and speculative since its value depends on our expectations of the consequences of some action *not* taken. If there genuinely is no alternative, then there is no opportunity cost, and no decision to be made. Presumably the opportunity cost of an hour spent watching television rises as examinations in economics loom closer!

It is the subjective and speculative nature of estimates of opportunity cost that lie behind difficulties in understanding and measuring the economic concept of profit. For the economist, economic profit is the value of the *surplus over opportunity cost*. Consider a simple example. An electrical engineer currently earns £10 000 per year working for a national company. He contemplates leaving the company to work for himself as an electrical repairer. He estimates that if he spent his £2000 savings (currently invested in a bank deposit account at 10 per cent interest) on equipment he could make a net income (cash inflows over cash outflows) of £12 000 year. From an accounting or taxation point of view this £12 000 is profit. From the decision-making or economic point of view, matters look somewhat different. From this surplus of revenue over direct costs the economist would deduct the opportunity costs to arrive at an economic profit on which the decision of whether or not to go independent would be based. The next best alternative to going independent is to work for the company, earning £10 000. Thus the opportunity cost in direct earnings is £10 000. Moreover, the £2000 savings currently generates £200 per year interest. Then the opportunity cost of using these savings to buy equipment is £200 a year, leaving an economic profit of £1800 per year (12 000 – 10 000 – 200), which is the economic value per annum of independence. It is this £1800 per year, the net benefit of independence, which needs to be compared to the extra effort and risk involved in independence.

Although the above example is much simplified, it does serve to underline the meaning of economic profit, as defined for decision-making purposes. In particular, economic profit needs to be carefully distinguished from the concept of accounting profit. The difference is largely due to a difference in purpose. It is the purpose of the accountant to present a 'true and accurate' record of the firm's activities. Given this criteria, it is inevitable that the accountant will be concerned with the precise recording of previous activities, dealing wholly in payments and receipts actually occurring. The measurement of profits for decision-making purposes is a rather different objective, involving especially the notion of opportunity cost, i.e. the conceptualisation of what might have happened but did not. 'In business problems the message of opportunity cost is that it is dangerous to confine cost knowledge to what the firm is doing. What the firm is not doing but could do is frequently the critical cost consideration which it is perilous but easy to ignore.'[2]

The measurement of profit

The notion of profit has developed a variety of meanings, some technical and some emotive. Defining profit as the surplus over opportunity cost is conceptually ideal from a decision-making point of view, but notoriously difficult to measure in any consistent and objective sense. It is time to take a closer look at the details of profit measurement, and to attempt to arrive at a working definition of profit that has operational value.

In a sense the firm can be considered as an organisation that transforms inputs into output. Any input–output mechanism can be evaluated in terms of the ratio of the output to input. For example, the efficiency of a motor car can be measured in terms of the ratio of output (miles) to input (petrol). Thus a car returning 40 miles per gallon is more fuel efficient than a car which gives 30 miles per gallon. Problems arise, however, when the inputs and outputs have more than one dimension. Continuing the motor car example, inputs include oil, servicing time, tyres etc. We could then have a wide range of efficiency indicators, such as miles per gallon of petrol, miles per tyre, etc. The problem is then which indicator, or combination of indicators, do we use to measure performance. Moreover, most of us are also concerned with other output dimensions, such as comfort, acceleration, etc. Rational evaluation of each motor car then becomes a complex matter involving the different input and output dimensions and our preferences between them. One way to overcome the variety of inputs problem is to measure inputs in terms of a common denominator, i.e. money. The economic efficiency of the car is then measurable in terms of output per £ spent. Conceptually at least, a value could be placed on each output dimension, weighted according to preference, and the car evaluated in terms of the ratio of output in £s to input in £s.

Returning to the business organisation, each has a variety of inputs and probably a variety of outputs. To measure the economic efficiency of the firm, take the value of output divided by the value of inputs. The value of output is called revenue (R), whilst the value of inputs is cost (C). The *rate of profit* is then the difference between revenue and costs divided by costs.

We should note that profit is a flow concept, which only has meaning when measured over some period. This contrasts with stock concepts, such as the value of the firm, which can be measured at some moment in time. Denote the time period by the subscript t. Then the rate of profit[3] is:

$$\pi \text{ rate} = \frac{R_t - C_t}{C_t}$$

The profit rate is determined by both technical and market factors. Technical factors include how good the firm is at transforming physical inputs into physical output (productive efficiency), and market factors in terms of the value placed upon both inputs and outputs.

As a performance indicator, the rate of profit concept is particularly useful when comparing profits in organisations of different size, and when the object of comparison is to obtain the best possible return on some limited sum of money. The rate of profit is then much used by those contemplating investment, such as stockbrokers, banks and other financial institutions.

As an object of pursuit, however, the owner of the organisation (to whom profit becomes income) is more likely to be concerned with the *absolute* amount of profit, defined over a period t as:

$$\pi_t = R_t - C_t$$

In both the absolute and rate forms, we appear to have a profit concept which is both simple and unambiguous. Unfortunately, matters are a little more complex. In particular there are two unresolved problems implicit in our definitions:

(a) the treatment of time;
(b) what to include in costs and revenues.

The time dimension of profit

At first sight, the time dimension problem is easily resolved. Simply define the time period that makes most operational sense. Thus for taxation or reporting purposes, profit is normally defined on an annual basis. For operating control, monthly, weekly or even daily profit measurement may be necessary to identify areas of opportunity and to take remedial action whenever performance falls below expectations. To some extent this is the practical solution to the time dimension. But there is a more serious and fundamental problem. The profit made in one period is unlikely to be independent of the profit made in subsequent periods. For example, profit in the immediate future can be increased by reducing or even abandoning current research and development, but probably at the expense of future profits. To take another example, excessive profits in the current period may induce the entry of competitors, reducing the scope for future profits.

The problem is that at any moment in time the organisation anticipates a stream of profits extending into the future. Actions taken now affect not only current but also future profits. How can comparisons be made between the reduction of current profits and a potential increase in future profits? Some mechanism is needed to make *intertemporal comparisons* of money sums. The solution to the problem lies once more with the concept of opportunity cost. The sacrifice of some sum of money now for future gain is a clear opportunity cost. The extent of that opportunity cost depends on what else could have been done with that sum of money. The obvious answer is that it could have been invested at the current interest rate. Hence a sum of money now has got a higher value than the equivalent sum of money one year hence, independent of inflation, because the present sum could be invested to grow into a larger sum in the future.

The comparison of money sums in different periods is achieved by discounting each sum to its present value.[4] If £100 now was invested at the interest rate of 12 per cent, it would grow to £112 in one year's time. Hence the expected sum of £112 in one year's time has a present value of £100 now.

Algebraically, £A invested now at the rate of interest i, will become £C in t years time, where

$$C = A(1+i)^t$$

hence $A = \dfrac{C}{(1+i)^t}$

and the worth of any future sum can be expressed in terms of its present value.

Suppose the firm anticipates a series of future profits over the next n years. Then the present value of that future profit stream is[5]

$$\frac{\pi_1}{1+i} + \frac{\pi_2}{(1+i)^2} + \ldots + \frac{\pi_n}{(1+i)^n}$$

$$= \sum_t^n \frac{\pi_t}{(1+i)^t}$$

We now have a mechanism for evaluating whether a loss in current profits is worth an anticipated gain in future profits. The present value of the anticipated extra profits can be compared to the current loss of profits on a straightforward cost and benefit comparison. The only difficulties remaining are the estimation of any future profit gain and the choice of an appropriate interest or discount rate. Each of these are characterised by uncertainty, since the future is unknown, while the choice of a discount rate is also affected by the firm's rate of time preference, i.e. its preference between current and future sums.

The inclusion of costs and revenues

Defining profit as the difference between revenues and costs over some time period raises the immediate question of what to include in costs and revenues. The problem is particularly acute over, although not completely confined to, costs. We have already noted that economists and accountants have differing objectives in the measurement of profit, with the economist being primarily concerned with decisions concerning the future, whilst the accountant's primary role is to provide an accurate record of previous activities. This difference in purpose has its most obvious manifestation in the problem of what to include in costs. In particular, there are substantial differences in the valuation of capital and the treatment of managerial earnings.

The valuation of capital

The absolute amount of profit over a period is defined as the absolute difference between costs and revenues in that period. Suppose however the firm sold one of its prime buildings in that period. Then revenue will have been increased (and possible costs decreased) out of all proportion to the firm's normal operating activities. Is the once and for all building scale to be treated as some sort of extra profit, giving a disturbed picture of the firm's performance? It would seem sensible to treat this item separately in some way, so that decisions are not made on the basis of distorted information.

The problem is basically that of separating the income of the organisation from the capital of that organisation. The firm that rashly spends any excess profit from the sale of its assets is ultimately going to find its worth substantially reduced. The concept was first and most succinctly expressed by Hicks.[6] 'We ought to define a man's income as the maximum value which he can consume during a week, and still expect to be as well off at the end of the week as he was at the beginning.'

Translating into organisational terms, the profit to the firm is the maximum value it can distribute over a period and still be worth at the end of the period what it was at the beginning. Thus to measure profit it is necessary to place a value on the organisation. Now the value of the organisation (or the sum of the values of its assets) is directly dependent on the future expected earning power of those assets. To decide to keep these assets in their present use it is necessary to compare this anticipated earning power to the next best alternative use. For most assets, the next best alternative to using the asset is to realise its market value, i.e. to sell it. Thus for decision-making purposes, the asset should be valued at its opportunity cost, normally measured by its market price. However, once more we have entered the realms of speculation, since in most cases the asset will not be sold, so that the market value is only an estimate. The accountant, of course, in the search for accurate reporting, is going to be more comfortable with the historical (or factual) value of the asset. Note, however, that in making decisions, the historical value of the asset is not only unimportant, it is irrelevant.

Similar problems arise in the treatment of depreciation. Over time, the value of an asset is likely to deteriorate, because of usage or obsolescence or both. In the measurement of profit, it is essential for good decision-making to take account of this change in asset value. The accountant will normally set a depreciation charge against current profit in terms of the initial cost of the asset and its anticipated economic life. The economist has differing information-al requirements, in that the asset has a value because of its anticipated earning power. The value of the asset is then the discounted earnings, which needs to be compared to the next best alternative (usually selling the asset) to determine whether the asset should continue in its present use. Depreciation then is the change in the net present value of anticipated earnings from the asset over time. As we have seen, valuation in these terms requires both forecasting skill and the adoption of an appropriate discount rate. However, depreciation can normally be approximated by changes in the market value (or replacement cost) of the asset.

A further complication is that of inflation. During the 1970s, inflation in Britain reached annual values of over 20 per cent, imposing severe strains on attempts to measure profits in terms of £s that were consistently decreasing in value. The accounting profession eventually responded with Current Cost Accounting, which attempts to take account of changes in the value of money by measuring values in terms of their current purchasing power. To date, accountancy practice has been slow to respond to this challenge. Fortunately the magnitude of this problem has fallen with the inflation rate in the 1980s.

Managerial earnings and capital

We saw earlier that the opportunity costs of setting up a business include earnings foregone, both on labour and capital. For the independent sole proprietorship, there is a problem of including these opportunity costs in the measurement of profit. Normally, accounting convention disregards these opportunity or implicit costs, so that reported profit exceeds economic profit. The problem is really whether allowance should be made for wage payment to the owner/manager, or whether this is a part of the profit of the firm, since this profit becomes the income of the owner. Once more, opportunity cost is the best guide. The foregone earnings of the owner/manager are an opportunity cost and should be deducted from reported profit. Any payment to the owner/manager over and above this is an element of profit (although it may represent the necessary inducement to incur the risk of operating the firm). This problem is considerably eased by the growth of the private or public company run by salaried managers with little or no ownership interest. Payment to the manager is then simply an exchange for services rendered, and forms part of the normal costs of operations.

Profit as an objective

Profit as an objective has emerged from over a century of economic theory. In this traditional economic theory, the typical firm was small, owner managed and competing with a large number of similar firms. Under these circumstances, profit is the rational objective because:

1.   The profit of the firm became the income of the owner. Maximisation of profit then ensured the self-interests of the owner/ manager, who both decided the actions that the firm should follow and made sure that these were carried out.

Note that if profit was positively related to the efforts of the owner, maximising profit would require maximum effort. Then extra effort would have to be traded off against profit in a manner which would not produce the maximum possible absolute profit.[7]

2.   The force of competition imposed profit maximisation upon the firm. Given the large number of other firms, any firm that did not maximise profit would not survive in business. It is interesting to note that the very pursuit of economic profit (in the sense of a surplus over opportunity cost) ensured that those profits could not persist over time. Any firm that made economic profits was, by definition, doing better than some other firms, who would enter the market and erode those profits. Thus any firm not maximising profit was necessarily making a loss, and could not survive.

The behavioural assumption of profit maximisation has served economic theory well. Because profit is the difference between revenue and costs, once revenue and costs are identified the assumption of profit maximisation enables predictions to be readily made about the consequence of any environmental change. Moreover, given identifiable profits, the techniques of classical optimisation can be used for decision-making.

Suppose a firm produces a single good. Given the cost and revenue functions described in Figure 3.1, the profit maximising price and output can be easily derived.[8] The vertical distance between total revenue (TR) and total cost (TC) at any output level defines the profit corresponding to that output. The difference between TR and TC describes the profit function π. Profit is then maximised at the output level Q, with total revenue TR_1 and total cost TC_1, giving a maximum profit of π_1.[9] Since total revenue is price times output, the resulting price can be found by dividing total revenue TR_1 by output Q_1, giving the slope of line $0a$.

Now suppose that total costs increase in a manner that makes the total cost curve everywhere more steep.

The increase in costs forces the profit function downwards and to the left. Profit maximisation implies that output falls from Q to Q_2, whilst price increases from $0a$ to $0b$.

The power of the model is such that we can immediately predict that output will fall and price increase (Figure 3.2).

However, in recent years, doubts have been expressed about the accuracy of the profit maximisation model as a description of current business behaviour. Two factors in particular have served to cast doubt on the validity of the model.

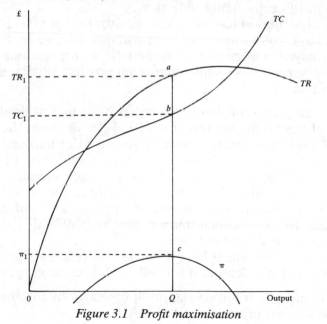

Figure 3.1   Profit maximisation

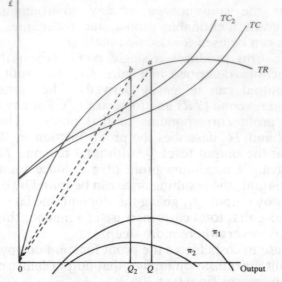

Figure 3.2   Predictions from the profit maximisation model

1.   The twentieth century has seen substantial changes in the ownership and organisation of business. The typical large company is owned by a diffusion of shareholders, and managed by salaried professionals with little or no ownership interest, paid salaries often unrelated to profits. Managers may then view profits as only one of a wide range of performance indicators.

2.   The same period has seen the concentration of markets dominated by large (often multinational) corporations, so that competition may have been severely weakened. Such corporations may well be able to survive at less than maximum possible profits, simply by virtue of their size.

The consequence of these factors has been to cast doubt on the validity of the profit maximisation model. In addition, the achievement of maximum profits imposes severe informational requirements on the manager. In particular, the equalisation of marginal cost and marginal revenue calls for precise measurements that are unlikely to be available. The business world is one of considerable uncertainty, characterised by discarded plans and unfulfilled expectations. In these circumstances, precise economic calculus becomes operationally meaningless.

As a result, economists have attempted to redefine the objectives of the firm. Such redefinition has followed three broad paths:

(i)   Attempts to resurrect the profit objective by placing profit in the context of an uncertain world.

(ii)   The replacement of profit with some other objectives, or group of objectives, that can be maximised in place of profit.

(iii) Abandoning the principle of maximising any objective, and consider instead the organisational context of the firm, normally expressed in terms of the satisfaction of some group of performance targets.

The rest of this chapter will consider each of these possible avenues in turn. The descriptions that follow are not intended to be a comprehensive guide to business motivation, but rather to impart a flavour of what may be called 'managerial' approaches to the firm.

Profit related objectives

According to this viewpoint, the true objective of the firm is something closely related to profit. Often the objective is tied to uncertainty, such as survival, security or the maintenance of liquid assets. Each of these objectives is *complementary* to profit, in that the maximisation of profit may ensure the attainment of that objective. The behaviour of the firm can then be modelled *as if* the firm was maximising profit.

Moreover, the informational problem inherent in the maximisation of profit is then an error of 'misplaced concreteness'. The essential condition is not that the manager knows with complete accuracy the estimated variables necessary for profit maximisation, but that the manager behaves *as if* the relevant variables were known, so that the decision-maker equates the subjectively assessed marginal revenue with the subjectively assessed marginal cost. It is then entirely possible that the manager's assessments are wrong. For the purposes of the theory this is irrelevant, since equating marginal revenue and marginal cost remains the operative rule. The manager merely strives in future to obtain better information, so that the decisions taken edge closer and closer to the absolute optimum.

The analogy often used is that of the decision to overtake when driving a motor car. The construction of a decision model would include the following variables:

(i)   the speed and anticipated behaviour of the car in front;

(ii)   the speed and accelerating potential of the car driven by the decision-maker;

(iii) the speed, distance from and anticipated behaviour of cars coming the other way;

(iv)   road and weather conditions;
(v)   the urgency of the journey expressed as a behavioural assumption.

Given this information, it would be possible to construct a decision-model, presumably involving both differential equations and some treatment of uncertainty.

The fact remains that when driving, we make overtaking decisions virtually instantaneously, without the appropriately defined explicit model or the use of some dashboard computer. Presumably some sort of Darwinistic law of survival ensures that the best decision-makers pass on this ability to their offspring!

Hence the behaviour of the firm is modelled as if the firm made perfect profit maximising decisions.

Other maximisation objectives

According to these approaches, the divorce of ownership and control, and the weakening of competition, have given managers the discretion to pursue other objectives. There are a large number of possibilities, but we shall confine our attention to the three most credible: the maximisation of sales revenue, the maximisation of growth, and the maximisation of managerial utility. Each of these theories suggests that the interests of the manager are most likely to be satisfied by the pursuit of some objective other than profit. Moreover, each of the alternatives is a substitute for, rather than complement to, profit, because they lead to behaviour that differs substantially from the predictions of the profit maximisation hypothesis. Each of the models is described in its simplest form – interested readers are invited to pursue their interest via the recommended readings.

1.   Sales revenue maximisation

This theory was developed by W. J. Baumol,[10] according to whom, the interests of the salaried manager are best served by the maximisation of sales revenue, which brings with it the benefits of growth, market share and status. Sales revenue can be used as a surrogate for the size of the firm, and the manager's income, prestige, and aspirations more closely identified with sales revenue than with profit. Moreover, by maximising sales revenue, managers avoid the risks inherent in the adoption of highly profitable but risky ventures. Steady performance is seen as a more comfortable alternative than the possibility of losses.

However, Baumol includes within his model the notion of a profit constraint, being some minimum absolute amount of profit necessary to satisfy shareholders (who are unlikely to know what maximum profit is possible anyway), and to prevent the possibility of a shareholder revolt endangering the security of managers.

By making some simplifying assumptions, the Sales Revenue model can be described in terms of a diagram. Assume a single period, with conventional cost and revenue functions. Figure 3.3 is then just a repeat of Figure 3.1. Given the cost and revenue functions, profit is maximised at the output level Qm. The point of maximum sales revenue is at the highest point on the total revenue curve, corresponding to output Qs. The profit constraint can be represented by a horizontal line, the height of which above the output axis is determined by the amount of profit necessary to satisfy shareholders. If the profit constraint is π_1, the absolute maximum sales revenue produces enough profit to satisfy this, and output will be Qs. Note that output is higher, and price lower, than with the objective of maximising profit (hence sales revenue maximisation is a substitute for profit maximisation).

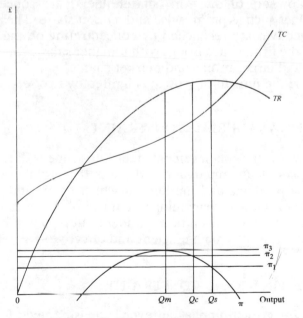

Figure 3.3   Sales revenue maximisation

However, if the profit constraint is above π_1 (say π_2) then output Qs does not produce enough profit to satisfy the constraint. Then output must be reduced, reducing total revenue but pushing the firm back up the profit function until π_2 is satisfied (at output Qc). Qc is then the output that maximises sales revenue, subject to the profit constraint π_2. Note that if the profit constraint is high enough (π_3), it can only be satisfied by producing to maximise profit (at Qm). In general, we expect behaviour somewhere between Qm and Qs, so that the firm gives up some profit to gain extra sales revenue. Note that beyond Qm, marginal revenue (or the slope of total revenue) is less than marginal cost (slope of total cost).

Baumol's model has been extended in a number of ways, principally to include advertising, multiple products and longer time periods.[11]

2. Growth maximisation

The model of growth maximisation was formulated by Marriss, who, like Baumol, saw managers as having both the ability and motivation to pursue objectives other than profit. According to Marriss, managers will seek the objectives which give them satisfaction, such as salary, prestige, status and job security. On the other hand, the owners of the firm (shareholders) are concerned with market values such as profit, sales and market share. These differing sets of objectives are reconciled by concentrating on the growth of the size of the firm, which brings with it higher salaries and status for managers and larger profits and market shares.[12]

However, the pursuit of growth is limited by two sets of factors:

(i)   THE MANAGERIAL CONSTRAINT

The ability of the management team to cope effectively with expansion is not unlimited. First, there is the problem of actually finding new products and markets in which to expand. Secondly, there is the problem of remaining in control of that expansion. The management team can itself be expanded, but only at a limited rate if management is to remain efficient and effective.

(ii)   THE FINANCIAL CONSTRAINT

The drive for growth implies an ever-increasing need for funds to finance investment. Funds can be obtained in two ways:

— internal investment by the use of retained profits;
— external investment by borrowing.

However, uncontrolled use of either of these sources of capital supply increases the risk of either takeover or shareholder revolt, each endangering the job security of management.

These constraints are satisfied simultaneously by maximising the *balanced* rate of growth, whereby the growth of demand is matched by an equal growth in capital supply. Growth in produce demand is achieved by diversification (entry into new products and/or markets) and research and development. However, each of these is limited by the need for profits (to satisfy shareholders and finance new investments).

The management desire for job security is achieved through the adoption of a prudent financial strategy, which involves achieving optimal values for three financial ratios.

(i) *The leverage ratio*

$$V = \frac{\text{value of debts}}{\text{value of assets}}$$

(ii) *Liquidity ratio*

$$L = \frac{\text{value of liquid assets}}{\text{value of total assets}}$$

(iii) *Retention ratio*

$$R = \frac{\text{retained profits}}{\text{total profits}}$$

Control of the leverage ratio keeps the extent of borrowing in check, while control of the liquidity ratio limits both the risk of insolvency (L too low), and the risk of takeover by firms looking for liquid assets (L too high). Via the retention ratio, sufficient profit must be distributed to keep shareholders reasonably content, whilst the distribution of profit in the form of dividends has an opportunity cost in terms of foregone investment funds.

The optimal solution is achieved when the balanced growth rate is maximised, with the growth in product demand (through diversification and research and development) matched by the growth in capital supply (through borrowing and reinvested profits).

The Marriss model is both ingenious and relevant, particularly in the way it highlights the constraints within which the salaried manager must operate. However, the optimal solution is contrived, depending as it does on some precise relationships between the diversification, profit and capital growth rates. Moreover, the model takes no explicit account of the behaviour of competitors, and has little to say about the decision-making processes involved in the determination of prices or outputs. The inclusion of diversification is a major achievement and helps to put the objectives of the organisation into the context of a world of risk and uncertainty.

3. The maximisation of managerial utility

The model of managerial utility was developed by Williamson,[13] and once more assumes that managers have both the desire and discretion to pursue objectives other than profit maximisation, subject to some minimum profit constraint. Managers achieve their objectives directly by spending any profits above the profit constraint on items that give rise to managerial satisfaction or utility. According to Williamson, managers can influence both the level of profits and how these profits are spent.

This is not a new idea, and is implicit in most of the managerial models. Williamson's contribution was to give operational value to the concept by identifying those variables he saw as giving rise to managerial satisfaction.

The basic Williamson model can be expressed in the form

$$Um = f(S, M, I_d)$$

where Um is the utility of managers, S is expenditure on staff, M denotes managerial emoluments and I_d measures the managers' discretionary power for investment. Managerial utility is then maximised subject to the minimum profit constraint. The identified variables can be justified as follows.

STAFF EXPENDITURE

Increased expenditure on staff generally increases profits by increasing output and/or sales, but expenditure is continued beyond the profit maximising level because staff expenditure represents both power and prestige to the manager.

MANAGERIAL EMOLUMENTS

These include expenditure in items such as expense accounts, luxury offices, company cars, etc. and give rise directly to managerial satisfaction. This non-salary expenditure on the personal comfort and well-being of managers appears in the company accounts as a necessary cost, but adds little to the operating efficiency of the organisation. Direct salary expenditure to managers is much more easily identified from company accounts, and may give rise to shareholder disquiet.

THE DISCRETIONARY POWER FOR INVESTMENT

The manager gains prestige and status by being able to finance capital projects beyond what is strictly necessary to the functioning of the firm. The manager is able to spend company money on 'pet' projects, often involving fashionable new technology in the form of computer based office equipment, justified as necessary but once more adding little to operating efficiency.

Each of these expenditure items remains hidden in the firm's accounts as necessary expenditure. The optimal solution involves a trade-off of expenditure from profits above the profit constraint on these items, depending on the preferences and power relationships within the management team. Note that the theory implies that production will be arranged in order to maximise economic profit, but that reported profit will be reduced by expenditure on these items above the profit maximising levels.

The theory goes on to explain that in times of rapid economic growth, expenditure on these discretionary items will increase rapidly, whilst in times of depressed markets, these items represent a cushion against economic adversity, in that expenditure in these items can be reduced without adversely affecting output. In normal circumstances, discretionary spending implies levels of staff, managerial emoluments and discretionary investment considerably in excess of profit maximising output.

One interesting corollary of the theory is that it may present an explanation for takeover activity, in that many takeovers are justified on the basis of cutting managerial expenditure and increasing profitability without affecting output. Thus merger occurs when the more profit-conscious management sees opportunities represented by firms indulging in discretionary expenditure.

Non-maximising objectives

The behavioural assumption of maximisation has got theoretical and mathematical advantages in that it enables models to be developed and optimal solutions to be found. However, from a practical point of view, the ability, need or even desire to maximise anything may be questionable. The business world is characterised by uncertainty, implying the absence of complete decision-information and the need to make forecasts which may well turn out to be wrong. Uncertainty about the variables within the firm's control interacts with uncertainty about the behaviour of rivals to make maximisation neither achievable nor desirable. The manager involved in complex and continual decision-making processes tries to simplify problems by the adoption of decision-making rules of thumb, which will have proved reliable in the past.[14]

Under these circumstances, some authors have abandoned the pursuit of maximisation in favour of some simpler and more achievable 'satisficing' objective.[15] Instead of pursuing a maximisation goal, the firm seeks some satisfactory solution. In a sense, of course, this merely shifts the problem to that of defining what is satisfactory. Satisficing objectives are set in terms of some aspiration level. In a particular period the actual performance is compared to the target goal. If the aspiration level is easily attained, then aspirations levels rise in the next period. If the target is not attained, search activity is undertaken to find out why. If the reasons are within the compass of the firm, action is taken to achieve the target in future. If not, or if no reasons are found, the aspiration level is simply revised downwards to what is achievable in future.

In some ways, the economic model of the firm treats the organisation as some sort of mysterious black box, with attention devoted to the inputs and outputs of the firm, and little attention paid to the *process* of transforming inputs into outputs. The satisficing approach generally goes beyond this and recognises that firms have an organisational structure, the form of which significantly influences the firm's conduct and performance.

The best known of the satisficing approaches to the firm is by Cyert and March.[16]

A behavioural theory of the firm

According to Cyert and March, the firm as an organisation is not a unified structure but a coalition of individuals, some organised into groups, each with varying interests and objectives. Decision-making within the firm is a continual political process of bargaining, in which side payments are made to ensure compliance or to entice individuals into some subgrouping. These side payments are over and above what is strictly necessary to keep the individual within the firm, and may include salary payments or commitments to various policies or projects. However, not all conflict is resolved.

The objectives of the firm are defined in terms of broad headings, of which Cyert and March identified five.

(i)   A production goal

This would ensure that output neither fluctuated wildly nor fell below some previously determined minimum acceptable level.

(ii)   An inventory goal

Sufficient stocks of raw materials, components and finished goods should be held to ensure that production is uninterrupted by shortages, and that there is enough stock to satisfy customer needs.

(iii)   A sales goal

The management of the firm, and particularly those responsible for marketing, are both judged and judge themselves by the ability to maintain and expand sales levels.

(iv)   A market share goal

Market share should not fall below an acceptable level. As a performance indicator market share is easily measured, and often used by shareholders.

(v)   A profit goal

Sufficient profit must be made to be able to finance investment and to distribute as dividends to shareholders.

Each goal is set in terms of an aspiration level, to which performance is compared with the results as outlined above. Some of the goals may be conflicting. For example, the maintenance of production may conflict with the profit goal in times of declining demand. The onus is then on management to restore both by seeking new products and new markets. The sales goal may conflict with the profit goal, with high sales requiring low and unprofitable prices. Conflict between goals or interest groups left unresolved by the bargaining and aspiration level processes is contained by the adoption of conflict–resolution mechanisms. Most important of these is the adoption of some overall objectives which can secure complete agreement but provide sufficient flexibility to be interpreted in different ways. Such broad objectives could include 'satisfying the customer' or 'making a good product'. Any residual conflict is then resolved by crisis management coping with problems sequentially as they occur, and by the adoption of standard operating procedures or decision-making rules of thumb.

As a description of the decision-making process, the Cyert and March model is likely to strike a chord in anyone familiar with the management process in a large organisation. As a theory of business behaviour, the Cyert and March model has several severe shortcomings. In terms of empirical validity, the theory is untestable. Almost any possible business behaviour can be explained by reference to at least one of the five organisational objectives. The use of aspiration levels does not allow objective predictions to be made about response to changing circumstances.

Most seriously the theory is inductive, in that it makes detailed generalisations about behaviour on the basis of observed performance of a small sample of firms. On the positive side, the theory does illustrate some of the organisational complexities of modern business behaviour, and makes a positive contribution to our understanding of decision-making as a political process.

Conclusion

This chapter began with the assertion by Joel Dean that profits are not merely an objective, they are the very reason for the existence of the business enterprise.

Subsequent investigation revealed not only a plurality of meaning for the concept of profit with substantial diversity of view about how profit should be measured, but also cast some doubt on the centrality of profit as the overriding objective of the modern firm. Having made some important qualifications to the notion of profit maximisation, and considered the merits of alternative objectives, the rest of this book will generally proceed on the assumption that the firm either seeks to maximise profit or that the true objective of the firm is some complement to profit. The reasons for this are generally functional. The assumption of profit maximisation has the enormous advantage of enabling decisions to be modelled simply and succinctly, and allows decision rules to be developed to cope with a variety of changing circumstances. This is not to doubt the attraction of the non-profit maximising theories, but more pragmatically to note that the development of unambiguous decision rules based on these approaches is a challenge yet to be met. If the content of this book stirs the reader to attempt to meet that challenge then this approach will have been entirely vindicated.

Application 3

Dominant shareownership and profitability[17]

1. Introduction

One of the dominant themes of Chapter 3 is that the diffusion of ownership of the modern corporation may give managers the discretion to pursue objectives other than profit maximisation. Freedom from shareholder or product-market constraints may enable managers to pursue sales maximisation, growth or other objectives as a substitute for profit maximisation. Under these circumstances, profitability can be expected to be a decreasing function of the extent of managerial control. Neun and Santerre set out to examine this hypothesis, by estimating the functional relationship between the percentage shareownership of the dominant (largest) shareholder and the profit rate.

2. Analysis

The dominant shareholder could establish control over the behaviour of the firm either by acquiring, or by threatening to acquire, majority shareownership. A shareholder can be expected to attempt to influence management behaviour when the projected costs of acquiring control are exceeded by the expected benefits. The expected benefit of acquiring control depends on the difference between the *actual* and *maximum* profit rates, and the share of shareownership (share of potential profits). The costs of acquiring control depends on the costs of obtaining additional shares, and the proportion of existing shareownership.

The problem for management is then to choose an actual profit rate, subject to a shareholder constraint. Neun and Santerre hypothesise the relationship between the holdings of the dominant shareholder and the profit rate shown in Figure A3.1.

Below DSO_1, managers have full control, and are free to pursue other objectives subject to a minimum profit rate sufficient to satisfy shareholders collectively. The cost of acquiring control for the dominant shareholder exceeds the anticipated benefits.

Over the range DSO_1 to DSO_2, obtaining additional shares by the dominant shareholder exerts pressure on managers to increase the profit rate. To pacify the dominant shareholder, managers must reduce the potential benefit of extra shareholding by increasing profits. Beyond DSO_2, the dominant shareholder exercises effective control and management must maximise profits.

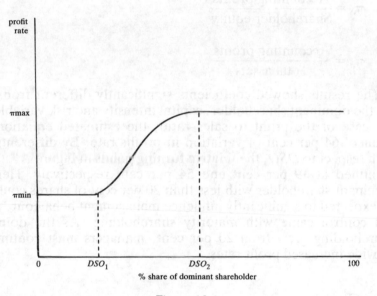

Figure A3.1

3. The results

To test this hypothesis, Neun and Santerre estimated the profit rate as a cubic function of the share of the dominant shareowner, for eighty-one US firms in four industries expected to be less than fully competitive. The actual equation estimated was:

$$\pi_i = b_0 + b_1 DSO + b_2 DSO^2 + b_3 DSO^3 + b_4 MSO$$
$$+ b_5 TA + b_6 K/S + b_7 D/E + b_8 I$$

with DSO = proportion of shares owned by dominant shareowner
    MSO = proportion of shares owned by managers
     TA = total assets (size)
    K/S = capital intensity (total assets divided by sales)
    D/E = debt to equity ratio (risk)
      I = dummy variable according to industry.

In view of the problems encountered in defining a profit rate, the study used three alternative measures;

$$\pi_s = \frac{\text{Accounting profits}}{\text{Sales}}$$

$$\pi_e = \frac{\text{Accounting profits}}{\text{Shareholder equity}}$$

$$\pi_a = \frac{\text{Accounting profits}}{\text{Total assets}}$$

The results showed coefficients significantly different from zero for the dominant shareholder, capital intensity and risk variables. In the case of the profit to sales ratio, the estimated equation 'explained' 64 per cent of variation in profits rate. By differentiating with respect to DSO, the relative turning points in Figure A3.1 were identified at 19 per cent and 54 per cent respectively. Hence a dominant shareholder with less than 20 per cent of shares could not be expected to significantly influence management behaviour, whilst full control came with majority shareholding. As the dominant shareholding grew from 20 per cent, managers must continue to provide increased profit rates.

4. Conclusion

The study showed that the dominant shareholder can exert increasing control over management once shareholding rises above 20 per cent. A positive association between dominant shareholding and profit rates suggests that, given the freedom to do so, managers will pursue objectives that result in less than maximum profits.

CHAPTER 4

Uncertainty – managing the future

Contents

Introduction

A fundamental problem for all decision-makers is the absence of complete information about the decision environment. If all possible actions, events and conditional outcomes could be predicted with complete confidence, then decision-making would be the simple mechanical exercise of calculating the optimal action according to some predetermined criteria. In practice, of course, the decision environment is characterised by uncertainty – or the absence of perfect and complete information. Decisions must be made on the basis of estimates and expectations, the former of which may be inaccurate, whilst the latter are often unfulfilled. The 'art' of management cannot be replaced by the 'science' of decision theory. What decision theory *can* do is to give structure to the decision-making process in a manner that focuses attention on the decision variables that are most important, so that resources can be devoted to their estimation. At the same time, a well-formulated decision model will not only provide a solution guide, it will also include some measure of the sensitivity of solutions to the estimated variables.

All decisions concern the future, which is 'imaginable but not knowable'. Actions are undertaken in anticipation of future benefits, which may or may not be realised. Thus all decisions contain an element of *risk* because of the unpredictability of outcomes, which imposes an opportunity cost on the decision-maker since different decisions would have been made if actual outcomes had been known beforehand. In certain circumstances, as we shall see, this opportunity cost of uncertainty can be measured directly. The cost of uncertainty will then be a guide to the amount of resources it is worthwhile spending to try to reduce uncertainty by the collection of further decision information.

Moreover, the risk that arises because of uncertainty will impact directly on the decision process through the decision-maker's *attitude towards risk*. The prudent or cautious manager may well choose different actions from the decision-maker who has the confidence (or resources) to take greater risks.

In Chapter 1 we encountered a simple framework for decision-making that ensured a logical and sequential approach to decisions. This framework can now be extended to include the uncertainty implicit in decision-making. Figure 4.1 is an extension of Figure 1.1, that includes both some subjective assessment of organisational variables and the estimation of how likely conditional outcomes are.[1]

Estimating probability

Each of us is familiar with the notion of estimating how likely different events are to happen. The decisions of what to wear tomorrow, whether to buy a new product, even whether to cross the road, are each exercises in decision-making under uncertainty that involve some estimation of the likelihood of chance events. To give

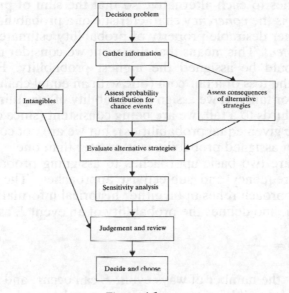

Figure 4.1

structure to decision-making, it is necessary to formalise this estimation procedure in a manner that is consistent, and which gives effect to our desire to evaluate the impact of likelihood estimates on the decision choice. The principle instrument for this formalisation is the concept of *probability*.

The probability of an event x is written as $p(x)$. If the event is certain to occur then its probability is one. If the event is certain not to occur then its probability is zero. Therefore, a decision must be made with incomplete information whenever the probability of an event is greater than zero and less than one.

Traditionally a distinction has been made between a situation of risk and that of uncertainty. Risk is a situation in which the probabilities of events are known beforehand, whilst uncertainty is a situation where the relevant probabilities are unknown. One of the techniques of decision analysis is to transform situations of uncertainty into risk by estimating the probability of chance events. Before examining methods of estimating probabilities it is useful to consider what are the desirable properties of a probability estimate for decision-making purposes.

One of the principles of decision-making outlined in Chapter 1 is that all the feasible alternatives should be considered. If we consider all alternatives, then by definition one must occur. Consequently, since the probability of a certain event is one, we should assign probabilities to each alternative so that the sum of probabilities is one. This is the *coherency* characteristic of a probabilities estimate.

The other desirable property of probability estimates is that they are *consistent*. This means that the event we consider most likely to occur should be assigned the highest probability. For example, consider the toss of a fair coin (one with an equal chance of landing on heads or tails). If we assign a probability of two-thirds to a head, and two-thirds to a tail, we are being consistent (since equally likely events are given equal probabilities), but we are not coherent, since the sum of assigned probabilities is greater than one.

There are two basic approaches to assigning probabilities – the relative frequency and subjectivist approaches. The relative frequency approach relies upon either historical information or logical deduction, and defines the probability of an event E as:

$$P(E) = \frac{n}{N}$$

where n is the number of ways event E can occur, and N is the total number of possible outcomes. These may be used either *a priori* (before the fact) or *a posteriori* (after the fact), depending on the available information. For example, consider rolling a die. The relative frequentist would consider there are six possible outcomes, each of which is equally likely. Thus the probability of scoring a three would be

$$P(3) = \frac{1}{6}$$

since there are six possible outcomes of which one outcome is a three. Alternatively, using the *a posteriori* approach, if the die had been rolled twenty times, with a three occurring four times, the probability of scoring three on one roll of the die would be:

$$P(3) = \frac{4}{20}$$

If the die was fair, and rolled a large number of times, the number of threes scored would tend towards 1/6 times the number of rolls.

The subjectivist approach regards probability as a measure of likelihood that reflects an individual's belief about the chance of an event. According to this approach, all probability estimates are subjective, and relative frequency is just a particular kind of subjective judgement – i.e. either that events are equally likely or that performance in the past will be continued into the future. This is not to claim that probability estimates are no more than guesses, but that experience and judgement can be used to generate probability estimates that are both consistent and coherent.

There is an important class of decision environments in which the relative frequency approach is difficult to sustain. These are unique events, such as launching a new product or purchasing a major new piece of capital equipment, for which there is neither historical information nor logically deductive guidelines. Assuming events are equally likely is clearly arbitrary, for then the probability of each event depends only on the number of events considered. The subjectivist would consider the unique event in terms of its own special circumstances, using whatever evidence is available combined with reasoned judgement to derive probability estimates. For the subjectivist, the distinction between risk and uncertainty disappears, since probability is subjective and probability estimates can always be made (with more or less confidence). A more useful distinction is one between situations where probability estimates can be relied upon, and ones in which probability estimates must be treated with caution. Recognising that probability is subjective forces attention upon the assumptions that underlie all probability estimates.

Probability distributions and expected value

A probability distribution is a list of possible outcomes, together with the probability associated with each. For example, suppose we are considering the likely return on a particular investment. We estimate that there is a 3 in 10 chance the return will be 8 per cent, a 6 in 10 chance of 10 per cent return and a 1 in 10 chance of 12 per cent return. Then the corresponding probability distribution of returns will be:

Table 4.1

Return	Probability
8%	0.3
10%	0.6
12%	0.1

Now decision implies a choice from alternatives, so that each alternative must be evaluated. However, each alternative action is unlikely to result in a unique outcome. Rather each action will be associated with a corresponding probability distribution of outcomes. The choice amongst alternatives is then dependent on the preference between different probability distributions. It is therefore necessary to be able to compare probability distributions.

For example, suppose we must choose between investment projects *A* and *B* (Table 4.2), where each has the estimated probability distribution of returns listed below.

Table 4.2

Project A		Project B	
Return %	*Probability*	*Return %*	*Probability*
8	0.3	6	0.1
10	0.6	8	0.2
12	0.1	10	0.4
		12	0.2
		14	0.1

One way to make the decision would be to enquire, 'Suppose I made the same decision a large number of times. If I always choose *A*, what would be my average return?' The answer is given by the *expected value* or *mean* of the distribution. The expected return on project *A* is just the average of all possible returns, using as weights for each outcome the probability of its occurrence.

More generally the expected value of *X*, written as $E(X)$, is given by the formula:

$$E(X) = \sum_{i=1}^{n} P(Xi).Xi$$

where $P(Xi)$ is the probability of event Xi, which is multiplied by the value of the corresponding event and summed over all events.

The expected return on each project can now be calculated:

$$E(A) = (8 \times .3) + (10 \times .6) + (12 \times .1) = 9.6\%$$

$$E(B) = (6 \times .1) + (8 \times .2) + (10 \times .4) + (12 \times .2) + (14 \times .1) = 10\%$$

Thus if I make the choice a large number of times, I can achieve a higher average return from project *B* than from project *A*. Note that the expected value is just an average, and is in no sense the return that is expected.

Moreover, choosing on the basis of expected returns ignores the *dispersion* of possible returns. The average return on project *B* may be higher than that of *A*, but returns to project *A* are less dispersed than project *B*. A measure of the dispersion of outcomes is the *standard deviation*, which is the square root of the sum of squared deviations from the average, measured by the formula.

$$S(X) = \sum_{i=1}^{n} \sqrt{(Xi - E(X))^2 . P(Xi)}$$

The standard deviation indicates how likely it is that the *actual* outcome is a given distance away from the *expected* outcome. The standard deviation of returns on projects A and B are:

$$S(A) = \sqrt{(8-9.6)^2 \times .3 + (10-9.6)^2 \times .6 + (12-9.6)^2 \times .1}$$
$$= \sqrt{0.768 + 0.096 + 0.576}$$
$$= \underline{1.2}$$

$$S(B) = \sqrt{(6-10)^2 \times .1 + (8-10)^2 \times .2 + (10-10)^2 \times .4 +}$$
$$\overline{(12-10)^2 \times .2 + (14-10)^2 \times .1}$$
$$= \underline{2.19}$$

Now although the expected return on B is greater than that of A, project B has returns which are more dispersed than those of A. The choice between A and B will then depend on the *attitude towards risk* of the decision-maker. This will be considered in more detail later. For the moment, we can note that if the projects have the same expected return, the project with lowest dispersion will normally be chosen. If the project with highest expected return has the same or lower dispersion than the other project, then the first project would be chosen. Only if one alternative has both a higher expected return and a greater dispersion of return is the choice more complicated, and rests basically upon how the decision-maker values expected return relative to dispersion.

The newsboy problem

The expected value concept is an important guide for decision-making with uncertain outcomes, particularly for repetitive decisions. One important set of decision situations is characterised as the 'Newsboy Problem' for reasons that will become obvious.

Suppose that I own a shop selling daily newspapers. Each day I must decide how many copies of the 'Daily Gossip' to order for tomorrow. The decision variables will be how many newspapers I think can be sold, the cost of each newspaper and the profit made on each sale. If I order too many, I shall be left with unsold stock, whilst ordering too few will result in missing profitable opportunities. My objective will be to make as much profit as possible, not just tomorrow but every day into the future. Consequently, the decision criteria adopted will be the maximisation of expected profit.

The 'Daily Gossip' is bought from a wholesaler for 15p per copy and sold at the retail price of 25p. Thus 10p profit is made on every sale, whilst unsold stock represents a unit cost of 15p. I consider that there are three possible levels of sales, 20, 30 or 40 newspapers. Then corresponding to the three possible events will be three possible actions – stocking 20, 30 or 40 newspapers.

Given the cost and revenue parameters, each combination of act and event will result in a unique outcome. Thus buying and selling 20 newspapers will give a profit of 200p, whilst buying 30 newspapers when 40 could be sold will result in a profit of 300p (since 40 newspapers cannot be sold if only 30 are stocked). Hence, the *conditional profit* or *payoff* table can be found, showing the net profit resulting from each act/event combination. This is illustrated in Table 4.3.

Table 4.3   Conditional profit table

		Act (Stock)		
		20	30	40
Event	20	200	50	−100
(Demand)	30	200	300	150
	40	200	300	400

Given the assumptions stocking 20 will always result in a profit of 200p, whilst stocking 30 will give either 50p or 300p profit. The choice between 20 and 30 then depends on how often stocking 30 results in a profit of 50p compared to how often it produces 300p, compared to the 200p assured from stocking 20. To choose between them requires information on how likely demands of 20, 30 or 40 are. Thus we need to estimate the probability of each demand level.

In these circumstances, the best guide to probability estimation will be previous experience. Suppose a record of sales over the past twenty days reveals the following:

Table 4.4   Previous sales

Sales	Frequency	P
20	5	0.25
30	10	0.50
40	5	0.25

Then, assuming that recent experience is likely to be repeated in the near future[2] the relative frequency approach can be used to generate the corresponding probability estimates. These probability estimates can be used with Table 4.3 to calculate the expected profit from each alternative action.

Let $E(\pi/x)$ represent the expected profit given action x. Then:

$$E(\pi/20) = (200 \times .25) + (200 \times .5) + (200 \times .25) = 200$$

$$E(\pi/30) = (50 \times .25) + (300 \times .5) + (300 \times .25) = 237.5$$

$$E(\pi/40) = (-100 \times .25) + (150 \times .5) + (400 \times .25) = 150$$

Therefore, to maximise expected profit, stock 30 copies per day, resulting in an average daily profit of 237.5p, which is higher than the expected profit from any alternative action. Note that the actual daily profit can never be 237.5p, but that some days 50p profit will be made and some days 300p profit.

Opportunity loss

We saw earlier that the fact of uncertainty imposes an economic cost on the decision-maker, because different actions would have been taken if the event was known beforehand. Thus decision-making under uncertainty involves opportunity losses. These opportunity losses may be of two types: obsolescence losses when stock exceeds demand, and foregone profit whenever demand exceeds stock. The newspaper stock decision can be made in terms of minimising opportunity losses, with results exactly equivalent to those from maximising expected profit.

In order to minimise the opportunity loss the conditional opportunity loss table must first be calculated. If stock exactly equals demand, then no opportunity loss is incurred. If stock exceeds demand, then each unsold newspaper has an opportunity loss of 15p, whilst if stock is less than demand, each foregone sale represents an opportunity loss of 10p profit. The conditional opportunity loss for the newsboy problem is shown below in Table 4.5.

Table 4.5 Conditional opportunity loss

		Act (Stock)			
		20	30	40	P
Event	20	0	150	300	.25
(Demand)	30	100	0	150	.50
	40	200	100	0	.25

The table can be combined with the probability estimates to calculate the expected opportunity loss from each action.

$$E(OL/20) = (0 \times .25) + (100 \times .50) + (200 \times .25) = 100p$$

$$E(OL/30) = (150 \times .25) + (0 \times .50) + (100 \times .25) = 62.5p$$

$$E(OL/40) = (300 \times .25) + (150 \times .5) + (0 \times .25) = 150p$$

Therefore, to minimise opportunity loss, 30 newspapers should be stocked. The minimum opportunity loss is the profit foregone because of uncertainty, and measures directly the *cost of uncertainty* (since this opportunity loss could be avoided if the event was known beforehand).

The expected value of perfect information

If the newsagent could predict perfectly the level of demand for tomorrow, then all opportunity losses could be avoided. The level of stock would exactly equal the level of demand. Table 4.6 shows the expected daily profit with this perfect information.[3]

Table 4.6

Stock	Profit	Probability	$E(\pi)$
20	200	.25	50
30	300	.50	150
40	400	.25	100
			300p

Given this perfect information, an average daily profit of 300p would be made. In the absence of perfect information, the best we could manage was an average daily profit of 237.5p. Thus the value of the perfect predictive powers, or the Expected Value of Perfect Information (EVPI) is 62.5p per day. Note that the Expected Value of Perfect Information is exactly equal to the minimum opportunity loss or the cost of uncertainty, since all opportunity losses would be avoided with perfect prediction.

The expected value of perfect information sets a *maximum* value on the worth of information. Given that perfect prediction is unusual, a more common problem is to estimate the worth of information that is likely to be valuable but less than perfect. Suppose, for example, the Welsh Business School offered to forecast the level of sales for tomorrow. Using the school's previous forecasts, we estimate that there is an 80 per cent chance that the forecast is correct. Given the three possible outcomes (demand for 20, 30 or 40 newspapers), if the forecast is incorrect then actual demand is equally likely to be either of the other two levels. Then what is the expected value of the forecast, and is it worth paying the 50p per day required for a daily forecast?

To evaluate the forecast it is necessary to consider the expected profit if we act on the forecast, and compare this to the expected profit without the forecast (already determined as 237.5p per day). Table 4.7 shows the conditional outcomes if the actual stock equals the forecast demand, whilst the bracketed numbers are the probabilities of each outcome.

Table 4.7   Act = Forecast

		20	30	40
Event	20	200 (0.8)	50 (0.1)	−100 (0.1)
(Demand)	30	200 (0.1)	300 (0.8)	150 (0.1)
	40	200 (0.1)	300 (0.1)	400 (0.8)

The expected profit for each act can be calculated.

$$E(\pi/20) = (200 \times .8) + (200 \times .1) + (200 \times .1) = 200$$

$$E(\pi/30) = (50 \times .1) + (300 \times .8) + (300 \times .1) = 275$$

$$E(\pi/40) = (-100 \times .1) + (150 \times .1) + (400 \times .8) = 325$$

Thus if the forecast is for a demand of 20, the average daily profit will be 200p, whilst if the forecast is 30, average daily profit will be 275p etc.

Now to find the expected profit after acting on the forecast, we need the probability of each forecast demand. According to our records a demand level of 20 has a probability of 0.25. Taking these *prior* probabilities as the likelihood of each forecast level, the expected profit after acting on the forecasts will be:

$$E(\pi/F) = (200 \times .25) + (275 \times .5) + (325 \times .25)$$

$$= \underline{268.25p}$$

Note that since the forecast is imperfect, this is less than the expected profit given perfect information (previously calculated as 300p). However, the forecasting service reduces the cost of uncertainty to 32.75p/day, and increases the expected profit from before the forecast (237.5p) by 30.75p. Thus the expected value of the forecasting service is 30.75p/day, so that it is not worth paying 50p/day for the forecast.

A digression – other decision criteria

The newsboy problem has been resolved via the estimation of event probabilities. As we saw earlier, in some situations probability estimation can be either impossible (relative frequentist view) or very difficult (subjectivist view). This is especially the case for one-off decisions, where there is neither the guiding hand of experience nor sufficient repetition to allow expected profit to be meaningful. In these circumstances the decision-maker must rely upon some other decision criteria. We shall briefly examine the mechanics and value of four alternative decision criteria, using the conditional profit table from the newsboy example, repeated as Table 4.8 below.

Table 4.8

		Act (Stock)		
		20	30	40
Event	20	200	50	−100
(Demand)	30	200	300	150
	40	200	300	400

(a)   The maximin strategy

This is a very pessimistic approach. For each possible action consider the *worst* that can happen. The worst outcome corresponding to the actions of stocking 20, 30 or 40 are 200, 50 and −100 respectively. Then simply choose the best of these, i.e. stocking 20 with a worst outcome of 200p/day. This is the maximin approach, because it involves selecting the maximum of the column minima. Note that this strategy ignores all outcomes other than the worst for each action.

(b)   The maximax strategy

This is the opposite of maximin, and involves choosing the overall best outcome from the best that can happen with each action. Thus we choose to stock 40, hoping for the daily profit of 400p. This is clearly very optimistic.

(c)   The equal-likelihood principle

In the absence of reliable probability estimates, this approach attaches an equal likelihood to each event. Given the three possible demand levels, each is assigned a probability of 1/3. These probabilities are then used to calculate expected profits, which are then maximised. If the probability of each demand level is 1/3, the expected profits from each action are:

$$E(\pi/20) = 200 \times 1/3 + 200 \times 1/3 + 200 \times 1/3 = 200$$

$$E(\pi/30) = 50 \times 1/3 + 300 \times 1/3 + 300 \times 1/3 = 216.67$$

$$E(\pi/40) = -100 \times 1/3 + 150 \times 1/3 + 400 \times 1/3 = 150$$

To maximise expected profit, the action of stocking 30 is chosen. Note that the assignment of probability is essentially arbitrary, and depends only on the number of events considered.

(d) Minimax regret

This strategy operates on the opportunity loss table (Table 4.5), examining the largest opportunity loss associated with each action and choosing the smallest of these. The largest opportunity losses for the stocking actions of 20, 30 and 40 are 200, 150 and 300 respectively, so that the least of these involves stocking 30 newspapers. Once more the approach is pessimistic, and ignores outcomes other than the worst for each decision.

Attitudes towards risk

We saw above that one of the elements in our decision choice is the attitude towards risk of the decision-maker, i.e. that the decision-maker who enjoys (or can afford) gambling may well choose a different alternative to the cautious decision-maker. Each of the decision criteria outlined above incorporates a particular attitude towards risk, expressed as a degree of optimism or pessimism. We shall see that even the use of expected profit or opportunity loss contains implicit assumptions about risk attitudes.

Consider a simple example. I am to toss a fair coin. If it lands on heads, I will pay you £1, whilst if it lands on tails you pay me £1. The expected value of the gamble is £0 $((\frac{1}{2} \times +£1) + (\frac{1}{2} \times -£1))$, and many readers would be prepared to take part. However, suppose I now change the sum involved to £1000. The expected value remains unchanged at zero, but now you must consider the consequence of losing £1000, and compare this to the pleasure of winning £1000.

The point is that we are no longer thinking in money terms, but of the *utility* of different outcomes. The loss of £1000 would cause considerably more anguish than the gain of £1000 would cause pleasure. Note that there will be some probability of winning £1000 (greater than $\frac{1}{2}$) that would induce you to take part.

The point was well made by Horowitz:[4]

If you and I were to stroll together and simultaneously spot a dime, I might suggest that we flip a coin for it. You provide a penny, toss it in the air; heads you win, tails I win. Most co-strollers would, I imagine, accept this offer. But what would you do if it were a thousand dollar bill? My guess is that you would suggest we split it, or at least accept my suggestion that we split it (unless you are much stronger and faster than I am). If I were particularly strong willed and could make very little use of an extra $500, I might refuse to split it evenly and instead offer you two choices; either we split the money on the basis of $600 for me, $400 for you or we flip for it. If I looked as if I meant it, you might object to the fact that I appear to be unfair and not speak to me thereafter, but I would probably get a goodly share of 600 : 400 splits.

This neatly introduces the concept of a *certainty equivalent*. By accepting the uneven split, you are revealing a preference for the certain $400 rather than the 50/50 chance of winning $1000. Any choice involving uncertainty can be considered as a gamble. The certainty equivalent of a gamble is a certain sum of money such that the decision-maker will be indifferent between the certainty equivalent and the gamble. If you would prefer to toss for the $1000 rather than accept a 601 : 399 split, then the $400 is the certainty equivalent of the 50/50 chance of winning $1000.

The certainty equivalent of any gamble will be subjective rather than objective and is determined by the individual's attitude towards risk. If the certainty equivalent is less than the expected value, then the decision-maker is averse to risk, with the gap between the expected value and certainty equivalent indicating the extent of risk aversion. We can now see that evaluating projects according to their expected profit is only appropriate in the absence of risk aversion, and is in fact equivalent to assuming *risk neutrality*. For many decisions that are repetitive or involve what are viewed as small sums of money, the use of expected profit or cost is quite appropriate. However, if the decision is unique or involves significant money sums, then the decision process must take explicit account of the attitude towards risk.

The decision-maker's attitude towards risk can be expressed, theoretically at least, in terms of the shape of the individual's utility function. A utility function plots the individual's view of the pleasure or pain associated with different money sums. Figure 4.2 shows the utility functions for individuals *A*, *B* and *C*. Individual *A* is neutral towards risk, since his pain or pleasure corresponding to different sums is strictly proportional to those money sums. Individual *B* is risk averse since the loss of a particular amount causes her more anguish than the gain of that amount would cause pleasure. Individual *C* likes taking risks, possibly considering that he has little to lose.

Note that for individual *B*, decisions involving small money sums can be made on the basis of expected profit, since the utility function is approximately linear around the origin.[5]

Despite the homely examples, the analysis of attitudes towards risk has so far been largely theoretical. The enquiring reader is entitled to ask about the practical relevance of this analysis. Clearly the concepts of utility or certainty equivalence can only be of use to the decision-maker if the appropriate functions or values can be

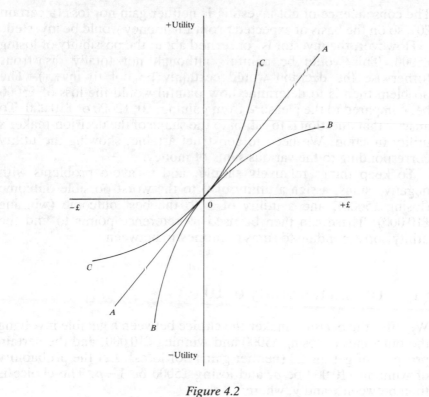

Figure 4.2

found. This is a reasonable question, and deserves the honest answer that in many cases they can't. Below a procedure is outlined to estimate the utility function, but its real value lies in forcing the decision-maker to be consistent and make some allowance for his attitude towards risk, rather than in finding precise utility values for money sums.

Suppose the decision-maker has to determine whether to invest £5000 in a new luxury restaurant, the success of which will depend on the local economic climate in one year's time. If the local economy is depressed, the £5000 will be lost. If there is little change in that climate, the investor will gain £2000, whilst an economic boom would mean £10 000 profit. The choice then depends not only on the probabilities of each event but also on the decision-maker's attitude towards risk. Suppose the probabilities of depression, little change or boom are estimated at 0.2, 0.5 and 0.3 respectively. Then the expected profit from investing is:

$$E(\pi/\text{invest}) = -5000 \times .2 + 2000 \times .5 + 10\,000 \times .3$$

$$= £3000$$

The consequence of not investing is neither gain nor loss (a certain £0), so on the basis of expected profit the money would be invested.

However, the investor is concerned about the possibility of losing £5000. This would be painful, although not totally disastrous (otherwise the decision would certainly be not to invest). The problem then is to determine how painful would the loss of £5000 be, compared to the pleasure from gaining, £0, £2000 or £10 000. To answer that question is to estimate the shape of the decision-maker's utility function. We need to construct a table, showing the utility corresponding to the various sums of money.

To keep things relatively simple, and to avoid problems with negative sums, assign a utility of 0 to the worst possible outcome (losing £5000), and a utility of 1 to the best outcome (winning £10 000). These can then be used as reference points to find the utility corresponding to sums of money in between.

(a)   To find the utility of £0

We offer the decision-maker the choice between a gamble involving the outcomes of losing £5000 and winning £10 000, and the certain prospect of getting £0 (neither gains nor loses). Let the probability of winning £10 000 be p, and losing £5000 be $1-p$. The choice is then between x and y, where:

$x = [(p, +£10\,000), (1-p, -£5000)]$

and $y = £0$

If the decision-maker was risk neutral, he would be indifferent when the expected profits were the same, i.e. when

$$0 = 10\,000p + (1-p)(-5000)$$

$$0 = 10\,000p - 5000 + 5000p$$

$$5000 = 15\,000p$$

$$\underline{p = 1/3}$$

However, given the choice between x and y when $p = 1/3$, the decision-maker chooses y, showing that he is risk averse.

The problem now is to vary p until the decision-maker is indifferent (unable to choose) between x and y.

Suppose $p = .5$, i.e. $x = [(.5, +10\,000), (.5, -5000)]$. The decision-maker still chooses y, preferring the certain £0 to the .5 chance of losing £5000. Consequently, p is increased. When $p = .7$ the decision-maker indicates that he would choose x rather than y. Hence there must be a value of p between .5 and .7 such that the decision-maker is indifferent.

Suppose that when $p = .6$, the investor is unable to choose between x and y. We can then infer that the expected utility of each must be the same. Since the utility of £10 000 has been assigned as 1, and the utility of £-5000 as 0, and at the point of indifference the expected utility of x must equal that of y, then

$$E(Ux) = E(Uy)$$

$$.6U\,£(10\,000) + .4U\,£(-5000) = U(0)$$

$$.6(1) + .4(0) = U(0)$$

$$U(0) = .6$$

On the relative scale between 0 and 1, the utility of £0 must be 0.6.

(b)   To find the utility of £2000

Now offer the choice between:

$x =$ probability p of winning £10 000, probability $1-p$ of losing

   £5000 $= [(p, £10\,000), (1-p, -£5000)]$

and $y =$ certain £2000.

Again vary p until the investor is indifferent. Suppose indifference occurs when $p = 0.8$. Then

$$E(Ux) = E(Uy)$$

$$.8U(10\,000) + .2U(-5000) = U(2000)$$

$$(.8 \times 1) + (.2 \times 0) = U(2000)$$

$$U(2000) = .8$$

The utility function can then be plotted in Figure 4.3.

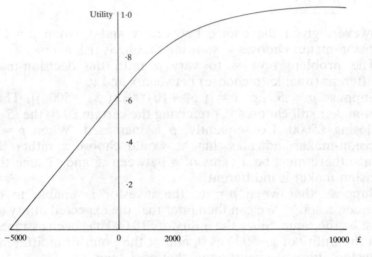

Figure 4.3

Note that Figure 4.3 differs from 4.2 in that negative utilities have been defined away.

We can now return to the investment problem, and make the decision on the basis of expected utility rather than profit, using Figure 4.3.

The consequence of not investing is the certain £0 now given a utility of 0.6. The expected utility of investing is found by replacing the conditional outcomes by their corresponding utilities. Hence,

$$E(U/\text{invest}) = .2U(-5000) + .5U(2000) + .3U(10\,000)$$

$$= .2(0) + .5(.8) + .3(1)$$

$$= .4 + .3$$

$$= \underline{0.7}$$

Therefore, on the basis of expected utility, the decision-maker should invest in the restaurant.

Note that once more certainty has not been introduced with the problem. Rather the procedure has taken explicit account of the attitude towards risk, through a series of hypothetical choice-situations.

Posterior probability analysis

Since uncertainty is the absence of complete decision information, one way to reduce uncertainty is to devote resources to the collection of decision information. Earlier we examined the value of predicted information about chance events, and saw that perfect predictive powers would eliminate the opportunity cost of uncertainty. In the absence of perfect predictive powers, the approach adopted was to estimate the probability of chance events. However, probability estimation is itself fraught with difficulties, and small variations in probability estimates may lead to substantial differences in decision choice. The purpose of this section is to examine a procedure which enables probability estimates to be updated in the light of further information. Since probability estimates are essentially subjective, decision making is likely to be improved by using the best available information in a consistent manner to derive probability estimates.

The Institute of Certifiable Accountants sets resit examinations each November for students failing the July examinations. The Institute is a profit-seeking organisation, which charges a fee to enter its examinations and pays a refund of £20 to each failing student. Previous experience suggests that the proportion of students failing the resit examination has the probability distribution outlined in Table 4.9 below.

Table 4.9

Failure rate	Probability
0.1	0.2
0.2	0.3
0.3	0.3
0.4	0.2

In this particular year, 1000 students have paid to resit the examination. Hence if the failure rate turns out to be 0.1, 100 students can be expected to fail, etc.

We can then find the expected cost of refunds by finding the number of students expected to fail at each failure rate, multiplying each by its corresponding probability to find the overall expected number of failures, which can then be multiplied by the £20 refund.

$$E \text{ (no. of failures)} = (0.1 \times 1000 \times 0.2) + (0.2 \times 1000 \times 0.3) +$$
$$(0.3 \times 1000 \times 0.3) + (0.4 \times 1000 \times 0.2)$$
$$= 20 + 60 + 90 + 80$$
$$= 250$$

$$E \text{ (Cost of failures)} = 250 \times 20 = £5000.$$

The course tutor is confident that if she ran an intensive revision course, at a cost to the Institute of £2000, the failure rate for the examination was sure to be 0.1. On the basis of expected cost, is it worthwhile for the Institute to pay for the course?

Since the expected cost without the course is found above, this must be compared to the expected cost with the course. After the course takes place, the failure rate will be 0.1, resulting in an expected 100 failures, each entitled to a refund of £20. Since the course costs the Institute £2000, the expected cost after the course is:

$$E \text{ (} C/\text{after course)} = \text{Cost of course} + E \text{ (Cost refunds/course)}$$
$$= 2000 + 100 \times 20$$
$$= £4000.$$

On the basis of expected cost, holding the course would save the Institute £1000.

However, the Institute is aware that the failure rate in the resit exams fluctuates from year to year, according to the quality of intake, the toughness of each exam, some random factors, etc. Hence the Institute's Director would like to improve the quality of the probability estimates outlined in the table above. To gather more information he sets a class test for a random sample of five students entered for the resit, designed to be as tough as the resit examination. Of these five students, one fails the class test. The problem is then to use this sample information to update the previous (prior) probability distribution in order to find a posterior probability distribution.

To do this we must first find the chance that for each of the failure rates (0.1, 0.2, 0.3 and 0.4) one student out of five would fail. The chance of one failure in five for a given failure rate is found from the *Binomial Distribution*.

The Binomial Distribution

Suppose an event X can either occur or not occur in a particular experiment, which is repeated n times. Then the probability of a particular number (x) occurrences is given by the Binomial formula –

$$P(X = x) = {}^nC_x p^x(1-p)^{n-x}$$

Where ${}^nC_x$ is the number of ways x items can be combined out of n, calculated as ($n!$ is read as n factorial)

$$^nC_x = \frac{n!}{x!\,(n-x)!}$$

with $n! = n \times (n-1) \times (n-2) \times \ldots (n-(n-1))$

and $0! = 1$

For example, suppose a fair coin is tossed ten times. We seek the probability of achieving just one head in these ten tosses.

Since the coin is fair, $p(H) = \frac{1}{2}$, and the probability of not getting a head is $1 - \frac{1}{2} = \frac{1}{2}$. Hence, in terms of the formula, $x = 1, n = 10$ and $p = \frac{1}{2}$, so that

$$P \text{ (1 head in 10 losses)} = {}^{10}C_1(\tfrac{1}{2})^1(1 - \tfrac{1}{2})^9$$

$$^{10}C_1 = \frac{10!}{1!\,9!} = \frac{10 \times 9 \times 8 \times 7 \times 6 \times 5 \times 4 \times 3 \times 2 \times 1}{1 \times 9 \times 8 \times 7 \times 6 \times 5 \times 4 \times 3 \times 2 \times 1} = 10$$

Therefore, P (1 head in 10) $= 10(\tfrac{1}{2})(\tfrac{1}{2})^9$

$$= 10 \times 0.5 \times 0.001953$$

$$= 0.00977$$

Hence there is less than one chance in 100 that ten tosses of a fair coin would result in just one head. If only one head did occur in ten tosses, it may be advisable to doubt the fairness of the coin being tossed!

Returning to the Institute problem, we seek the chance of one student in five failing the class test for each of the given failure rates. To avoid confusion, call this the likelihood (L).

If the failure rate is 0.1, the likelihood of one student in five failing ($p = 0.1, x = 1, n = 5$), is

$$L = {}^5C_1(0.1)^1(0.9)^4$$

$$= 5 \times 0.1 \times 0.6561$$

$$= 0.3281$$

Similarly,

if f.r. = 0.2,

$$L = {}^5C_1(0.2)^1(0.8)^4$$

$$= 5 \times 0.2 \times 0.4096$$

$$= 0.4096$$

if f.r. = 0.3,

$$L = {}^5C_1(0.3)^1(0.7)^4$$

$$= 5 \times 0.3 \times 0.2401$$

$$= 0.3602$$

if f.r. = 0.4,

$$L = {}^5C_1(0.4)^1(0.6)^4$$

$$= 5 \times 0.4 \times 0.1296$$

$$= \underline{0.2592}$$

These are then the *likelihoods* of the various failure rates, given that one student in five failed the test. Note that these likelihoods by themselves do not define a probability distribution, since they are not coherent (and in fact sum to more than one).

The problem is now to combine these likelihoods with the prior probabilities, in order to derive a posterior probability distribution which takes consistent account of both. This is achieved via *Bayes Theorem.*

Bayes Theorem

Bayes Theorem provides a consistent and relatively simple means of combining probability distributions and likelihoods. Moreover, the theorem is convergent in that if the procedure is repeated over and over for subsequent sample information, the final probability estimates will be the same, irrespective of the initial probability distribution.

The theorem states that the posterior probability of event A (*PoPA*) is:

$$PoPA = \frac{\text{Prior Probability of } A \times \text{Likelihood of } A}{\underset{\text{Overall events}}{\Sigma(\text{Prior probabilities} \times \text{likelihoods})}}$$

In the Institute example, we have the following information:

Failure rate	Prior probability	Likelihood		Posterior probability
F.r.	P.	L.	$P \times L$	PoP
0.1	0.2	0.3281	0.0656	0.1883
0.2	0.3	0.4096	0.1229	0.3528
0.3	0.3	0.3602	0.1081	0.3103
0.4	0.2	0.2592	0.0518	0.1487
			$\Sigma PL = 0.3484$	1.0001

To apply Bayes Theorem, then, for each failure rate multiply the prior probability by the likelihood (to find $P \times L$). Then find the sum of the prior probabilities times likelihoods. Finally, divide each product by the sum of the products, i.e.

$$PoP\,(f.r. = 0.1) = \frac{0.0656}{0.3484} - 0.1883$$

etc.

As a check, the sum of the posterior probabilities should equal 1. Note that the result of one student failing in a sample of five has made the middle failure rates more likely (and failure rates of 0.1 and 0.4 less likely). If no students had failed the sample test, the lower failure rates would have been made more likely.

All that remains is to use this new probability distribution to re-evaluate the decision. The expected cost of running the revision course remains the same at £4000. To find the expected cost without the course, the new expected number of fails must be found.

E (no. of fails)
$$= (0.1 \times 1000 \times 0.1883) + (0.2 \times 1000 \times 0.3528)$$
$$+ (0.3 \times 1000 \times 0.3103) + (0.4 \times 1000 \times 0.1487)$$
$$= 18.83 + 70.56 + 93.09 + 59.48$$
$$= \underline{242}$$

Hence the expected cost without the course is

$242 \times 20 = £4840$

To minimise expected cost, the course will still take place.

Decision trees

A decision tree is a diagrammatic representation of the decision problem, that enables the decision-maker to examine the relationship between sequential decisions. In many cases the decision-tree is just a useful way of describing decision problems. For example, the decision for the investor in the 'Attitudes towards risk' section above, was whether to invest £5000 in a restaurant, the outcome of which depended on the future economic climate. In a decision tree, squares are used for decisions whilst circles denote outcomes.

The problem can be represented by Figure 4.4.

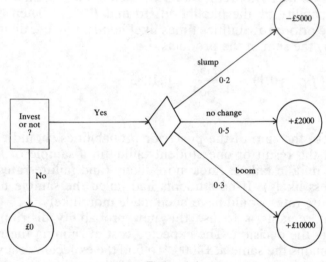

Figure 4.4

The decision tree can then be used to calculate expected returns, or even expected utilities (if the conditional outcomes in money terms are replaced by their corresponding utilities).

However, although the decision tree is a useful descriptive device, its value for decision-making purposes increases considerably when decisions are sequential.

The outcomes shown in Figure 4.4 refer to the net return next year consequent upon different events. Suppose, however, that if a slump occurs next year, the restaurant can be converted into a community centre for £2000, yielding a return of £4000 if the slump continues and losing the £2000 if the slump turns into a boom. Moreover, *given* that there is a slump next year, the chances of a further slump, no change or boom are assessed at 0.4, 0.4 and 0.2 respectively.

However, if the restaurant is extremely successful next year because of a boom, spending a further £5000 could convert it into a country club, offering the prospect of losing the £5000, making an extra profit of £2000 or even £10 000, depending upon whether there is a slump, no change or further boom the year after. Given a boom next year, the chances of a further boom, no change or slump are assessed as 0.4, 0.4 and 0.2.

The investor now faces a two-stage decision process, with further decisions dependent on both the initial choice and outcome. The decision tree can then not only keep track of the options available, it can offer an optimal path through the variety of decision situations.

The decision problem is now represented by Figure 4.5. The problem now is that the decision to invest initially cannot be sensibly made until the decision-maker considers the later decisions. Clearly the option of converting the restaurant to country club does not arise unless the initial decision is to invest. However, although the decision about conversion only occurs after the initial decision, logically it is sensible to consider what the investor would do *if* given the later choice, since the outcome of that decision will affect the viability of the earlier decision. This is the principle of *backwards induction*, whereby the last decision temporally is considered first. Once the decision-maker knows the conversion decision choice, the initial choice can be made in view of the expected later outcomes.

Again, to keep things relatively simple we shall assume the investor is now risk neutral (although note that the methodology remains unchanged if the utility function illustrated in Figure 4.3 is used to replace money sums by their respective utilities). Consider first the conversion decision given an initial slump (see Figure 4.5).

The expected net return from investing the extra £2000 to convert to a community centre is:

E (return/conversion after slump)

$= 0.4(4000) + 0.4(2000) + 0.2(-2000)$

$= £2000$

Hence the decision to maximise expected profit would be to convert to a community centre after an initial slump, reducing the expected initial losses from £5000 to £3000.

The expected return from converting the restaurant to a country club following a boom is:

E (return/conversion after boom)

$= 0.2(-5000) + 0.4(2000) + 0.4(10\ 000)$

$= £3800$

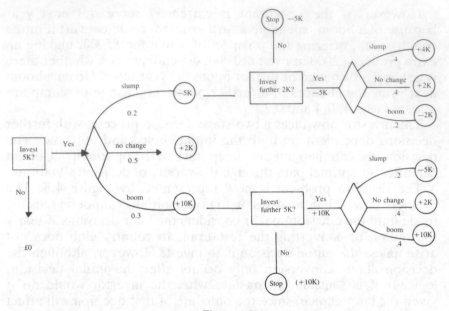

Figure 4.5

Converting the restaurant after an initial boom would add £3800 to the expected profit after the first period of £10 000.

The initial decision can now be reconsidered. The table below sets out the conditional outcomes.

	Don't invest	Initial return	Subsequent expected return	Probability
Boom	0	10 000	3800	0.3
No change	0	2 000	0	0.5
Slump	0	−5 000	+2000	0.2

Expected return/invest = 13 800 × 0.3 + 2000 × 0.5 + −3000 × 0.2
= 4540

The addition of the conversion possibilities has considerably enhanced the expected value of the investment. Moreover, even if a slump occurs in the first year, the chance of recouping at least some of the initial losses is high (0.8), whilst the chance of losing because of a slump followed by a further slump is very low (0.2 × 0.2 = 0.04 or 1 chance in 25). Note that if the expected profit of either conversion option had been negative, the decision tree would have been blocked at that point.

The decision could have been extended to cope with subsequent decisions, posterior probabilities, expected utilities, the time value of money, etc., each at the expense of further complexity. Indeed, because the decision tree approach is logical and sequential, it is highly amenable to computer programing, so that the computer can handle decision trees involving a multiplicity of options and events.

Conclusions

This chapter has examined a variety of techniques for handling the absence of complete decision information. However, it would be a mistake to consider that decision-making under uncertainty can be reduced to a mechanical exercise. The value of decision analysis, like the decision framework outlined in Chapter 1, lies in the way it forces the decision-maker to make assumptions explicit, and approach the decision problem in a systematic manner. A common informational requirement of the approaches outlined in this chapter is the probability estimate. We have seen that probability estimates are essentially subjective. Yet this does not undermine the validity of the decision analytic approach. In considering the choice amongst alternatives, not only do we need to estimate the likely conditional outcomes, we must also estimate how likely these outcomes are. Much intuitive or 'seat of the pants' management involves a decision process, which if made explicit, would be readily recognisable to the reader of this chapter. What we are insisting is that we make that explicit leap and actually formulate the hunches and predictions that allow us to examine the consequence of various scenarios. Only then can we examine the sense or otherwise of those predictions, and consider the consequence of alternatives.

Take a simple example. You have the option to continue into postgraduate education. If you take this route and achieve a higher degree, your lifetime earnings will be £1 000 000, compared to the £750 000 anticipated if you don't take that option. However, if you fail the postgraduate degree, your expected earnings fall to £600 000. Clearly this is an important decision, and rests upon the unknown probability of passing the higher degree. Subjectively you consider your chances of passing are good but not certain.

You could examine your recent and historical performance, seek the guidance of tutors, etc., but the probability estimate ultimately lies with you.

One way to focus on the range of probabilities is to suppose that the expected return from each action was the same. If the probability of success is P, and hence failure $1 - P$, then if:

$$E \text{ (return/postgrad course)} = E \text{ (return/without course)}$$
$$P(1\,000\,000) + (1 - P)(600\,000) = 750\,000$$
$$400\,000\,P = 750\,000 - 600\,000$$
$$P = 15/40$$
$$= 3/8$$

Hence, if you consider the chance of passing the postgraduate exams exceeds 3/8, then the expected return is greatest from taking the course. This is an easier question to answer than asking what is the probability of passing. Of course, we are taking no account of your attitude towards risk!

Application 4

Sainsbury's and a haul of contraband butter[6]

1. Introduction

The application that follows is an example of how a little analysis backed by intuitive reasoning can help the firm to take profitable advantage of unusual circumstances, even in conditions of considerable uncertainty. The description and analysis that follows is a stylised abstraction from the real situation, but serves to illustrate the benefits of the decision analytic approach, even in a climate of little information.

2. Background

J. Sainsbury Ltd were invited to tender for a consignment of butter impounded by HM Customs and Excise. At the time, butter imports were subject to a quota system, and the shipper of this consignment had unsuccessfully attempted to evade customs by packaging butter as sweetfat and including some sweetfat. Both the ratio of butter to sweetfat and the future market prices of sweetfat and butter were unknown. Moreover, Sainsbury's could only guess at the number of competitors submitting tenders, and at what level.

Estimating the consignment value

The true value of the consignment depended on three variables: the butter/sweetfat ratio, and the prices of butter and sweetfat at the time delivery would be made to the successful tenderer.

95

The probability distribution of future buying prices of sweetfat and butter were estimated using market experience, and are shown in Table A4.1.

Table A4.1   Estimated probability distribution of future prices

Butter, £/ton	200	220	240	260	280	300
probability	.05	.10	.10	.20	.50	.05
Sweetfat, £/ton	110	130	150	170	190	210
probability	.05	.40	.20	.20	.10	.05

Estimating the butter/sweetfat ratio was more problematical. Representatives from each company invited to tender were able to inspect a sample of the haul chosen by a Customs officer at random from the deep freeze. Two hundred and fifty cases were withdrawn from the freezer, and Sainsbury's chief buyer was given ten, without choice, to inspect. Of the ten, eight contained butter and two were sweetfat, each of satisfactory quality.

The chief buyer considered that the proportion of butter was unlikely to be below 50 per cent or above 90 per cent because of the risks and rewards involved. Given the sample information, the likelihood of having eight cartons of butter in a sample of ten could be estimated from the Binomial distribution for proportions between these values (Table A4.2). These likelihoods could be converted into a probability distribution by dividing each by the sum of likelihoods. However, the buyer was concerned both by the small size of the sample and its randomness.

Intuitively, the proportion of butter could be estimated by considering the geometry of the ship the consignment came from. It seemed likely that in the hold, butter would be separated from sweetfat, either by placing the sweetfat on pallets above the butter, or by separating the two by having sweetfat on pallets surrounding the butter on all sides, so that cursory inspection would reveal just sweetfat. Given the rough dimensions of the hold, the proportion of butter could be subjectively estimated. Hence the distribution from the Binomial was subjectively adjusted to give the probability distribution used for analysis (column 4, Table A4.2).

Given the prices of butter (b) and sweetfat (s), and the proportion of butter (p), the value of the consignment per ton (v) is:

$$v = pb + (1-p)s$$

Combining Table A4.1 and A4.2, the probability distribution of value per ton could be estimated, resulting in the histogram shown in Figure A4.1.

Table A4.2   Assessing the probability distribution of butter proportion

Likelihood of sample results, given the proportion of butter $p = {}^{10}C_8(p)^8(1-p)^2$

Proportion of butter	Likelihood	P	Estimate used
0.55	.0763	.0521	0.05
0.60	.1209	.0825	0.05
0.65	.1756	.1198	0.05
0.70	.2335	.1593	0.20
0.75	.2816	.1921	0.40
0.80	.3020	.2060	0.20
0.85	.2759	.1882	0.05
	$\Sigma L = 1.4658$		

The marginal cost of stockholding and administration was estimated at £8/ton, leaving a net expected value per ton of:

$$233 - 8 = £225$$

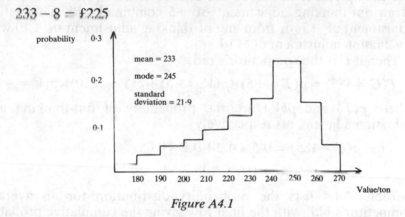

mean = 233
mode = 245
standard deviation = 21·9

Figure A4.1

Source: Bunn and Thomas, 'J. Sainsbury and the Haul of Contraband Butter'.

Competitor behaviour

The final and most complex part of the problem remained – to determine a tender price that took account of competitor behaviour.

In the absence of any information about how other buyers would estimate the value of the consignment, Sainsbury's adopted a symmetry assumption – i.e. that Sainsbury's own estimate of value was their best estimate of how others would estimate its value. Sainsbury's chief buyer anticipated that competitors would expect a 20 per cent profit margin on this sort of business. Then £185/ton seemed a reasonable base point. (Since at £185, the expected profit margin was (225 – 185)/185 = 21.6%.)

However, this base point needed adjustment for two reasons – competitors may have different estimates of value, and they may try to 'out-think' Sainsbury by raising their bids. Then Sainsbury had to estimate a probability distribution for these adjustments – Table A4.3.

Table A4.3

Out-thinking adjustment: Base = 185, probability	+5	+10	+15	+20	
	0.5	0.2	0.2	0.1	
Valuation adjustment: probability	−10	−5	0	+5	+10
	0.05	0.2	0.5	0.2	0.05

Given Table A4.3, and the base point of £185, a probability distribution for the average competitor's bid could be estimated. For example, a competitor's bid of £185 could be the consequence of an out-thinking adjustment of +5 combined with a valuation adjustment of −5, or from an out-thinking adjustment of +10 with a valuation adjustment of −10.

Then if C is the competitor's bid,

$$P(C = 185) = p(T = +5) \times p(V = -5) + p(T = +10) \times p(V = -10)$$

where $p(T)$ and $p(V)$ are the probability of out-thinking and valuation adjustments respectively,

i.e. $p(C = 185) = 0.5 \times 0.2 + 0.2 \times 0.05$

$$= 0.110$$

Table A4.4 lists the probability distribution for an average competitor's bid, with the final row giving the cumulative probability distribution.

Table A4.4   Average competitors bid

$x =$	180	185	190	195	200	205	210	215
Probability	.025	.110	.300	.245	.185	.100	.030	.005
$P(C \leqslant x)$	.025	.135	.435	.680	.865	.965	.995	1.000

Then if Sainsbury's bid £190, the probability that a random competitor bids higher is equal to:

$1 - p(C \leqslant 190)$

$1 - 0.435 = .565$

However, to win the contract Sainsbury's had to outbid all competitors. There was a large number of *potential* competitors, although only about three were expected to make a bid. In these circumstances, the actual number of competitors can be assumed to have a *Poisson*[7] distribution with mean of three.

Then if Sainsbury's made a bid of £x, and *p* is the probability of an average competitor bidding higher, then Sainsbury's probability of winning (outbidding all competitors) is $e^{(-3p)}$. If the expected value of the consignment was £225, a bid of £x leads to an anticipated profit per ton of $225 - x$. Multiplying this by the probability of Sainsbury's' winning gives the expected profit per ton at each bid (Table A4.5). Maximising the expected profit per ton led Sainsbury's to make a bid of £203/ton.

Table A4.5 Expected profit/ton at each bid

Bid £x =	190	195	200	205	210
p	.565	.320	.135	.035	.005
$e^{(-3p)}$	.19	.39	.77	.90	.99
π/ton = 225 − x	35	30	25	20	15
$E(\pi/\text{ton})$	6.6	11.7	19.2	18	14.8

Sainsbury's were awarded the contract, and subsequently realised an actual profit of £40/ton.

Conclusion

This application illustrates a number of points from the chapter, including the use of expected value, the estimation of probabilities and the uncertainty arising from competitors' behaviour. It is a good example of squeezing the maximum of information from the knowledge and experience available, and explicitly using that information to make reasoned judgements. As Bunn and Thomas point out: 'The success of the model in this particular instance is a vindication but not a justification. The essential feature of the analysis is that of providing a "thinking structure" with which the protagonist can build up his subjective probability distribution on competitive strategies.'[8]

CHAPTER 5

Demand theory and estimation

Contents

Introduction

In a commercial environment, the success of the organisation is dependent on its ability to produce the goods customers want, and sell them at a price customers are prepared to pay. A knowledge of the firm's demand conditions is then essential decision information, controlling the decisions of what and how much to produce, as well as the more obvious marketing decisions such as price and advertising. New investment decisions, whether to replace equipment, the quantity of labour to employ, are each related to the anticipated level of sales. It is then vital that the decision-maker understands the relationship between the likely level of sales and the internal and external variables that influence sales. Moreover, any decision involves a comparison of the anticipated costs and benefits of following a particular action. In the business context, the benefits from that action are usually expressed in the form of revenues.

Hence, estimating the future level of sales must play a major role in defining the decision environment.

Thus the analysis of demand for decision-makers is in two parts. The first part is the analysis of the variables that can be expected to influence demand. The second is an examination of how the *precise* relationship between demand and those variables can be estimated in a manner that has operational value for decision-making.

Demand theory

It is not the intention of this chapter to summarise the vast body of knowledge that makes up the economic theory of consumer demand. Our purpose, rather, is to extract those parts of demand theory that can act as guides for commercial decision-making – a much more limited objective.

The starting point for demand theory is an understanding of why consumers buy particular goods. The motivation of individual consumers is a complex psychological matter involving the development of consumer preferences and tastes, habit formation, the desire to conform to social norms, etc. For our purposes it is sufficient to note that goods are purchased for the satisfaction (or utility) they yield, and that the satisfaction from a particular good is generated by the various characteristics of that good.

The principal tool used to analyse demand is the concept of a demand function, written as

$$Da = f(X_1 \ldots X_n)$$

where Da is the demand for good a, f is a general (unspecified) function, and $X_1 \ldots X_n$ are the variables that influence demand. Our first task is to identify the particular variables that influence demand. The problem later will be to transform this general function into a specific one, not only including the variables that influence the demand for a particular good but also measuring the *extent* to which demand is affected.

Given the demand function, the influence of a particular variable upon demand can be measured by the partial derivative,

$$\frac{\delta D}{\delta Xi}$$

If this partial derivative is positive, an increase in Xi will lead to an increase in demand, and conversely for negative partial derivatives.

The demand influencing variable that dominates consumer demand theory is the price of the product. The simplest demand function is

$$D = f(Pa)$$

which can be plotted as the *demand curve*. There is an inverse relationship between demand and price, so that $\delta Da/\delta Pa$ is negative, and the demand curve slopes down from left to right. When the price of a good changes, consumer demand theory points to two effects:

1.   Income effect

When the price of a particular good increases, the real income (measured in terms of how much that real income will purchase) falls. For example, maintaining consumption of the good whose price has risen implies the consumer has less to spend on other goods. Alternatively, maintaining consumption of other goods means the consumer has less to spend on the original good. Hence, when the price of a good rises, the real income of the consumer falls.

2.   The substitution effect

When the price of a particular good changes, then its relative price (compared to other goods) also changes. If the price of the good falls, other goods become relatively more expensive. In terms of opportunity cost, the consumer now has to forgo less of the other goods in order to buy the good whose price has fallen.

The net effect of a change in price is then the sum of the income and substitution effects. The substitution effect always implies that more of a good whose price has fallen will be demanded. The income effect depends upon the nature of the good in question. If the good is *normal*, the increase in real income consequent to a price fall will further increase the demand for that good. However, if the good is *inferior*, the increase in real income following a price fall will lead to a fall in the demand for that good (and an increase in the demand for other normal goods).

Consequently, for a normal good, both effects imply that demand will increase after a price fall, and the demand curve is downward sloping.

For an inferior good, the net result depends on the relative strengths of the income and substitution effects. If the income effect (now reducing demand for the good whose price has fallen) is less than the substitution effect, the demand curve will still slope down.

Only in the unusual case of the income effect outweighing the substitution effect will the demand curve slope upwards.[1]

The above analysis illustrates the fact that the demand for one particular good is not independent of the demands for other goods. When the price of one good changes, the demand for other goods will be affected via both the income and substitution effects.

In the recent past, price has begun to lose its dominant position as the major demand determinant, as evidence mounted that other variables may have an equal or greater effect on demand. In graphical terms, a change in some other variable that affects demand will cause a shift in the demand curve, compared to movement along the demand curve caused by a change in price. Figure 5.1 illustrates the difference, where an increase in price from p_1 to p_2 causes a fall in demand from d_1 to d_2, whilst a change in another variable that increases demand shifts the demand curve to D_2 so that demand is restored to d_1 at the new price. Note that a particular demand curve is drawn on the *ceteris paribus* assumption that all other variables affecting demand remain unchanged.

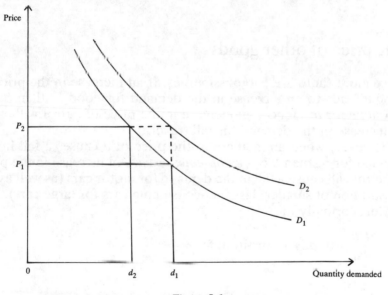

Figure 5.1

Other variables affecting demand

The preceding analysis pointed to the importance of both income and the existence of other goods.

Income

The definitions of normal and inferior goods can be expressed in terms of the partial derivatives. Let Y represent income

If $\dfrac{\delta Da}{\delta Y} > 0$, then a is a normal good

If $\dfrac{\delta Da}{\delta Y} < 0$, b is an inferior good.

In each case, a change in incomes cause a shift in the demand curve.

Inferior goods are usually those for which there are more expensive preferred substitutes. Then an increase in income causes a switch away from the inferior good to its preferred alternative. Typical examples include black and white television sets and down-market motor cars. Note that whilst a particular good may be inferior for a certain consumer, it is possible that the good is normal when demand is aggregated over all consumers.

The price of other goods

Once more there are two possibilities. If an increase in the price of good a leads to an increase in the demand for good b, then b is a *substitute* for a. Hence, an increase in the price of petrol will cause an increase in the demand for rail travel.

However, when an increase in the price of a causes a fall in the demand for b, then b is a *complement* to a. An increase in the price of petrol will cause a fall in the demand for motor cars (as well as the substitution of smaller, less fuel-consuming cars for large cars).

More formally, if

$$\dfrac{\delta Db}{\delta Pa} > 0, \ b \text{ is a substitute for } a$$

and if $\dfrac{\delta Db}{\delta Pa} < 0, \ b$ is a complement to a

Note that neither substitute nor complementary goods need to be directly related in terms of use or characteristics. An increase in the cost of housing may well cause a fall in the demand for motor cars, as each are ultimately substitutes in the competition for family expenditure.

Advertising

The purpose of advertising is to increase demand, either by informing consumers of the existence and characteristics of the good and the seller, or by attempting to change the preferences of the consumer.

Hence we expect that:

$$\frac{\delta Da}{\delta Aa} > 0$$

where Aa is advertising expenditure for good a. Similarly, the advertising of complementary or substitute goods will affect the demand for the initial good, where

$$\frac{\delta Da}{\delta Ab} < 0 \text{ for substitute goods,}$$

and $\dfrac{\delta Da}{\delta Ac} > 0$ for complements.

The nature of the good

Economists make two distinctions between types of goods:

(a) Durables and non-durables

A durable good yields a flow of services or utility over time. The demand for the durable good can be split into two market segments – ownership extension and replacement demand. For example, as the number of households owning telephones reaches saturation level, the marketing approach of the telephone seller has changed to the replacement market. Hence the emphasis of telephone advertising is on convincing the buyer that his present telephone is either functionally inadequate or unfashionable. Because consumption of the durable good occurs over an extended period, consumers are more willing to finance payment over time. Hence the cost and availability of credit is an important demand determinant for items such as houses, cars and washing machines.

For non-durable goods purchase is likely to be repetitive and hence given little thought. Then clever or attractive packaging may be an effective selling strategy to induce impulse buying.

(b)   Consumer and producer goods

Producer goods are those not bought for their intrinsic satisfaction but for the goods or services they help to produce. No one buys a fork-lift truck to polish it on their drive on Sunday mornings, but for the goods or services it can help to produce. Hence the demand for producer goods is a function of the anticipated demand for some other final product. For example, an expected increase in the future demand for houses will increase the current demand for cement mixers.

The general demand function outlined earlier can now be made more specific.

$$Da = f(Pa, Pb, Y, Aa, Ab)$$

Particular goods such as consumer durables may well have other important demand determinants that warrant inclusion. Note also that we are still considering the demands of an individual. The demand function for the firm is found by adding together the individual demand curves of relevant consumers, and may include some potential market size variable. For example, the demand function for this book would include some measure of the total number of students engaged in the study of managerial economics.

Elasticity

Given a particular demand function, the marginal effect of a unit change in one demand influencing variable Xi can be measured by the partial derivative $\delta Da/\delta Xi$. Thus given the simplest linear demand function

$$D = a + bP$$

where a and b are parameters, then a change in price of one unit will affect demand by b units. This is a useful measure of the sensitivity of demand, but is surpassed by a *relative* measure of the responsiveness of demand to a change in one variable, called the *elasticity of demand* with respect to that variable, where

$$\frac{\text{Elasticity of demand}}{\text{with respect to } Xi} = \frac{\text{percentage change in demand}}{\text{percentage change in } Xi}$$

Note that demand elasticity can be positive (when Xi and demand change in the same direction) or negative (when an increase in Xi

causes demand to fall). Note also that when the percentage change in demand is greater than the percentage change in the variable (Xi) demand is said to be *elastic* with respect to Xi, whereas if the demand change is proportionately less than the change in Xi then demand is *inelastic* with respect to Xi.

Suppose that Xi increases from $X1$ to $X2$, and as a consequence demand changes from $D1$ to $D2$. Then the elasticity of demand with respect to $Xi(\varepsilon X_i)$ is:

$$\varepsilon xi = \frac{\dfrac{D2 - D1}{D1} \times 100\%}{\dfrac{X2 - X1}{X1} \times 100\%}$$

if ΔD is the change in demand, and ΔX_i the change in Xi,

$$\varepsilon xi = \frac{\dfrac{\Delta D}{D} \times 100}{\dfrac{\Delta X}{X} \times 100} = \frac{\Delta D}{\Delta Xi} \cdot \frac{Xi}{D}$$

For very small changes in Xi, $\Delta D / \Delta Xi$ will tend towards the partial derivative, so that

$$\varepsilon xi = \frac{\delta D}{\delta Xi} \cdot \frac{Xi}{D}$$

Note that even if $\delta D / \delta Xi$ is constant, the elasticity of demand will vary with Xi/D and also the direction of change.

Elasticity of demand is a completely general concept, which can be applied to any measurable variable that affects demand. Thus, for example, we can estimate the income elasticity of demand or the advertising elasticity of demand, but not the elasticity of demand with respect to changes in tastes, unless those changes in taste can be identified with some measurable variable. The most common elasticity indicator, and one with substantial decision value, is the price elasticity of demand (εp).

Price elasticity

The price elasticity of demand measures the responsiveness of demand to a change in price, where

$$\varepsilon p = \frac{\delta D}{\delta P} \cdot \frac{P}{D}$$

Consider the demand function illustrated in Figure 5.2.

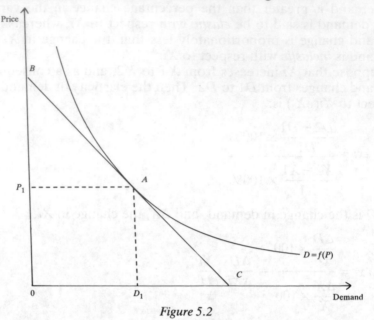

Figure 5.2

Our objective is to find the price elasticity of demand at point A. This can be achieved a number of ways.

(i)   MATHEMATICALLY

Since $\varepsilon p = \dfrac{\delta D}{\delta P} \cdot \dfrac{P}{D}$,

if we know the precise form of the function $D = f(P)$, the elasticity at point A can be found by differentiating the function $f(P)$ and then multiplying the partial derivative by P_1/D_1 to find the *point elasticity* at A.

(ii)   GRAPHICALLY

First find the tangent to the demand function at A, i.e. the line BC. The slope of BC measures $\Delta P/\Delta D$, and at A is equal to AD_1/D_1C. Now the relevant elasticity formula is:

$$\frac{\Delta D}{\Delta P} \cdot \frac{P}{D}$$

The first part of the elasticity formula is the inverse of the slope of BC, and hence equals D_1C/AD_1. At point A, the second part of the elasticity formula (price divided by demand) is $OP_1/OD_1 = AD_1/OD_1$. So at point A,

$$\varepsilon p = \frac{D_1C}{AD_1}\frac{AD_1}{OD_1} = \frac{D_1C}{OD_1}$$

(iii)   BY EXPERIMENT

Both the previous methods have required precise and accurate information. The first method implies that the demand function is known and differentiable, whilst the second requires exact information about where the tangent to the demand curve cuts the quantity axis.

A method of estimating elasticity with rather less information is available. Figure 5.3 repeats the demand function from Figure 5.2.

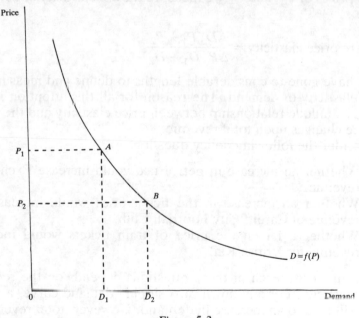

Figure 5.3

Since that price changes slightly to P_2, resulting in the observed demand D_2, at point B.

Recall the elasticity formula:

$$\varepsilon p = \frac{\Delta D}{\Delta P} \cdot \frac{P}{D}$$

Considering the price fall from P_1 to P_2,

$$\varepsilon p = \left(\frac{D_2 - D_1}{P_2 - P_1}\right) \cdot \frac{P_1}{D_1}$$

Since P_1, P_2, D_1 and D_2 are known, the values can be substituted into the formula to find εp_1.

However, consider also the price increase from P_2 to P_1.

$$\text{Now} \quad \varepsilon p = \left(\frac{D_1 - D_2}{P_1 - P_2}\right) \cdot \frac{P_2}{D_2}$$

to find εp_2.

The first half of the formula is equivalent in both cases, but P_1/D_1 is unlikely to equal P_2/D_2. Hence the price elasticity of demand depends not only on the *size* of the price change but also on the *direction* of the price change.

To overcome this problem, when considering the elasticity between prices of P_1, and P_2 we measure the *arc* elasticity of demand, where

$$\text{Arc price elasticity} = \frac{\Delta D \cdot P_1 + P_2}{\Delta P \cdot D_1 + D_2}$$

We have gone to considerable lengths to define and measure the price elasticity of demand. The reason for all this attention is that there is a unique relationship between price elasticity and the effect of price changes upon total revenue.

Consider the following policy questions:

(a) Whether an increase in petrol tax would increase Exchequer revenue.
(b) Whether an increase in the ticket price would increase the revenue of Cardiff City Football Club.
(c) Whether a fall in the price of train tickets would increase revenue for British Rail.

The answer to each of these questions depends on the relevant price elasticity. For any downward sloping demand curve, a fall in price will lead to an increase in demand. However, total revenue to the firm is the product of the price of the good and the quantity sold at that price. By cutting price the firm will increase *sales quantity*, but what happens to *sales revenue* depends on price elasticity. If the proportionate increase in demand is greater than the proportionate fall in price, i.e. if demand is price elastic, total revenue will rise when price falls. Alternatively, if demand is price elastic and price rises, demand will fall by proportionately more than price has risen, and total revenue must fall. Table 5.1 summarises the elasticity, price change and total revenue relationship.

Table 5.1 Elasticity, price change and total revenue

		Price	
		Decrease	*Increase*
Demand is price	*Elastic*	Total revenue increases	Total revenue decreases
	Inelastic	Total revenue decreases	Total revenue increases

Hence the increase in petrol tax will increase Exchequer revenue if demand for petrol is price inelastic. In fact, the price elasticity of demand tells us how marginal revenue is related to price.

Recall that $TR = P \cdot Q$.

and $MR = \dfrac{\delta TR}{\delta Q}$

Using the product rule of differentiation,

$$\frac{\delta TR}{\delta Q} = P \cdot \frac{\delta Q}{\delta Q} + Q \cdot \frac{\delta P}{\delta Q}$$

Therefore, $MR = P + Q \cdot \dfrac{\delta P}{\delta Q}$

Now multiply the top and bottom of the second part by P,

$$MR = P + P \cdot \frac{Q}{P} \cdot \frac{\delta P}{\delta Q}$$

$$= P \left(1 + \frac{Q}{P} \cdot \frac{\delta P}{\delta Q} \right)$$

Price elasticity was defined earlier as $\varepsilon p = \delta Q / \delta P \cdot P / Q$, so the second part of the above equation is just the reciprocal of price elasticity, and

$$MR = P \left(1 + \frac{1}{\varepsilon p} \right)$$

Some behavioural generalisations can be made solely on the basis of price elasticity alone:

1.   If demand is inelastic, it is never profitable to decrease price, since total revenue would fall as quantity (and hence costs), rise.

However, if demand is inelastic, an increase in price would increase total revenue, even though sales (and hence costs) were lower. Hence, the firm can always increase profit by increasing price if demand is price inelastic. Therefore a profit maximising firm will never sell at a price whereby demand is price inelastic.

2.   If demand is elastic, the pricing strategy will depend on costs. A price reduction would increase total revenue, but the extra revenue would need to be compared to the extra costs of producing more. Alternatively, a price fall would decrease total revenue but may be profitable if costs fall at a faster rate than revenue.

3.   If the objective is to maximise sales revenue, this will be achieved by pricing so that demand is neither price elastic nor inelastic – i.e. at the point of *unit elasticity*, where the proportionate change in demand exactly matches the proportionate change in price. Only at this point will it not be possible to increase revenue simply by changing price. Note that if the demand curve is a downward sloping straight line, the point of unit elasticity occurs exactly halfway down the demand curve (since elasticity equals QD/OQ) (Figure 5.4). By the same logic, demand must be price elastic between points B and C (since $QD > OQ$), and inelastic between C and D.

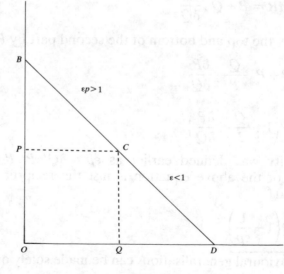

Figure 5.4

Given the importance of price elasticity, it is necessary to examine the factors which influence it. It is clearly in the interests of the profit-seeking firm to attempt to reduce the price elasticity of demand for its products.

Factors affecting price elasticity

1. The price elasticity of demand for a good will be larger, the greater and closer the number of available substitutes. Hence, the demand for salt is less price elastic than the demand for cornflakes since salt has few substitutes whilst cornflakes have many. Generally, a good will have closer substitutes, and hence a higher price elasticity, the more narrowly the good is defined. The demand for fountain pens will be more elastic than the demand for pens, and the demand for Parker fountain pens more elastic still.

2. The price elasticity of demand for a good will be larger, the longer the period of time in which the consumer can adjust to the change in price. Thus an increase in the price of petrol will have little immediate effect on consumption, since many drivers are committed to car journeys in the short term. Over time, however, if the high price persists consumers will begin to adjust their travel patterns, and make longer term decisions (buy smaller car, relocate near railway station) on the basis of the high petrol price.

Table 5.2 reports short and long run price elasticity estimates for a variety of commodity groups in the USA.[2]

In each case, the long run price elasticity exceeds the short run. For household electricity, for example, the dearth of substitutes mean that in the short run a 10 per cent increase in price would only reduce demand by 1.3 per cent. In the long run, however, consumers would switch to other energy sources so that demand would fall by 19 per cent.

Table 5.2 Estimated price elasticities for commodity groups, USA

Commodity group	Short-run elasticity	Long-run elasticity
Cinema tickets	0.87	3.67
China and glassware	1.54	2.55
Tobacco	0.46	1.89
Electricity (household)	0.13	1.89
Local bus transport	0.20	1.20
Stationery	0.47	0.56

Other elasticity measures

Recall that elasticity is a generalised concept, applicable to any measurable variable which influences demand. Table 5.3 defines some other useful demand elasticities.

Table 5.3   Non-price elasticities

		Expected sign
Income (Y) elasticity	$\dfrac{\delta D}{\delta Y} \cdot \dfrac{Y}{D}$	>0, normal goods <0, inferior goods
Cross price elasticity	$\dfrac{\delta Da}{\delta Pb} \cdot \dfrac{Pb}{Da}$	>0, if a, b substitutes <0, if a, b complements
Advertising elasticity	$\dfrac{\delta D}{\delta A} \cdot \dfrac{A}{D}$	>0

In each case demand may be elastic or inelastic with respect to the relevant variable. For example, demand is income elastic if a rise in income leads to a greater proportionate rise in demand. In an economy of rising incomes, it is unfortunate to be producing a good that is either inferior (negative income elasticity) or income inelastic. Houthaker and Taylor[3] estimated that cinema tickets had an income elasticity of 3.41, household electricity 1.94, china and glassware 0.77 and margarine −0.20. Hence a 10 per cent rise in income would lead to a 34 per cent increase in cinema ticket demand, a 19 per cent increase in the demand for household electricity, a 7.7 per cent rise in china and glassware demand, and a 2 per cent fall in the demand for margarine.

The characteristics approach to demand

One useful alternative approach to demand has been to define a product in terms of its characteristics. Then, for example, a motor car embodies characteristics such as comfort, speed, efficiency, safety, etc. Taking the first two, and assuming each to be measurable enables a particular car to be located in characteristics space (Figure 5.5). Model A, therefore, combines C_1 of comfort and S_1 of speed, whilst B has C_2 of comfort and S_2 of speed.

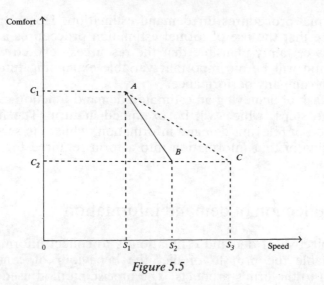

Figure 5.5

Suppose cars A and B are the same price. Then the choice between them will depend on the consumers' preferences for comfort against speed. In theory the consumer can divide his expenditure along budget line AB (so many months of car A, so many of car B). Suppose a new car C is introduced, at the same price, with comfort level C_2 and speed S_3. Then the budget line becomes AC, and car B will never be purchased.

This characteristics space analysis may allow the valuation of particular characteristics. For example, if two houses differ only in their location, any price difference must reflect only the locational difference. Practical problems arise, of course, because most products have a large number of characteristics, most of which can only be subjectively assessed. Nevertheless, characteristics space analysis has an important role in explaining the introduction of slightly differentiated products.

Estimating demand functions

In order to make plans, and to adjust to changes in the economic environment, every business organisation needs to estimate its likely future sales. The form and substance of these estimates varies considerably, according to resources, custom and perceived need. The situation is similar to that concerning decision analysis in Chapter 1. There are many successful and profitable firms that have few formal procedures for demand estimation. However, there is evidence that the use of formal estimation procedures is growing, and it is certainly plausible that the resources devoted to demand estimation will be an important variable explaining future differences in company performance.[4]

The task of achieving an estimated demand function can be split into two steps, which will be examined in turn. The first is the collection of relevant demand information, whilst the second is the processing of that information into a form required for successful forecasting.

The collection of demand information

The objective of demand estimation is to collect information that will enable the firm to predict the behaviour of consumers in relation to the firm's products. The precise method used to collect and process information will depend upon the specific forecasting purpose. For example, the development of a long-term corporate plan covering an entire product range is a very different forecasting exercise from estimating the likely sales of a particular product in a specific location over the next three months. In each case, a decision must be made about the resources to devote to estimation that will reflect the importance of the forecast.

Amongst the methods available to collect demand information for forecasting are interview techniques, market surveys, consumer and market experiments. Each of these will be considered in turn. However, the most important source of demand information, particularly for established products and markets, will be the records of previous sales, both internally generated and available externally, often from government publications.

Interview techniques

Since the purpose is to discover the future buying intentions of consumers, the most obvious approach is to ask them! Consumer interviews can be conducted by the firm, asking present customers about their anticipated future behaviour, or by commissioning one of the many market research organisations to conduct interviews on the firm's behalf, using a sampling strategy that identifies the potential market. Such interviews can enquire not only about anticipated buying, but about reactions to possible price or product changes, reactions to rivals' products, etc. As an example, consumers can be asked to state the current price of the product. The absence of knowledge may suggest that the demand for the product is relatively price inelastic!

The basic problem with all interview approaches is the hypothetical nature of the questions being asked. There may be little reason to suppose that consumers will behave in the manner they suggest, often simply because they may not know their future behaviour, as well as more conscious motives. Consumer interviews may be better at providing qualitative information, about reactions to the product, rather than the hard quantitative data required for concrete estimates.

Market surveys

A refinement of the consumer interview approach is to survey those closest to the market, i.e. the buying staff of major customers or even the firm's own sales staff, on the grounds that these people have the greatest knowledge available.

However, these interviews are once more hypothetical, with the added danger that respondents may have a vested interest in giving particular answers. For example, the firm's own salesforce may have an interest in providing cautious estimates, so that their own performance looks good when estimates come to be reviewed.

Consumer experiments

One answer to the hypothetical nature of most consumer interviews is to replace the hypothetical question with an actual one. For instance, the firm marketing chocolate bars could give a selection of consumers a small sum of money to spend on chocolate, and then monitor subsequent purchases of its own and rivals' products in a particular 'consumer clinic'. The sum of money could then be varied to estimate income elasticity, and prices changed to work out price and cross price elasticities.

However, such experiments are rare for a number of reasons. First and foremost they are expensive to set up and administer, so that sample sizes may be too small to be reliable. Secondly, these experiments are difficult to control as in a laboratory, so that other variables affecting demand (e.g. the weather) may change. Consequently, such consumer experiments tend only to be conducted to help decisions concerning the introduction of new non-durable consumer products.

Market experiments

With this approach the consumer clinic is replaced by the actual market. For example, the firm marketing chocolate bars may sell them at one price in a particular area, and another price in some other area. Alternatively, an advertising campaign may be conducted in one TV region to gauge its effectiveness. Once more the problem is to attribute differences in demand solely to the controlled variable (price or advertising campaign). Again the experiment may be expensive to run, although market experiments may be the only reliable source of demand information for new products, which can be given a 'trial run' in a market segment judged to be representative of the full market.

Statistical demand estimation

The most common source of demand information is the historical record of sales collected by the firm itself. This may be augmented by other internal records (such as price and advertising) and by external records collected by the industry (such as industry sales) or by public bodies (such as consumer income, average prices, etc.). The processing of such information, or that provided by any of the other methods, involves moving from the general demand function

$$Da = f(X1 \ldots Xn)$$

to a specific one including both the variables that influence demand and some measure of how much each variable affects demand.

The problem is then to get from a mass of data information useful for decision-making. Once more the process used will depend on the importance of the forecast, but there are also conceptual difficulties to be overcome. Before attempting such difficulties, the decision-maker must consider which of two alternative approaches is most relevant to the decision problem.

These approaches can be labelled as *explanatory* and *extrapolatory*. With the explanatory approach the intention is to explain variations in demand by reference to the variables (such as price and income) which affect demand. Once a specific demand function has been generated, values of these demand influencing variables need to be estimated before a demand forecast can be made. Then the *sensitivity* of the forecast can be found by varying the *independent* variables to examine their influence on demand. The ultimate reliability of the demand forecast will depend not only on the accuracy of the estimated demand function but also on the accuracy of the explanatory variable estimates.

Using the extrapolatory approach, a *time-series* of data can be used to establish a pattern of demand change over time, which can then be extrapolated into the future to generate forecasts. Since time changes in a regular fashion, once the relationship between demand and time has been estimated there is no uncertainty over the values of the independent variable. However, all the extrapolatory approach can do is to establish a pattern – it offers no explanation of why that pattern occurs, and forecasts based on extrapolation implicitly assume that the established pattern of change will be continued into the future.

Hence the explanatory approach establishes a demand function of the form $Da = f(X1 \ldots Xn)$
whilst the extrapolatory demand function is

$$D = g(t)$$

Note that the two approaches can be combined by the inclusion of a time variable into the explanatory demand function.

Given the provision of sufficient data, the first conceptual problem is to choose the functional form that best fits the available data, and which can be used to make forecasts. Figure 5.6 shows a hypothetical collection of observed data on price and demand.

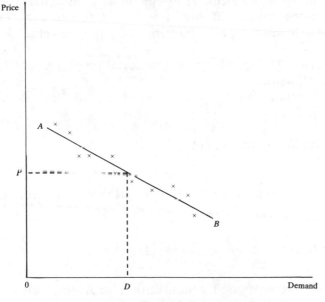

Figure 5.6

Given the observations, there are an infinite number of possible equations defining the relationship between demand and price. Moreover, we know that price is not the only demand determinant – some of the demand variation in Figure 5.6 will have been caused by changes in some other variable. To impose a relationship between demand and price onto these observations is to assume that these other variables affecting demand change in some strictly random manner.

The simplest function form will be the linear demand function,

$$D = a + bP$$

where a is the intercept and b the slope of the demand curve. Fitting this function to the observations involves some explicit definition of what constitutes a 'best-fitting' function, and then using these observations to estimate the values of a and b that satisfy that definition.

The definition of best fit conventionally accepted is that that minimises the sum of squared deviations from the line. Clearly, given the observations in Figure 5.6, no straight line can go exactly through all points. Suppose that the line of best fit is straight line AB, defined as

$$(1) \; \hat{D} = \hat{a} + \hat{b}P$$

where $\hat{a}$ and $\hat{b}$ are the estimated values of a and b corresponding to line AB, and $\hat{D}$ is the estimated demand at a particular price. Then the deviations from that line are the differences between the estimated demand at a particular price ($\hat{D}$) and the actual demand at that price (D).

i.e. $(2) \; e = D - \hat{D}$, where e is the deviation of the actual demand from the estimate.

From equation (2)

$$D = \hat{D} + e$$

Substitution into equation (1),

$$D = \hat{a} + \hat{b}P + e$$

We seek to minimise the sum of squared deviations, summed over all n observations,

i.e. Minimise $\sum_{i=1}^{n} e_i^2 = \sum_{i=1}^{n} (D - \hat{D})^2$

This is an unconstrained minimisation problem, solved by differentiating with respect to a and b, since

$$\sum_{i=1}^{n} e_i^2 = \sum_{i=1}^{n} (D - \hat{a} - \hat{b}P)^2$$

and then setting each partial derivative equal to zero.

The resulting equations are called the normal regression equations, solved for a and b, to give:

(A) $\hat{a} = \bar{D} - \hat{b}\bar{P}$

and (B) $\hat{b} = \dfrac{\Sigma DP - n\bar{D}\bar{P}}{\Sigma P^2 - n\bar{P}^2}$

where $\bar{D}$ is the mean of demand ($\Sigma D/n$) and $\bar{P}$ is the mean of price ($\Sigma P/n$). Equations (A) and (B) can then be used to estimate $\hat{a}$ and $\hat{b}$ for any straight line through a series of observations.

Company X is concerned to estimate the demand for its computer printer for the month of August. The firm's record of demand over the previous six months are listed in the table below.

(1) Month	(2) Demand	(3) t	(4) Dt	(5) t^2
Feb.	25	1	25	1
Mar.	28	2	56	4
Apr	32	3	96	9
May	35	4	140	16
June	42	5	210	25
July	43	6	258	36
Total	$\Sigma D = 205$	$\Sigma t = 21$	$\Sigma D_t = 785$	$\Sigma t^2 = 91$

The company is confident that demand is following a regular pattern over time, and seeks to fit the extrapolatory demand function

$Dt = a + bt$

to this data, and use that to estimate demand for August. The tabulated data are plotted in Figure 5.7.

Equations (A) and (B) enable the data to be transformed into estimates for a and b. First translate the calendar months into linear time by letting February $= 1$, March $= 2$ etc. (column 3).

Then $\bar{D} = 205/6 = 34.17$, and $\bar{t} = 3.5$. Now to apply equation (B), we need ΣD_t and Σt^2, shown in columns 4 and 5.

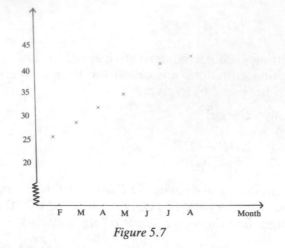

Figure 5.7

Then

$$\hat{b} = \frac{785 - 6(34.17)(3.5)}{91 - 6(3.5)^2}$$

$$= \underline{3.853}$$

and $\hat{a} = 34.17 - 3.853 \times 3.5$

$$= 20.685$$

Hence the estimated equation is

$$Dt = 20.685 + 3.853t$$

For the month of August, $t = 7$ and the estimated demand is:

$$D_7 = 20.685 + 3.853 \times 7$$

$$= \underline{47.656}$$

Note that the estimation of the linear function between demand and time may not be the best method in this case since demand for the printer may be seasonal, or demand may have varied due to exogenous (outside the model) variables. For instance, the large rise in demand between May and June may have been precipitated by a price reduction, or the collapse of a competitor. It is important to adjust the estimate according to the knowledge and experience of the decision-maker.

One measure of the accuracy of the estimated equation is the coefficient of determination (R^2), where

$$R^2 \frac{\Sigma(\hat{D} - \bar{D})^2}{\Sigma(D - \bar{D})^2}$$

Hence R^2 measures the proportion of total variation $(D - \bar{D})$ explained by the estimated equation. As R^2 approaches one, the estimated equation becomes better in terms of explaining (in a statistical sense!) variations in demand. For the example worked above, $R^2 = 0.88$, showing that the fitted equation explains 88 per cent of the variation in demand over the period.

The accuracy of the estimate can often be improved by the inclusion of other demand influencing variables. For example, we may wish to estimate the explanatory function

$$D = a + bP + cY$$

where Y is consumer income. In terms of estimation procedure this presents no particular problem, since the normal regression equations (A) and (B) can be extended to cover two or more independent variables, if at the cost of a little complexity. However, these computational complexities are easily overcome by computer usage, and there is a wide range of statistical packages available (such as SPSS, TSP and SORITEC) capable of performing these calculations in seconds. A more important problem with the inclusion of further variables into the simple straight line is that the estimation procedures assume that these further variables are independent of each other. If this is not the case (for example, if Price and Income are related in some way) the problem of *multicollinearity* arises, and the estimation process is liable to divide the joint effect of the related variables in some arbitrary way. The solution to multicollinearity is to specify the precise form of the relationship between demand influencing variables, and include this in the model.

A related problem occurs when a time variable is included in the estimated equation, or when the data used refer to observations over time. The estimation procedure assumes that deviations from the line in one period are unrelated to deviations in a previous period. When error terms are time-dependent, the problem of *autocorrelation* exists, and the estimates are liable to serious error. If autocorrelation is present, the equation must normally be re-specified by dropping one or more of the present independent variables, or by introducing some variable to account for the pattern of deviations.

Even if these statistical problems can be overcome, the straight line demand function may not be the most appropriate form.

Consider the general straight line function:

$$D = a + bP + cY$$

Specification in these terms is equivalent to assuming that the marginal impact of a change in price is constant (since $\delta D / \delta P = b$), and hence unrelated to either the size of price or the level of income. In terms of the extrapolatory function

$$D = a + bt,$$

this assumes that demand always changes in subsequent periods by the same constant amount.

One alternative is to estimate instead the exponential or logarithmic demand function, such as:

$$D = a \,.\, P^b \,.\, Y^c$$

For example, Richard Stone estimated the demand for beer in the UK to be

$$D = 177.6 \,.\, P^{-1.04} \,.\, Y^{-0.023} R^{0.939}$$

where P = price of beer
$\quad\quad\; Y$ = aggregate real income
$\quad\quad\; R$ = average retail price for all other goods

The exponential demand function has several important advantages. First it is *intrinsically linear*, so that the equation can be estimated by linear regression. This means that the equation can be transformed into the simple straight line, in this case by taking logarithms of both sides, i.e.

$$\log D = \log a + b \log P + c \log Y$$

Then if $D^1 = \log D$ etc.,

$$D^1 = a^1 + bP^1 + CY^1$$

which can be estimated in the usual way. Secondly, the coefficients of the exponential equation have an important interpretation. First, find the partial derivative with respect to price:

$$\frac{\delta D}{\delta P} = b \,.\, (a \,.\, P^{b-1} Y^c)$$

Hence the marginal effect of a change in price is now dependent on the level of P and the level of income.

Now multiply both sides by P/D

$$\frac{\delta D}{\delta P} \,.\, \frac{P}{D} = b(a \,.\, P^{b-1} \,.\, Y^c)\frac{P}{D}$$

$$= \frac{b(a \,.\, P^b \,.\, Y^c)}{D}$$

Now substitute $D = aP^bY^c$

to get $\dfrac{\delta D}{\delta P} \cdot \dfrac{P}{D} = b$

The left-hand side of the equation is, of course, the elasticity of demand. Hence, the coefficients of price and income are estimates of the relevant demand elasticities. Thus, whilst the straight line demand function implicitly assumes the partial derivatives are constant, the exponential function assumes that elasticities are constant. Referring to Stone's demand for beer function, the price elasticity of demand for beer is −1.04, the income elasticity is −0.023 and the cross price elasticity of demand is 0.939. Thus a 10 per cent rise in beer prices would reduce demand by 10.4 per cent (demand is just price elastic), a 10 per cent rise in income would reduce demand by 0.23 per cent (beer is just about an inferior good) and a 10 per cent rise in the price of other goods would increase beer demand by 9.39 per cent, presumably by driving everyone to drink (hence beer is a substitute to other goods).

The identification problem

One serious problem to be overcome in the estimation of an explanatory demand equation is that of identifying the demand function.[5] The difficulty is that *sales* of a product, rather than *demand* are observed at different prices. Now economic theory suggests that sales and prices are simultaneously determined by the interaction of both supply and demand. Hence from a series of price/sales observations, it is impossible to determine whether the estimated equation is the demand curve, or the supply curve, or more likely a combination of both. Figure 5.8 illustrates the point.

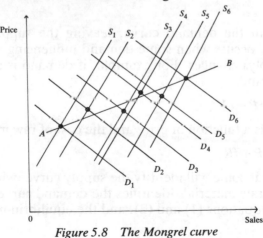

Figure 5.8   The Mongrel curve

Observations of sales and price are plotted, and the line of best fit estimated (AB). Without further information it is impossible to know whether this line is the demand curve or the supply curve, or some mixture. For example, the observations in Figure 5.8 are consistent with the shifting demand curves $D_1 \ldots D_6$, and the shifting supply curves $S_1 \ldots S_6$, so that the line AB is neither a demand nor supply curve, but is a Mongrel curve.

The line of best fit will only identify the demand curve if we know that the supply curve has shifted over the observation period whilst the supply curve has not (Figure 5.9). Equally the supply curve can only be identified if it has stayed constant whilst the demand curve shifts.

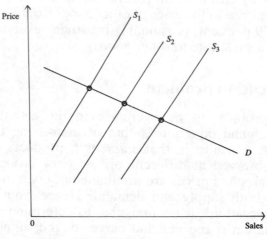

Figure 5.9   *Identifying the demand curve*

Now a shift in the demand curve, leaving the supply curve unchanged, only occurs when some demand influencing variable (not affecting supply) changes. For example, if demand is a function of price and income.

$$D = a + bP + cY \tag{1}$$

whilst supply is a function of price and the cost of raw materials (R).

$$S = d + eP + fR, \tag{2}$$

any change in income will identify the supply curve, whilst a change in the cost of raw materials identifies the demand curve.

Given the equations (1) and (2), and the equilibrium condition.

$$D = S$$

the parameters of (1) and (2) can be estimated by solving (1) and (2) in terms of price and quantity, to get the *reduced form* equations, i.e.

if $S = D$

$$a + bP + cY = d + eP + fR$$

$$bP - eP = d - a + fR - cY$$

$$P = \left(\frac{d-a}{b-e}\right) + \left(\frac{f}{b-e}\right)R - \left(\frac{c}{b-e}\right)Y \qquad (3)$$

Since the bracketed values are constants, equation (3) can be estimated by linear regression.

If the equilibrium quantities are denoted by Q, so that

$$D = S = Q$$

then $Q = a + bP + cY$

and $Q = d + eP + fR$

These two equations can be manipulated to eliminate P to give

$$Q = \left(\frac{ae-db}{e-b}\right) + \left(\frac{ce}{e-b}\right)Y - \left(\frac{fb}{e-b}\right)R, \qquad (4)$$

where once more the bracketed values are constants and can be estimated by linear regression.

Given estimated numbers for the bracketed values, there are then six simultaneous equations which can be solved for the six co-efficients $a \ldots f$. The demand and supply functions (1) and (2) have then been identified and estimated.

Longer term forecasting

Whilst the demand functions estimated earlier are of considerable value for forecasting the potential sales of particular products, the prudent decision-maker is also concerned with the development of a long-term organisational strategy, definable as the task of planning and directing resources to place the organisation in the most advantageous long-run position. Thus the company's long-run plan will include policies for developing new products and markets, acquisitions and mergers and long-term capital investment projects inside the framework of a corporate budget. Given the objective of formulating a corporate planning strategy, the manager will be concerned to look at trends in both the *remote* environment – the set of political, social and demographic factors beyond the influence of the firm, and the *task* environment which is the set of competitive conditions in which the firm operates. Then, for example, the building company will be keen to establish long-term trends in household formation, population growth, household income and all of the other factors which will influence long-run demand for houses, as well as with the more local developments in land availability, operating costs and competitors' actions.

The problem in longer term forecasting is to seek prior indication of changes that affect the demand and supply conditions. There are a number of possible alternatives for seeking longer term information, the choice of which will depend on the particular informational requirements of the firm.

Judgemental forecasts.

The intention of this approach is to establish qualitative and/or quantitative information via a survey of expert opinion – either internal or external to the firm. For example, academic economists are often approached to give their views on likely long-term trends – a rewarding experience in many ways since untoward forecasts can always be blamed on random fluctuations (or government intervention)! One variant of a simple survey of expert opinion is the *Delphi* method, whereby questionnaires are submitted to a group of experts for their views, results analysed and then summaries resubmitted to the same experts requesting that they modify their initial positions or defend them against the weight of average opinion. Thus the Delphi method overcomes the various interdependencies which can occur whenever groups of experts gather to give views.

Leading indicators

Various published economic time-series have been discovered to be reliable indicators of future economic conditions. For example, raw material price changes are a leading indicator for future manufacturing costs, since it takes time for these price changes to work through to manufacturing costs. However, the relationship between leading indicators and other economic variables need not be intuitively obvious – for example, the growth of the money supply is often considered a leading indicator of price changes, despite causal links that appear to surpass human understanding!

Time-series analysis

Once more the intention is to establish a pattern of change over time that can be extrapolated into the future. In addition to the simple linear function considered earlier, the exponential or logistic functions can be estimated to suit particular circumstances, where the functions take the forms:

$$Dt = ab^t$$

or $\dfrac{1}{Dt} = K + ab^t$

with a, b and K as estimated parameters.

These functions are illustrated in Figure 5.10. The exponential function is useful for rapidly expanding markets, whilst the logistic function exhibits the life-cycle of many consumer durable products, with slow initial growth followed by rapid expansion and finally growth tailing off as the market approaches saturation.

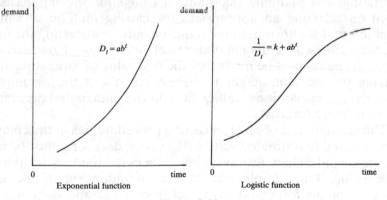

Figure 5.10

In addition to curve-fitting techniques, long-term time-series can be analysed in terms of moving averages or difference equations. The moving average is simply the average observation over a number of periods, used to smooth out short-term variations and establish underlying trends. Difference equations are used when sales in one period are considered to be a function of previous sales, with previous sales given weights that vary with their distance in time from the present.

Econometric models

Econometric models are growing in their importance to longer term forecasting, with one recent US survey finding 90 per cent of sampled corporations subscribing to an external econometric model.[6] Econometric models are systems of simultaneous equations used to represent the real economy, with parameters estimated from economic time-series. The models can then be manipulated to produce forecasts or to examine the impact of exogenous changes. Models vary in their complexity and forecast accuracy, with the largest models using hundreds of simultaneous equations and thousands of explanatory variables, based on powerful computer systems. In the UK, major econometric models are run by the Treasury, the City Business School, the Cambridge Economic Policy Group and others.

Forecast review: summary and conclusions

This chapter has summarised salient points from demand theory and emphasised the importance of demand estimation to successful operating and planning decisions. Throughout the emphasis has been on selecting an appropriate forecasting method to suit the decision-makers informational requirements. Forecasting the future is costly, time-consuming and ultimately unreliable. However, once more the point must be made that the real value of forecasting lies in forcing the decision-maker to be explicit about the assumptions underlying expectations, rather than in the anticipated accuracy of any particular forecast.

The ultimate test of any forecasting procedure lies in the comparison of actual to estimated values. However, decisions must be made before actual values are available, otherwise there is no point in forecasting. One simple way to get an indication of the likely accuracy of any forecast is to extract from the sample data on which the forecast is built a small subsection of data which can then be used to compare forecast with actual values.

For example, suppose the manager has twenty observations on price and demand. First remove every fifth observation. The remaining sixteen observations can then be used to estimate a demand function, the actual prices from the reserved observations can be substituted to generate forecast demands, which are then compared to the actual demands observed at those prices. Thus the forecasting procedure can be evaluated prior to the actual forecast use. The prediction errors from the reserved values are an indication of the accuracy of the forecast method, which can then be adjusted accordingly.

One final point – as elsewhere in this book, techniques have been encountered which give the appearance of sophistication and accuracy. Once again, however, successful forecasting is an art in which the forecasters' experience and judgement need to be combined with forecasting technique. If predictions were easy to make and always reliable, there would be little point in forecasting! The decision analysis of Chapter 4, with regard to the value of further information, can be easily used to demonstrate that inaccurate forecasts may be worse than useless.

Application 5

Chris Patrick, Cardiff Business School, UWIST

Case study: estimating and forecasting demand

Both firms and government bodies at some stage require demand estimates and forecasts in an effort to make optimal economic decisions. These decisions range from topics concerning sales or profit maximisation to government policy designed to promote national welfare and efficient resource allocation within the economy.

There is a wide variety of techniques for estimating and obtaining forecasts of demand. This application will be confined to an example of the econometric estimation of a demand curve and its subsequent use for forecasting purposes, followed by a brief illustration of forecasting using a simple trend equation.

Background

The example chosen here is from a journal article by Fujii[7] in which he estimates the following demand equation for cigarettes in the USA.

$$Q = 2656.1 - 13.677P + 0.271Y + 2.997A$$

$$+ 0.330Q_{-1} + 215.580D1 - 33.986D2 - 139.590D3$$

$$1929-1973$$

where Q = annual per capita cigarette consumption per person over 14;

P = relative cigarette wholesale price index (1967 = 100);

Y = real per capita disposable personal income in 1972 dollars;

132

A = aggregate corporate cigarette advertising expenditure index (1967 = 100)

Q_{-1} = per capita cigarette consumption lagged one year;

$D1$ = dummy variable = 0 for 1929–52;

            = 1 for 1953–73.

$D2$ = dummy variable = 0 for 1929–63;

            = 1 for 1964–73.

$D3$ = dummy variable = 0 for 1929–67;

            = 1 for 1968–73.

The variable Q_{-1} reflects the well-known tendency of cigarette smoking to be habit forming. The dummy variables $(D_1 - D_3)$ capture the influence of various public information campaigns about cigarettes and their effects on health (see Fujii, pp. 479–82). Excluding these dummy variables, all the variable coefficients are of expected sign. For example, an increase in cigarette prices decreases consumption, whilst an increase in income increases consumption.

This equation could now be used to generate forecasts of the demand for cigarettes. For example, suppose we wish to forecast values for Q after 1973. Data for the explanatory variables would have to be substituted into the estimated equation. In order to forecast cigarette consumption for 1974, we would have to calculate the following:

$$Q = 2656.1 - 13.677P_{74} + 0.271Y_{74} + 2.997A_{74}$$
$$+ 0.330Q_{73} + 215.580 - 33.986 - 139.590;$$

where P_{74}, Y_{74}, and A_{74} are the values of price, income and advertising for 1974 and Q_{73} is cigarette consumption for 1973.[8]

The only difficulty in using such an equation for forecasting purposes is in finding the values for the explanatory variables. If one were to estimate an equation using data up to the current period and then wished to calculate forecasts for the next few years it would be necessary to forecast the explanatory variables first. This would add a further source of error to the overall forecast. In this situation, it is easier to use some form of time-series analysis, especially if the main purpose is to obtain forecasts as opposed to finding the determinants of cigarette consumption.

Simple trend estimation

Time-series analysis may take several specific forms, ranging from simple trend equations to more complex forms such as Box–Jenkins type estimation. The following example illustrates the use of a simple trend to obtain forecasts of annual consumer expenditure on alcoholic drink and tobacco in the UK from 1948 to 1984. In this example, two trend equations are estimated using Ordinary Least Squares (OLS):

(i) $Q = 7164.4 + 220.3t$

   (30.33) (20.33)

(ii) $Q = 8788.5 + 5.39t^2$

   (35.98) (13.98)

where Q = annual consumer expenditure on alcoholic drink and tobacco;[9]
         t = time trend (= 0, 1, 2, . . ., 37).

The figures in brackets are the ratio of the estimated coefficient to its standard deviation, which is distributed as 't' and referred to as a t-score. It is therefore possible to conduct a t-test to see whether each coefficient is significantly different from zero in a statistical sense. This test is set up as follows:

Null Hypothesis $H_0 : \beta i = 0$

Alternative Hypothesis $H_A : \beta i \neq 0$

If we are willing to live with a 5 per cent chance of rejecting the null hypothesis when it is in fact true, then the decision rule is as follows:

If t-score 2.042 then *do not* accept H_0
(i.e. Reject H_0 in favour of H_A)
Otherwise, *do not* reject H_0.

Here we can conclude that each of the coefficients in both equations is significantly different from zero.

In order to decide which of the two equations is likely to provide better forecasts, we proceed to compare the mean absolute deviation (MAD), mean square error (MSE) and Theil's U statistic (U) for each equation. These are computed as follows:

$$\text{MAD} = \frac{\Sigma |e_i|}{37} \qquad\qquad \text{MSE} = \frac{\Sigma (e_i)^2}{37}$$

$$U = \frac{\sqrt{\dfrac{1}{37} \Sigma (e_i)^2}}{\sqrt{\dfrac{1}{37} \Sigma \hat{Y}_i^2 + \dfrac{1}{37} \Sigma Y_i^2}}$$

where Y_i = observed value of Y

$\hat{Y}_i$ = predicted value of Y

$e_i = Y_i - \hat{Y}_i$.

The better the equation in terms of its predictive accuracy, the smaller will be the computed value of each statistic.

Table A5.1   Error analysis statistics

	First order trend (Equation 1)	Second order trend (Equation 2)
MAD	509.94	748.50
MSE	468754.50	912072.00
U	0.03	0.04

These statistics suggest that the linear equation provides more accurate predictions within the sample period and hence is the appropriate one of the two to use for generating forecasts.

The forecast for 1985 is as follows:

$$Q_{85} = 7164.4 + 220.3(38)$$

$$= 15536.$$

The 95 per cent prediction interval is 15536 +/− $t_{.025}(7424)$.

That is, we are 95 per cent sure that the true value of consumption of alcoholic drink and tobacco for 1985 lies between 14028 and 17044 million pounds.

Production

Contents

Introduction

The previous chapter took a close look at demand theory and estimation, on the grounds that decision-making requires careful consideration of the likely benefits of any action, usually expressed in terms of revenue. The other side of the decision equation is evaluation of the *costs* of an action, to which the benefits can be compared. It is to the costs that we now turn, using as a starting point the economic analysis of *production*. The primary activity of any commercial organisation is the transformation of inputs into outputs. It is this transformation process that now concerns us. In a general sense 'production includes all economic activity, other than ultimate consumption'.[1]

Thus teaching, writing this book, driving to work, are all production activities involving the transformation of inputs into output, and creating value that will ultimately be reflected in final consumption. However, the analysis will be somewhat simpler if we restrict attention to the production of manufactured goods. Note that the production of physical commodities differs only from the production of services in that produced goods can be stored, whereas services can only be produced at the point and time of sale. Note also that production is the process of transforming physical inputs into physical outputs – production theory deals with the physical volume of inputs and outputs without any mention of money values. It is only later that we shall consider the economic decisions of what to produce or how much, for the moment we are only concerned with the possibilities of how to produce a given output.

The production function

The starting point for the analysis of production is the production function, analogous to the demand function of the previous chapter, where

$$Q = f(X_1, X_2 \ldots X_n)$$

with Q = quantity of output of a particular good and Xi = the quantity of the particular input i used in the production of Q.

Once more the effect of a change in a particular input can be measured by the partial derivative

$$\frac{\delta Q}{\delta Xi} = MPi$$

which can now be labelled as the *marginal product* of the input i, since it shows the effect on output of an extra unit of input i. At the same time, the *average product* of input i can be defined as the ratio of output to that input, so that

$$APi = \frac{Q}{Xi}$$

Moreover, we can also define the output elasticity (ei) with respect to a given input, where:

$$ei = \frac{\% \text{ change in output}}{\% \text{ change in input } i}$$

or $\quad ei = \dfrac{\delta Q}{\delta Xi} \cdot \dfrac{Xi}{Q}$

Thus output can be elastic or inelastic with respect to a particular input, depending on whether the relevant output elasticity is greater or less than one.

Note that since

$$MPi = \frac{\delta Q}{\delta Xi} \text{ and } APi = \frac{Q}{Xi}$$

then $ei = \frac{\delta Q}{\delta Xi} \cdot \frac{Xi}{Q} = MPi \times \frac{1}{APi} = \frac{MPi}{APi}$

So that output elasticity is equal to the ratio of marginal to average products.

Input substitution

For simplicity, assume that output (Q) is produced by combining just two factors of production – capital (K) and labour (L). Then the production function is simply:

$$Q = f(K,L)$$

Once more, the problem is to move from the general unspecified function to a specific one, defining exactly how output is related to the inputs. The shape of this production function will depend on the degree of substitution between the factors, located somewhere within a range from zero to perfect substitution.

Zero substitution

With zero substitution, output can only be increased by increasing the quantity of both inputs by a fixed proportion. For example, suppose that the inputs for bicycle production are frames and wheels. Then each bicycle will require one frame and two wheels – increasing the number of wheels cannot increase bicycle output without a correspondingly proportionate increase in the number of frames. The production function for bicycles is then just a series of vertical lines above the input plane – illustrated in Figure 6.1.

Note that Figure 6.1 uses three dimensions – two inputs and one output. Three dimensional diagrams soon become very complicated, so it is useful to abstract the output dimension, as in Figure 6.2, which shows the same production function as a series of points against the two input axis.

A variation on zero substitution occurs when a product can be made via a limited number of techniques, each of which has zero substitution. For example, with a given area of agricultural land

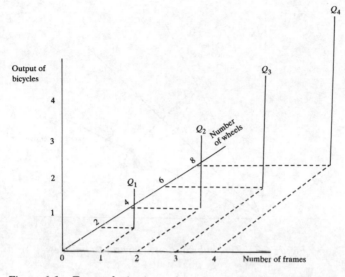

Figure 6.1 Zero substitution – frames and wheels to make bicycles

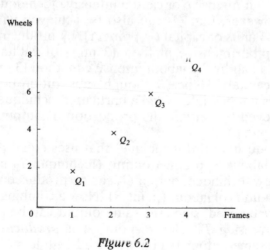

Figure 6.2

potatoes can be grown using either a labour intensive technique (men with spades) or a capital intensive technique (men with tractors). For each technique, increasing the amount of equipment (spades or tractors) will not affect output unless there is the same proportionate increase in labour. The production function is illustrated in Figure 6.3, measuring equipment in terms of its money value (to allow spades and tractors to be shown on the same axis).

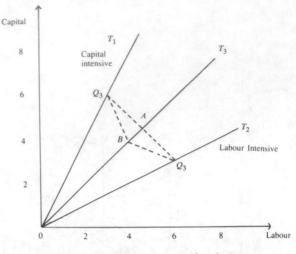

Figure 6.3   Zero substitution – several techniques

From Figure 6.3, output level Q_3 can be achieved with 6 units of labour, 3 of capital or with 6 units of capital and 3 of labour, by using the labour intensive or capital intensive techniques respectively. Note, however, that Q_3 can also be achieved with $4\frac{1}{2}$ units of labour and $4\frac{1}{2}$ units of capital (at point A), by producing a half of Q_3 with the capital intensive method (3 units of capital, $1\frac{1}{2}$ units of labour) and a half by the labour intensive method (3 units of labour, $1\frac{1}{2}$ units of capital). Hence, although substitution between capital and labour is not possible *within* a particular technique, substitution can be achieved by varying the proportion of output produced by each technique.

Now introduce a third technique, that uses equal proportions of capital and labour to product output (technique T_3 in Figure 6.3). Using the new technique, output Q_3 can be produced with 4 units of capital and 4 units of labour (point B). Now a combination of T_1 and T_2 will *never* be used, since the same output can be produced with less input by using T_3. Hence, point A is *productively inefficient* because the same output can be produced with less of each input at point B. The decision-maker must now choose how to produce Q_3 along the lines $Q_3 B Q_3$.

The locus of productivity efficient input combinations to produce a given output level is called an *isoquant*. By productively efficient is meant that same output cannot be produced using less of all inputs, or equivalently that the same inputs cannot be used to produce more output.

Perfect substitution

The other extreme to zero substitution is perfect substitution, whereby output can be produced with all capital, or all labour, or any linear combination in between. Hence, to keep output constant (i.e. to move along the isoquant), capital can be substituted for labour at a constant rate. A family of isoquants with perfect substitution is shown in Figure 6.4.

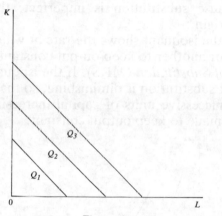

Figure 6.4

Between the extremes of zero and perfect substitution is the case of limited substitution possibilities, with the resultant production function illustrated in Figure 6.5.

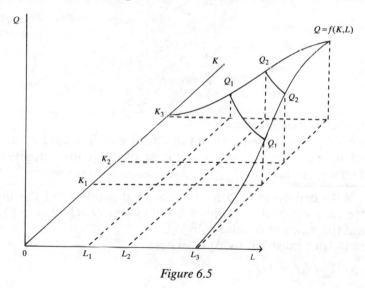

Figure 6.5

In Figure 6.5, output Q_1 can be produced with combinations L_1 K_3, K_1 L_3 or anywhere along curve $Q_1 Q_1$. The family of isoquants is obtained by passing a series of planes, horizontal to the input plane, through the production surface at various heights. Each plane then represents a different output level. In geographical terms, if the production surface is a hill, then the isoquants are the contour lines of that hill with different heights corresponding to different output levels.

The isoquants derived from Figure 6.5 are shown in Figure 6.6. Note that because substitution is imperfect, the isoquants are convex to the origin.[2]

The slope of the isoquant shows the rate at which one factor can be substituted for another to keep output constant and is called the *Marginal Rate of Substitution* (MRS). If the isoquant is convex, the marginal rate of substitution is diminishing, so that, for example, if we take away successive units of capital increasing increments to labour must be made to keep output constant.

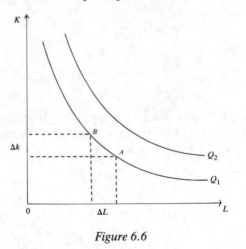

Figure 6.6

Marginal rate of substitution
The MRS_{KL} (marginal rate of substitution capital for labour) is the change in capital necessary to keep output constant, given a unit change in labour.

The MRS can be related to the marginal products of the inputs. Suppose that we start at point A on isoquant Q_1 (Figure 6.6), and decrease the amount of labour by ΔL.

Then output must fall by $\Delta Q1$, where

$$-\Delta Q1 = \Delta L \times MP_L$$

To restore output (get back to the isoquant at point *B*), more capital must be added. If capital increases by *K*, output will increase by ΔQ_2, where

$$\Delta Q2 = \Delta K \times MP_K$$

To keep output constant, the fall in output due to decreasing labour $(-\Delta Q1)$ must be offset by the increase in output due to increasing capital $(\Delta Q2)$ such that

$$-(-\Delta Q_1) = \Delta Q_2$$

i.e. $-(\Delta L \times MP_L) = \Delta K \times MP_K$

or $\dfrac{\Delta L}{\Delta K} = -\dfrac{MP_K}{MP_L}$

Now $\Delta L/\Delta K$, keeping output constant, is just the inverse of the slope of the isoquant in Figure 6.6 (the marginal rate of substitution).

i.e. $MRS_{KL} = \dfrac{\Delta K}{\Delta L} = \dfrac{1}{\Delta L/\Delta K} = -\dfrac{MP_L}{MP_K}$

Hence the marginal rate of substitution is equal to the ratio of marginal products of the factors.

Efficient production

We have so far only considered the technical possibilities for input substitution, described by the isoquant corresponding to a particular output level. Given that a particular output level has been judged desirable, the problem is now *how* to produce that output level, i.e. to choose a particular point along the isoquant. Hence, we seek the optimal input combination to produce a given output level. The choice will, of course, depend on the definition of optimal. The profit-maximising objective implies that a given output level must be produced at *least* possible cost. Note, however, that the logical link does *not* run both ways – minimising the cost of producing a particular output level does not imply profit maximisation: such behaviour is consistent with a range of possible objectives.

The costs to be minimised are usually expressed in money terms. Hence money is introduced into the analysis, via the prices of the input. If labour is relatively expensive, the least cost output combination is likely to involve a capital intensive production method, and conversely if labour is relatively cheap. The optimal input combination will then depend on two things:

— the relative prices of the factors
— the technical substitution possibilities.

Technical substitution possibilities are described by the isoquant, showing the productively efficient input combinations to produce a given output. The relative prices of the factors can be described by the budget line or *isocost* curve, showing the input combinations that can be purchased with a given amount of money.

Suppose, in our two input case, capital has a cost per unit of £r, whilst labour has a cost per unit equal to £w. Further suppose that the firm has a budget of £m to spend on inputs. If all £m was spent on capital, m/r units would be bought, whilst if all £m was spent on labour, m/w units would be purchased. Moreover, given that the prices of capital and labour are fixed, any linear combination of inputs between these two points can be purchased. Hence these two points describe the intercepts of the isocost line corresponding to £m at those prices, drawn in Figure 6.7.

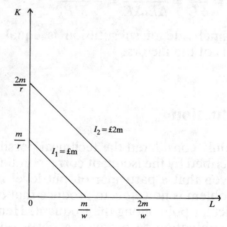

Figure 6.7   The isocost corresponding to £m, $P_L = W$, $P_K = r$

The *location* of the isocost depends on the amount of money being spent. An increase in expenditure to £2m would move the isocost out parallel to itself, to I_2. The *slope* of the isocost depends on the relative prices of the factors or the *factor price ratio*. If the price of labour increased to w^1 spending £m on labour would result in less labour being bought $(m)/w^1$, and the isocost line has become steeper.

The determination of the optimal input combination is now the simple matter of putting the isocost and isoquant together. To produce the given output at least cost, the isocost is pushed inwards as far as possible (reducing expenditure), consistent with still being able to produce the given output. Thus the optimal input combination occurs when the isocost is tangental to the isoquant. Further expenditure reductions would prevent the attainment of the given output (Figure 6.8).

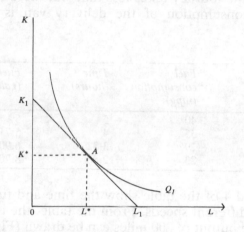

Figure 6.8   Optimal input combinations

In Figure 6.8, the least cost method of producing Q_1 is with K^* of capital and L^* of labour. At point A the slope of the isoquant (MRS) is equal to the slope of the isocost (factor price ratio), i.e.

$$MRS_{KL} = -\frac{P_L}{P_K}$$

Now the slope of the isoquant is also equal to the ratio of marginal products, so that, at the optimum

$$-\frac{MP_L}{MP_K} = MRS_{KL} = -\frac{P_L}{P_K}$$

or $$\frac{MP_L}{P_L} = \frac{MP_K}{P_K}$$

At the optimum, the last £1 spent on labour adds as much to total output as the last £1 spent on capital. Any input combination violating this rule must be suboptimal, since a change in input proportions could then lead to producing the same output at lower cost.

Efficient production: an example

A component manufacturer is contracted to make weekly deliveries
of the component to a car assembly plant 100 miles away. Delivery
of the components is subcontracted to a local haulier, at a price
determined by the time and fuel used. Time and fuel are substitut-
able inputs in the production of output (delivery mileage). By
driving faster the journey takes less time but more fuel. The speed
related fuel consumption of the delivery van is shown in the
following table.

Speed (mph)	Fuel consumption (mpg)	Time (hours)	Fuel (gallons)
40	40	5	5
50	35	4	5.71
60	29	3.33	6.90
70	23	2.86	8.70

Columns 3 and 4 of the table show the time and fuel used for the
round trip at different speeds. From the table, the isoquant corresponding to the output of 200 miles can be drawn (Figure 6.9).

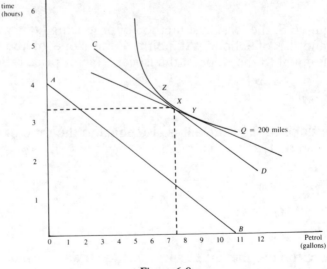

Figure 6.9

Suppose the price of fuel is £2 per gallon, whilst the cost of driver
time is £5 per hour. Then a trade-off must be made between speed

and fuel. Note that loading and unloading time remains the same whatever the journey speed, and need not enter the speed decision.

At the relative prices given, the isocost line can be located by choosing an arbitary expenditure. If expenditure is £20, the isocost is located at line *AB* in Figure 6.9. The journey cannot be achieved at this cost level, so expenditure must be increased, moving the isocost line outwards parallel to itself. The least cost position occurs at the point of tangency *X*, with isocost line *CD*. At point *X*, 6.9 gallons of fuel and 3.33 hours or driver time are used, resulting in a least cost of £30.45 (and a speed of 60 mph).

Suppose now that the cost of driver time increases to £7 per hour. The isocost line becomes less steep, resulting in the tangency point *Y*, with a minimum journey cost of £38.85 and an average speed of 200/3.15 = 63.5 mph.

To solve this problem we have made a number of simplifying assumptions. In particular, we have assumed no constraints such as traffic jams and speed limits. The imposition of a 50 mph speed limit on delivery vans would move the input combination to point *Z*, resulting in a total cost of four hours driver time at £7 per hour plus 5.7 gallons of fuel at £2 per gallon equals £39.40. Hence the imposition of the speed limit would increase cost by £0.55 or approximately $1\frac{1}{2}$ per cent.

Efficient production – an alternative derivation

The optimal input combination can also be found as the solution to a constrained optimisation problem (Chapter 2). Let x_i be the quantity of input i, p_i be the corresponding price per unit of input i, and Q be the desired output.

Then total cost is just the sum of expenditures on each input:

$$TC = p_1 x_1 + p_2 x_2 + \ldots + p_n x_n = \sum_{i=1}^{n} p_i x_i$$

The problem is then to minimise total cost, subject to the output constraint, i.e.

$$\text{Min } TC = \sum_{i=1}^{n} p_i x_i$$

$$\text{s.t. } Q = f(x_1, x_2 \ldots x_n)$$

This is a constrained minimisation problem solved by the method of Lagrange multipliers. First set the constraint in its implicit form, i.e.

$$Q - f(x_1, x_2 \ldots x_n) = 0$$

Then multiply the implicit constraint by an artificial variable (λ) and add to the objective function to form the Lagrangean function (L), where

$$L = \Sigma p_i x_i + \lambda(Q - f(x_1, x_2 \ldots x_n))$$

Then find the partial derivatives with respect to $x_1, x_2 \ldots x_n$ and λ, set equal to zero and solve.

$$\frac{\delta L}{\delta x_1} = p_1 - \lambda \frac{\delta f}{\delta x_1} = 0$$

$$\frac{\delta L}{\delta x_i} = p_i - \lambda \frac{\delta f}{\delta x_i} = 0$$

and $\dfrac{\delta L}{\delta \lambda} = Q - f(x_1, x_2 \ldots x_n) = 0$

Taking the general case,

$$p_i - \lambda \frac{\delta f}{\delta x_i} = 0$$

Now $\dfrac{\delta f}{\delta x_i} = MPi$ (marginal product of i)

so $p_i - \lambda . MPi = 0$

$$P_i = \lambda . MPi$$

and $\dfrac{MPi}{p_i} = \dfrac{1}{\lambda}$

Now λ (and hence $1/\lambda$) is the same for all n inputs, hence

$$\frac{MPi}{p_i} = \frac{MPj}{p_j}$$

and the ratio of marginal product to price must be the same for each input.

Production in the short run

We saw earlier that economists distinguish between the short- and long-run time periods in terms of adjustment to change. In the short run, adjustment to change is only partial, whilst the long run allows total adjustment to change. Within the context of production, a short-run period is one in which at least one of the inputs is fixed. Factor fixity occurs because of physical obstacles to change (e.g. the time taken to build a new factory) or because of contractual obligations (such as employment contracts). In each case factor fixity occurs not because it is impossible to change the quantity of a factor, but because it may be inordinately expensive to do so.

In the two input case, the fixity of one factor implics that output can only be changed by varying the quantity of the non-fixed (variable) factor. The question is then *how* does output change when the variable factor changes. Clearly in the case of zero substitution, output cannot change at all. With perfect substitution, output changes in proportion to the change in the variable factor. With the more interesting case of limited substitution possibilities, the answer is given by the *law of diminishing returns*. If the amount of capital is fixed, adding more and more labour to that capital will lead to increases in output. According to the law of diminishing returns, there is a point at which the increases in output, corresponding to successive additional units of labour, will start to fall. Returning to the agricultural example, with a given amount of land and a given number of spades, the addition of a few units of labour will lead to large increases in potato output. As more labour is added, the spades can be used more intensively (e.g. a shift system). However, continuing additions to labour start to get in each other's way, so that the increase in output starts to tail off, and may even reach zero.

The law of diminishing returns
As more of the variable factor is added to the fixed factor, the marginal product of the variable factor will eventually fall.

The production function for potatoes, for a given number of spades, is shown in Figure 6.10, together with the corresponding marginal and average product of labour curves.
Note that:

(i) total output can only be increased by increasing the number of men;

(ii) average product is at a maximum when the marginal product equals the average product (and the tangent slope in the upper diagram coincides with the line from the origin to the curve);

(iii) the total, marginal and average product of labour curves are drawn on the assumption of a particular fixed amount of the other factor. A different fixed amount of capital would result in differing product curves for labour.

(iv)   if $Q = f(L)$

$$MP_L = \frac{\delta Q}{\delta L}$$

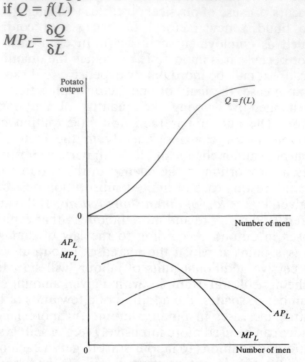

Figure 6.10   The short-run production function

Increases in labour increases output, so $\delta Q/\delta L > 0$, but the law of diminishing returns implies that $\delta^2 Q/\delta L^2 < 0$ (i.e. the marginal product of labour falls).

The way that output changes in response to changes in the variable factor defines the returns to that factor. If the marginal product of labour increases with the quantity of labour, then the returns to labour are increasing ($\delta^2 Q/\delta L^2 > 0$). The law of diminishing returns implies that returns to the factor must ultimately diminish.

Production in the long run

Since the long run is a period of complete adjustment to change, in the long run all factors are variable. The firm cannot only choose the optimal input combination, it can also determine the optimum scale of operations, i.e. not only the factor combination for a given output level but also the scale of that output level. Large-scale production is achieved by increasing the quantities of all inputs, and brings with it particular production advantages and disadvantages. With large-scale production inputs can become specialised (and hence more productive) by concentrating on just one stage of the production process. For example, the small printing firm needs general printing equipment which can be used for a variety of printing tasks, whilst the large printing firm can have special printing machines devoted to printing business cards, letterheads, etc. The specialised machinery can then produce the output with less inputs per unit of output, i.e. be more productively efficient. However, large-scale production may bring its own disadvantages, in terms of the loss of managerial control, or the 'dehumanisation' of labour that may increase the incidence of labour disputes. The point is that the *nature* of production changes as the *scale* of production changes.

The effect of scale changes is reflected in the nature of *Returns to Scale*. Recall that returns to a factor were measured in terms of the effect on output of changing just that input, keeping other inputs constant. Returns to scale are measured by examining the effect on output of changing *all* inputs in the same proportion. For example, suppose that all inputs increase by the proportion α. If output increases by more than α, there are *increasing returns to scale*. If output increases by less than α, *returns to scale are decreasing*.

Finally if a proportionate change in all inputs leads to the same proportionate change in output, returns to scale are constant.

Returns to scale
Returns to scale measure the empirical relationship between changes in *all* inputs and changes in output. If output changes at a faster rate than inputs, returns to scale are increasing. If output changes at a slower rate than inputs, returns to scale are decreasing. Finally, if output changes at the same rate as output, returns to scale are constant.

Consider the production function;

$$Q = 5L^2 + 4K^2 + 2LK$$

To examine the nature of returns to scale, multiply each input (K and L) by a constant proportion (α). Let the new output level be Q^1.

Then $Q^1 = 5(\alpha L)^2 + 4(\alpha K)^2 + 2(\alpha L)(\alpha K)$

$\qquad = 5\alpha^2 L^2 + 4\alpha^2 K^2 + 2\alpha^2 LK$

$\qquad = \alpha^2(5L^2 + 4K^2 + 2LK)$

$\qquad = \alpha^2 Q$

Hence, if $\alpha = 2$, doubling all inputs will lead to four (α^2) times the initial output, and returns to scale are increasing.

Whilst the reasons for returns to scale were briefly touched on earlier, the nature of returns to scale is essentially an empirical matter of the actual relationship between inputs and output.

Returns to scale and input elasticities

We have $X = f(K, L)$

and $\varepsilon L = \dfrac{\delta X}{\delta L} \cdot \dfrac{L}{X} = \dfrac{MP_L}{AP_L} \qquad \varepsilon K = \dfrac{\delta X}{\delta K} \cdot \dfrac{L}{K} = \dfrac{MP_K}{AP_K}$

Returns to scale can be measured by the total output elasticity (ε) or the percentage change in output divided by the percentage change in *all* inputs. Suppose both inputs change by a small amount (ΔK and ΔL). Then output must change according to the marginal products of the inputs, i.e.

$\qquad \Delta X = \Delta K \cdot MP_K + \Delta L \cdot MP_L$

Now multiply the first term by K/K, and the second by L/L

Then $\Delta X = K\dfrac{\Delta K}{K} \cdot MP_K + L \cdot \dfrac{\Delta L}{L} \cdot MP_L$

Divide throughout by X,

$\qquad \dfrac{\Delta X}{X} = \dfrac{\Delta K}{K} \cdot \dfrac{K}{X} \cdot MP_K + \dfrac{\Delta L}{L} \cdot \dfrac{L}{X} \cdot MP_L$

Since $\dfrac{K}{X} = \dfrac{1}{AP_K}$, and $\dfrac{MP_K}{AP_K} = \varepsilon K$

then $\dfrac{\Delta X}{X} = \dfrac{\Delta K}{K} \cdot \varepsilon K + \dfrac{\Delta L}{L} \varepsilon L$

The proportionate change in output depends on the proportionate change in inputs and the elasticity of output with respect to each input.

Now assume both inputs change by the same proportion, so that

$$\frac{\Delta K}{K} \times 100\% = \frac{\Delta L}{L} \times 100\% = \text{say } \beta\%$$

Then $\dfrac{\Delta X}{X} \times 100\% = \beta\varepsilon K + \beta\varepsilon L$

$$\text{and } \frac{\dfrac{\Delta X}{X} \times 100\% = \varepsilon K + \varepsilon L}{\beta}$$

The left-hand side of this equation is just the percentage change in output divided by the percentage change in inputs, or the output elasticity (ε).

i.e. $\varepsilon = \varepsilon K + \varepsilon L$

The total output elasticity is the sum of the output elasticities with respect to each input. Note that if $\varepsilon > 1$, returns to scale are increasing, and if $\varepsilon < 1$, returns to scale are decreasing.

Empirical production functions

The estimation of an empirical production function is an attempt to relate the actual quantity of output to the actual input levels used to produce that output, and is fraught with similar difficulties to those encountered in the estimation of demand curves in the previous chapter. In addition, there are particular problems with the implicit assumption of productive efficiency, and special difficulties in the quantification of capital inputs. However, despite these difficulties, empirical production functions have been estimated for a variety of industries. The functional form commonly adopted is the Cobb–Douglas production function, whereby

$Q = aK^bL^c$ (note the similarity to the exponential demand function)

The Cobb–Douglas function has been chosen for a variety of empirical and analytical reasons. Most obviously, the Cobb–Douglas production function is intrinsically linear, so that the parameters a, b and c can be estimated by linear regression. In addition, the Cobb–Douglas function has a number of interpretative properties listed below.

(i) The marginal product of each factor is equal to the factor exponent times its average product.

For example,

$$MP_K = \frac{\delta Q}{\delta K} = b \cdot a \cdot K^{b-1} L^c$$

$$= b(a \cdot K^b L^c) K^{-1}$$

$$= b \cdot \frac{(Q)}{K}$$

$$MP_K = b \cdot AP_k$$

(ii) The marginal rate of substitution (slope of the isoquant) is equal to the ratio of the exponents times the factor utilisation ratio.

$$\text{e.g. } MRS_{KL} = \frac{\delta Q/\delta K}{\delta Q/\delta L} = \frac{b\left(\dfrac{Q}{K}\right)}{c\left(\dfrac{Q}{L}\right)} = \frac{b}{c} \cdot \frac{L}{K}$$

(iii) The output elasticity with respect to any input is equal to the exponent of that input.

Recall that $\varepsilon K = \dfrac{\delta Q}{\delta K} \cdot \dfrac{K}{Q}$

Now $\dfrac{\delta Q}{\delta K} = MP_K = b \dfrac{Q}{K}$

So $\varepsilon K = b \cdot \dfrac{Q}{K} \cdot \dfrac{K}{Q}$

$$= b$$

Similarly, $\varepsilon L = C$

Finally, (iv) The nature of returns to scale is measured by the sum of the exponents, i.e.

if $b + c > 1$,   Returns to Scale are Increasing
  $b + c < 1$,   Returns to Scale are Decreasing
  $b + c = 1$,   Returns to Scale are Constant.

Let each output be multiplied by the constant proportion α. The new output (Q^1), will be

$$Q^1 = a(\alpha K)^b(\alpha L)^c$$
$$= \alpha^b \alpha^c a K^b L^c$$
$$= \alpha^{b+c}(Q)$$

Hence if $b+c>1$, output increases at a faster rate than the inputs.

An example of an empirical Cobb–Douglas production function is considered in the Application at the end of this chapter. In a more general analysis, Moroney (1967) estimated Cobb–Douglas exponents for a variety of US manufacturing industries (Table 6.1).

Table 6.1 Estimated Cobb–Douglas exponents for selected US industries
$(Q = a . K^b L^c)$

Industry	Capital (b)	Labour (c)
Chemicals	0.20	0.89
Printing	0.46	0.62
Electrical Machinery	0.37	0.66
Textiles	0.12	0.88
Petroleum	0.31	0.64

Source: J. Moroney (1967), 'Cobb–Douglas Production Functions and Returns to Scale in US Manufacturing Industry', *Western Economic Journal*, December pp. 39–51.

According to Table 6.1, in the chemical industry the output elasticity of capital is 0.20, and of labour 0.89. Hence a 10 per cent increase in labour would lead to an 8.9 per cent increase in output. Note that since the sum of exponents is greater than one, returns to scale are increasing (and a 10 per cent increase in each input would lead to a 10.9 per cent rise in chemical output). Further down the table, however, returns to scale in the petroleum industry are decreasing.

Linear production technology

Recall the case of zero substitution possibility within a particular production process but with a number of possible production processes. Figure 6.11 below is a repeat of Figure 6.3.

We noted earlier that the isoquant for the output level Q_3 was the dashed line $Q_3 B Q_3$. We can now make several additional comments.

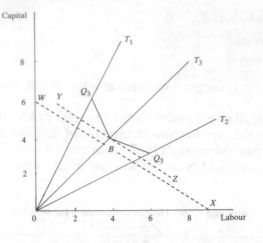

Figure 6.11

(i)   Along each productive process line, returns to scale are constant. For example, along T_1, a doubling of each input will always lead to a doubling of output.

(ii)   If there is just one productive process, there is no production decision to be made. For example, if T_3 was the only process available, the optimal input combination to produce Q_3 would always be at B. Whatever the relative prices of the inputs, the least cost method of producing Q_3 would be where the isocost line passes through point B.

(iii)   With a number of zero substitution production processes, the least cost input combination will always require that just one process is used. Whatever the slope of the isocost (relative price ratio of the factors) the tangency of the isocost line to the isoquant Q_3BQ_3 must always occur at a corner of the isoquant.[3]

What we are leading up to is that cost minimisation with a number of zero substitution production techniques is in fact a *linear programming* problem, whereby the input requirements of a particular production process to produce a given output define the linear constraints, whilst the prices of the inputs define the objective function to be minimised.

Referring back to Figure 6.11, suppose that the objective is to produce Q_3 at minimum cost, whilst the price of capital is £3 per unit and the price of labour is £2 per unit. These prices define the slope of the isocost (or objective function). Proceeding as in Chapter 2, we choose an arbitary amount of expenditure to locate the isocost curve. For example, suppose expenditure was £18. If this was all spent on capital 6 units could be bought, whilst spending it all on labour would purchase 9 units of labour. These two points define the intercepts for the isocost line *WX* in Figure 6.11, corresponding to £18 expenditure. It is clear that output level Q_3 cannot be achieved at that cost level, and expenditure must be increased, moving the isocost line outwards parallel to itself, until it just touches the isoquant at point *B* (line *YZ*). Hence to produce Q_3 at minimum cost, the optimal input combination is 4 units of capital and 4 units of labour, with a minimum total cost of £20.

More complex cost minimisation problems with linear technology involving a greater number of inputs can be solved by the sort of computer software package illustrated in Chapter 2. Such programs have the added advantage of computing a shadow price for each input which shows the value to the decision maker of having more of each input available.

Application 6

The flow of oil

The flow of oil of a given density and viscosity through a pipeline is a function of two variables – the internal diameter of the pipeline and the hydraulic horsepower used to pump the oil. In 1975, Pearl and Enos[4] estimated the Cobb–Douglas production function to be:

$$Q = 24.95 \times H^{0.36} \times D^{1.72}$$

where Q = flow of oil in barrels per day
H = hydraulic horsepower
D = internal pipe diameter in inches

This equation can be used to derive the isoquants for oil flow, drawn in Figure A6.1 for oil flows of 50 000, 100 000 and 150 000 barrels per day. The isoquants are continuous and convex, showing that pipe diameter and horsepower are imperfect substitutes.

From the production function, the marginal products of the two factors can be found by partial differentiation.

$$MP_H = \frac{\delta Q}{\delta H} = 0.36 \times 24.95 \times H^{0.36-1} \times D^{1.72}$$

$$= 8.982 \times H^{-0.64} \times D^{1.72}$$

$$MP_D = \frac{\delta Q}{\delta D} = 42.914 \times H^{0.36} D^{0.72}$$

The negative exponent for horsepower in the marginal product of horsepower equation shows that as it is increased, keeping diameter constant, output will increase at a diminishing rate (i.e. diminishing returns to horsepower). This is confirmed by the negative sign of the second derivative with respect to horsepower.

$$\frac{\delta^2 Q}{\delta H^2} = -0.64 \times 8.982 \times H^{-1.64} \times D^{1.72}$$

158

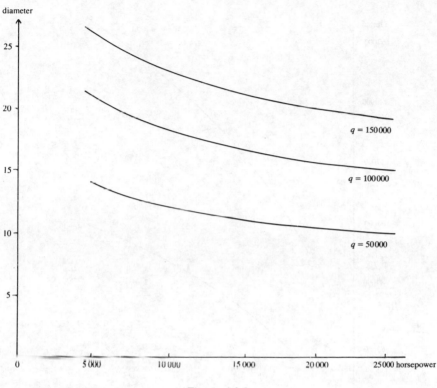

Figure A6.1

In fact, given the production equation, the short-run production function can be found by examining the effect of horsepower on output, keeping diameter constant. This is illustrated in Figure A6.2. In each case, as horsepower increases, oil flow increases at a falling rate.

The horsepower–output relationship

However, the marginal product of pipe diameter equation shows that the returns to the factor pipe diameter are increasing, since the marginal product increases at an increasing rate. This is confirmed by Figure A6.3.

Finally, the sum of exponents in the production function is greater than one, showing that returns to scale are increasing. For example, if each input was doubled, the new output would be:

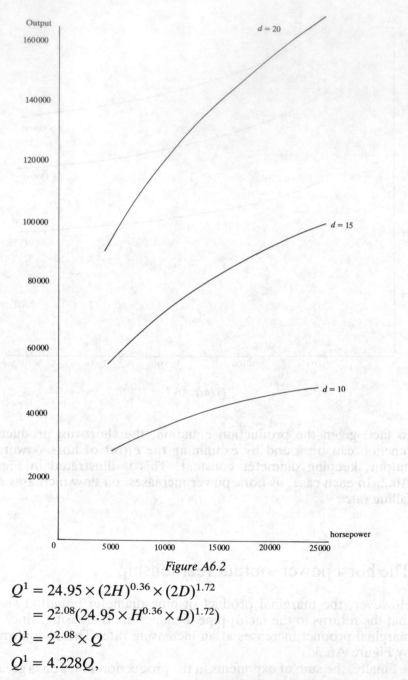

Figure A6.2

$$Q^1 = 24.95 \times (2H)^{0.36} \times (2D)^{1.72}$$
$$= 2^{2.08}(24.95 \times H^{0.36} \times D)^{1.72})$$
$$Q^1 = 2^{2.08} \times Q$$
$$Q^1 = 4.228Q,$$

so the doubling of inputs has increased output to more than four times its initial level.

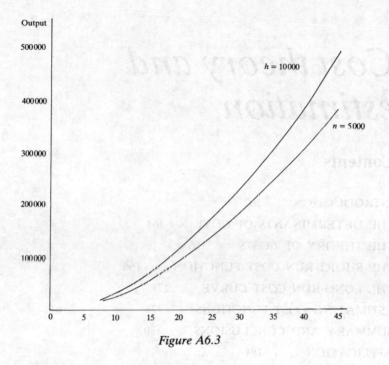

Figure A6.3

CHAPTER 7

Cost theory and estimation

Contents

Introduction

The motivation in considering the theory and estimation of costs is to provide cost estimates that are relevant to decision-making. Optimal decision-making requires the careful comparison of the costs and benefits of any action. In evaluating these costs, it is essential to have regard to the cost concept relevant to decision-making. The adoption of any particular course of action or the use of any resource imposes a cost in terms of opportunities foregone. It is this opportunity cost which is the relevant cost concept in deciding on a particular course of action.

The traditional source of cost information is the company accounts. However, company accounts are composed to meet the legal and financial requirements for which they are designed. Before those accounts can be used for decision-making purposes, a process of revision, deletion and adjustment is necessary to conform to the economic concept of opportunity cost. A number of these points

were made in Chapter 3 (Profits and Objectives) but their importance is such that no apology is necessary for their reassertion here.
As Dean points out, 'It is better to have a rough approximation of
the concept of cost that is correct for a particular decision than to
have an accurate estimate of an irrelevant concept.'[1] The adjustment of accounting figures for decision-making is a far from simple
process, but one that is essential for sensible decisions.

Consider a simple example. What is the cost of undertaking the
twelve-month MBA programme at the Cardiff Business School?
The simple answer is the sum of tuition fees and living expenses for
the year in Cardiff. In terms of the student's household accounts or
a tax return entry, this is sufficient. In terms of the decision of
whether to take the programme or not, this cost estimate may well
lead to incorrect decisions, because it ignores the opportunity costs
of attending the course. Depending on the circumstances of the
particular individual, the opportunity costs could well include
forgone earnings and interest, which sum to considerably more
than the out-of-pocket expenses considered earlier. Table 7.1 lists
the author's estimates of the full costs of the MBA programme.

Table 7.1   Costs of the MBA programme in Cardiff

Expenditure incurred	
Tuition	£1680
Accommodation and living expenses	4500
Books and equipment	500
Explicit costs	£6680
Forgone income	
Salary	£8000
(net of statutory deductions for a	
graduate with 5 years experience)	
Forgone interest (£3340 at 10%)	334
	£8334
Total cost	£15 014

In Table 7.1, interest costs are calculated by assuming that fees
and other expenses are paid half yearly, and an interest rate of 10
per cent. It is the full cost of £15 014 that needs to be compared to
the anticipated earning power of the asset (MBA degree) to
determine whether taking the degree would be profitable (but note
the comment in Chapter 4 regarding the possibility and consequences of taking the degree and not passing).

The determinants of cost

The level of costs is determined by a range of variables, captured in the form of a general cost function

$$C = f(X_1 \ldots X_n)$$

Once more the methodological approach is to identify the variables that influence cost, introduce some measure of the sensitivity of costs to changes in a particular variable and then consider ways of estimating a specific cost function.

The variable that has received most attention in economic literature is the level of output. Much of our effort in this chapter will be devoted to examining the cost–output relationship, in both the short and long run. We should note, however, that output is a multidimensional concept, where each output dimension has a relationship to the level of costs. Armen Alchian[2] identified the relationship between output dimensions in the form of an equation:

$$V = \sum_{T}^{T+m} x(t) \, . \, dt$$

where   V = total contemplated volume of output
   $x(t)$ = rate of output at time t
   T = start time of production
   m = length of time period over which output is produced.

Greater output is associated with both a higher rate of output and a larger planned volume of output – however, the methods used to achieve each could be significantly different. A faster rate of output implies using existing plant at a more intensive rate, whereas a larger planned volume of output may be consistent with a larger scale of production. Hence, costs will be affected by each in different ways. Producing over a longer planned time period involves greater maintenance costs, but lower set-up costs. With a given plant and equipment, varying the rate of output may well increase costs considerably. Alchian summarised the relationship between costs and output dimensions in the form of four propositions.

1. $\dfrac{\delta C}{\delta x} > 0$ The faster the rate of output, the higher the total costs of that output.

2. $\dfrac{\delta^2 C}{\delta x^2} > 0$ As the rate of output increases, total cost increases at an increasing rate.

3. $\dfrac{\delta C}{\delta V} > 0$ Total costs increase with contemplated volume of output (for a given output rate).

4. $\dfrac{\delta^2 C}{\delta V^2} < 0$ As planned volume of output increases, total cost increases at a decreasing rate.

Hence the rate of output, the size of plant, the contemplated volume of output and the stability of output will each have a significant effect on the level of costs. The time period over which output is produced is the key to an understanding of the importance of output dimensions to costs. We shall go on to consider the relationship between the level of costs and the rate of output in a given time period, but before then there are two other cost determinants that need to be considered.

(a)   The price of inputs

Variations in the relative prices of inputs affect both short-term operating decisions and longer term planning decisions. For the latter, forecasting the future relative prices of inputs is important decision information for the choice of future productive facilities and capacity. Changes in input prices affect costs both directly in terms of current expenditure, and indirectly in terms of the choice of production method. Dean gives the following illustration:[3] 'High wages and low materials prices warrant a larger amount of wastage and rejects than the reverse relations does, since the cost of conserving materials is the labour time spent in careful planning and precise operation.'

(b)   Technology

Technology is the sum of human knowledge and experience. The relationship between cost and output is examined on the implicit assumption that technology remains constant. However, human knowledge and experience advances in a continuous (and possibly accelerating) process that can have profound implications for the production process and hence the economic decisions made by the firm. This is especially obvious in the choice of capital equipment, which may well be out of date before construction is completed. Advances in technology occur when output can be produced with less inputs. However, changes in technology may affect demand as well as supply, rendering products as well as production facilities obsolete and providing new market opportunities. Some forecast of the rate of technological change, despite the obvious difficulties implied, will need to be built into the planning process.

The theory of costs

The theory of costs concentrates on the relationship between the level of cost and the rate of output in a particular period, assuming that *shift parameters* such as the planned volume of output and the level of technology remain constant.

Recall that optimal input combinations (i.e. production of output at least cost) occur when the isoquant is tangental to the isoquant. Figure 7.1 shows the optimal input combinations for a variety of output levels, given limited production possibilities, constant input prices and just two inputs (capital and labour). The locus of optimal input combinations is the *Expansion Path*. From the Expansion Path, and the given assumptions, the total cost of any output level can be determined as just the sum of the cost of inputs used to produce that output. From Figure 7.1, the cost of producing Q_1, given that the price of labour is £w per unit, the price of capital is £r per unit, will be $wL_1 + rK_2$, etc. Hence the relationship between cost and output has been completely determined.

However, we can as yet say little about the shape of the cost–output relationship, which will depend on the precise location of these isoquants and the relationship between them. Figure 7.1 offers no guide to the levels of output represented by $Q_1 \ldots Q_3$, other than $Q_3 > Q_2 > Q_1$. Moreover, Figure 7.1 implicitly assumes that the input combination is continuously variable. In reality, of course, input combinations are likely to be freely variable only in the long run. Once a production method has been chosen, changing the input proportions is liable to be both difficult and expensive.

The short-run cost function

The short run was defined earlier as a period of time within which at least one of the inputs is fixed. Then output can only be raised by

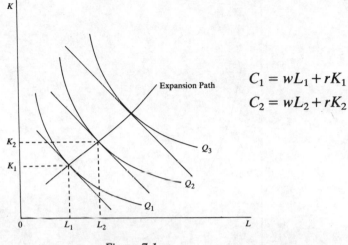

Figure 7.1

increasing the quantity of the variable input. The relationship between the variable input and the output level was examined in the previous chapter, and depends upon the nature of returns to that factor.

Assume just two inputs (capital (K) and labour (L)), and fixed input prices (at r and w respectively). Then the cost of producing an output level x will be:

$$C_x = wL_x + rK_x$$

where L_x and K_x are the quantities of labour and capital used to produce x.

Assume that the quantity of capital is fixed, at say $\bar{K}$.

Then $C_x = wL_x + r\bar{K}$.

Since capital is fixed, output and total cost will vary only with the quantity of labour. Fixed costs (FC) will equal $r\bar{K}$, and variable costs (VC) equal wL_x.

The *average cost* of output is simply total cost divided by output. Hence, the average cost of producing $x(AC_x)$ will be:

$$AC_x = \frac{wL_x}{x} + \frac{r\bar{K}}{x}$$

The second part of the average cost equation is *average fixed cost*, and will depend only on the level of output (since both r and K are constant). As output increases, the average fixed cost must fall, and in fact $r\bar{K}/x$ describes a rectangular hyperbola (Figure 7.2).

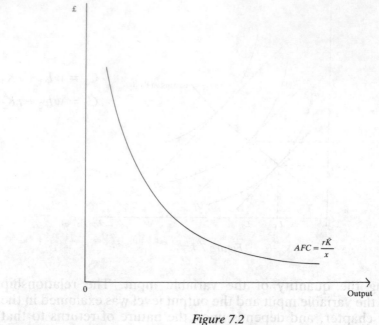

Figure 7.2

The first part of the average cost equation is the *average variable cost* (AVC) and

$$AVC = \frac{w \cdot L_x}{x}$$

Now the average product of an input was defined earlier as total output divided by the quantity of that input. Hence the average product of labour (APL) is total output divided by labour, or

$$APL = \frac{x}{L_x}$$

Since the price of labour is constant at w, substituting the equation for average variable cost gives:

$$AVC = w \cdot \frac{1}{APL}$$

$$AVC = \frac{w}{APL}$$

The average variable cost varies inversely with the average product of labour. If the average product rises, the average variable cost must fall, and conversely.

The marginal cost of output, or the cost of producing an extra unit, can be approximated by the derivative of total cost with respect to output.

If $C_x = wL_x + r\bar{K}$

$$MC = \frac{\delta C_x}{\delta x} = W \cdot \frac{\delta L_x}{\delta x}$$

since r and K are both constant. Now the marginal product of labour (MPL) is the derivative of output with respect to labour, i.e.

$$MPL = \frac{\delta x}{\delta L_x}$$

Substituting into the equation for marginal cost:

$$MC = w \cdot \frac{1}{MPL}$$

$$MC = \frac{w}{MPL}$$

The marginal cost of output varies inversely with the marginal product of labour. If the marginal product of labour falls, marginal cost must rise, and conversely.

Figure 7.3 reproduces the average and marginal products of labour curves from Figure 6.9, with shapes determined by the Law of Diminishing Returns on the assumption of a fixed amount of capital. Given the relationships now established between average cost and average product, and marginal cost and marginal product, the average and marginal cost curves can now be drawn for a fixed wage rate. As marginal product rises, marginal cost must fall etc.

Note that:

(i)   Each short-run curve is drawn for a particular fixed level of capital (size of plant). A larger size of plant would probably shift the average and marginal product curves upwards and hence average and marginal cost curves downwards.

(ii)   The average total cost curve is found by including the average fixed cost curve, and then adding the average fixed cost at any output level to the average variable cost. The effect is to shift the average cost upwards by a decreasing amount as output expands.

(iii)   At the minimum point on the average cost curve, marginal cost is equal to average cost. The relationship between average and marginal cost is explored in Table 7.2.

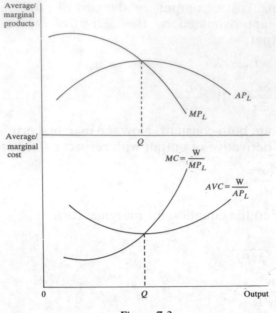

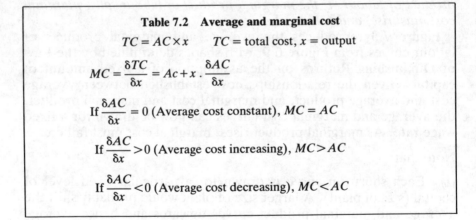

Figure 7.3

Table 7.2   Average and marginal cost

$$TC = AC \times x \qquad TC = \text{total cost}, \; x = \text{output}$$

$$MC = \frac{\delta TC}{\delta x} = Ac + x \cdot \frac{\delta AC}{\delta x}$$

If $\dfrac{\delta AC}{\delta x} = 0$ (Average cost constant), $MC = AC$

If $\dfrac{\delta AC}{\delta x} > 0$ (Average cost increasing), $MC > AC$

If $\dfrac{\delta AC}{\delta x} < 0$ (Average cost decreasing), $MC < AC$

(iv)   We saw earlier that the output elasticity with respect to a particular input was equal to the ratio of marginal to average product, i.e.

$$\varepsilon L = \frac{MPL}{APL}$$

In Figure 7.3, the marginal product of labour exceeds labour's average product up to output level Q. Hence up to Q, $\varepsilon L > 1$ and average variable cost is falling. Beyond $Q, \varepsilon L < 1$ and *AVC* rises. The size of the output elasticity with respect to the variable input therefore determines the shape of the average variable cost curve (on the assumption of a constant price for the variable input).

The long-run cost curve

In the long run all factors are variable. The decision-maker is free to determine the optimum scale of production, at the same time as the optimal input combination. Hence the long-run average cost curve (LRAC) is sometimes called the planning curve.

The shape of the long-run average cost curve can be analysed in a number of ways that lead to the same conclusion – that LRAC is determined by the interaction of the nature of returns to scale and the nature of input prices.

First consider an intuitive argument. *Assume that input prices are constant.* Then the LRAC curve is completely determined by the nature of returns to scale.

Suppose that returns to scale are constant. Then to double output requires a doubling of all inputs. Since the input prices are constant, buying twice as many inputs *must* cost twice as much money. Output has doubled, and so have total costs. Hence average cost has remained the same.

Now suppose that returns to scale are increasing. To double output requires *less* than twice as much inputs. If input prices are fixed, this must cost less than twice as much money. Hence average cost has fallen.

Finally, if returns to scale are decreasing, it should now be obvious that with constant input prices, average cost must rise. Figure 7.4 plots a Long Run Average Cost Curve assuming returns to scale are first increasing, then constant, and then decreasing.

A digression – output elasticities, returns to scale and LRAC

Recall that

$$\varepsilon = \varepsilon L + \varepsilon K \qquad \text{(p. 153)}$$

where $\quad \varepsilon$ = output elasticity with respect to all inputs
εL = output elasticity with respect to labour
εK = output elasticity with respect to capital

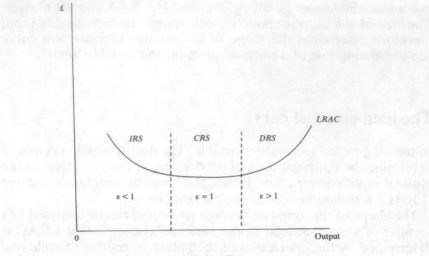

Figure 7.4

and that $\varepsilon L = \dfrac{MP_L}{AP_L}$ $\varepsilon K = \dfrac{MP_K}{AP_K}$ (p. 138)

Hence $\varepsilon = MP_L \cdot \dfrac{L}{x} + MP_K \cdot \dfrac{K}{x}$

where x = output, L, K the quantities of capital and labour used to produce that output.

Introduce input prices, by multiplying the first part of the equation by w/w, and the second part by r/r.

$$= \frac{MP_L}{w} \frac{wL}{x} + \frac{MP_K}{r} \frac{rK}{x}$$

For least cost production, $\dfrac{MP_L}{w} = \dfrac{MP_K}{r}$ (p. 145)

So $\varepsilon = \dfrac{MP_L}{w} \dfrac{(wL + rK)}{x}$

We saw earlier that $w/MP_L = MC$, whilst the term in brackets is just the average cost.

Hence $\varepsilon = \dfrac{AC}{MC}$

and the output elasticity (or returns to scale) determines the relationship between average and marginal cost.

If $\varepsilon = 1$, $AC = MC$ and average cost is constant.

If $\varepsilon > 1$, $MC < AC$, average cost must be falling

$\varepsilon < 1$, $MC > AC$, average cost must be rising.

(Figure 7.4)

Factor prices

The analysis has proceeded on the assumption that factor prices are constant. We can examine this assumption in more detail.

Assume now that returns to scale are constant. Hence to double output requires a doubling of inputs. If input prices increase, then total cost must more than double, and average cost increases. Conversely, if output prices decrease, total cost must less than double and average cost decreases. Hence we need to examine how input prices change as the demand for that input changes.

Chapter 3 confirmed that prices are determined by the simultaneous interaction of supply and demand. An increase in demand can be represented by a shift in the demand curve. Figure 7.5 examines three possible consequences.

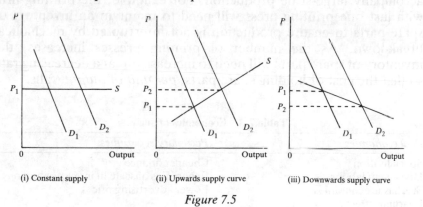

(i) Constant supply   (ii) Upwards supply curve   (iii) Downwards supply curve

Figure 7.5

In case (i) the supply curve for the input is perfectly elastic. An increase in demand has no effect on input price. Hence assuming that input prices are constant when demand changes is equivalent to assuming that input supply is perfectly elastic.

Case (ii) represents an upward sloping supply curve for the input. The increase in input demand leads to an increase in input price from P_1 to P_2.

In case (iii) the downward sloping supply curve for the input means that the increase in demand results in a fall in the input price.

Economies and diseconomies of scale

The preceding analysis has presented a technical explanation of the shape of the long-run average cost curve, showing how that shape is related to returns to scale and input prices. The economic explanation of the shape of long run average cost looks at the reasons *why* returns to scale are constant or not and why input prices may change as output expands.

Economies of scale provide the economic explanation why LRAC falls as output expands and may be subdivided into *real* economies and *pecuniary* economies.

Real economies of scale are the reasons why as output expands, less units of input are required per unit of output. *Pecuniary economies of scale* are the reasons why the price per unit of input falls *as* more of the input is purchased. Table 7.3 lists the main sources of each type of economy.

Under real economies, specialisation and the division of labour refer to the benefits of mass production, enabling a long and complex production process to be divided into a series of simpler and more manageable tasks, using highly specialised inputs. Stochastic economies refer to the reductions in uncertainty which accompany large-scale production. For example, the printing firm with just one printing press will need to maintain an inventory of spare parts to ensure production is not interrupted by mechanical breakdown. As the number of printing presses increases, the inventory of spare parts will need to increase but at a decreasing rate so that the cost of holding spare parts, *per unit of output*, falls.

Table 7.3   Economies of scale

Real economies	Pecuniary economies
Specialisation	Cheaper finance
Division of labour	Economies of scale in input production
Stochastic economies	Lower advertising prices
Learning effects	
Marketing economies	
Managerial economies	
Economies of increased dimensions	

Learning effects refer to the observed phenomenon that as experience of production increases, the cost of production falls. Learning effects are particularly important in the production of high technology products. For example, one study[4] estimated a *learning coefficient* in aircraft production of 80 per cent, implying that each doubling of aircraft output of a particular model reduced unit costs by 20 per cent.

Marketing economies occur when the marketing cost per unit of output falls as output expands. For example, a new product can often be added to the product range without increasing the number of salesmen, significantly reducing average selling cost. Managerial economies occur with the specialisation of each management function, and the mechanisation of information processing. Finally, economies of increased dimensions occur because of the geometric relationship between costs and capacity. For example, consider the construction of a warehouse, the cost of which is proportionate to the surface area (walls, floor and roof). A warehouse with a height, width and length of 10 metres has a surface area of $600m^2$ and a capacity of $1000m^3$. Increasing the height, width and length to 20 metres will increase surface area (and hence costs) to $2400m^2$, but capacity increases to $8000m^3$. Cost has increased by four times, whilst capacity has increased by eight times, implying that the cost per unit of capacity has halved.

Turning to pecuniary economies, larger firms are often able to obtain finance easier and cheaper (i.e. at a lower rate of interest) than small firms. The price of inputs may fall because of economies of scale in input production reflected in special discounts available to the large purchaser. Lower advertising rates may be attainable by the large (and regular) advertiser.

All these reasons point to a fall in long-run average cost as output expands, but there are reasons why LRAC may increase beyond a particular output level (diseconomies of scale). The most oft cited reason is the problem of control in large organisations (managerial diseconomies). This may be supplemented by an upward sloping supply curve for inputs and the alienation of labour if the division of labour is carried to extremes. Note, however, that diseconomies of scale at the plant level may be avoided by duplication. For example, if the average cost of electricity is minimised by a power station producing 10 billion kilowatt hours, with unit costs rising steeply thereafter, the cheapest way to produce 20 billion kilowatt hours will be to have two power stations. Nevertheless, diseconomies at the firm level cannot be avoided by duplication, although they may be reduced by decentralisation.

The significance of economies of scale

The shape of the long-run average cost curve has serious implications for the market structure of an industry. Market structure will be considered in detail in the next chapter, but for the moment, it is sufficient to note that an industry dominated by one large firm may have prices considerably higher than if competition was strong. Yet if long-run average cost falls continuously as output expands, the optimal market structure from a production cost point of view is to have just one large firm (a situation of *natural monopoly*). Table 7.4 examines the minimum efficient plant size (MEPS), as a share of UK produced sales for a variety of products, with MEPS defined as the lowest level of output compatible with producing at least cost.

Table 7.4   Minimum efficient plant size as a % of UK produced sales

Product group	MEPS as % of UK produced sales
Bread	1%
Refined sugar	18–20%
Cigarettes	21%
Sulphuric acid	26%
Diesel engines	56%
TV tubes	100%
Turbo-generators	120%

Source: Department of Prices and Consumer Protection (1981) *A Review of Monopolies and Merger Policy* (London: HMSO, 1978), reprinted in L. Wagner, *Readings in Applied Microeconomics* (Oxford: Oxford University Press, 1981), pp. 148–71.

According to Table 7.4, the UK market is large enough to support 100 efficient bread plants, 4 sulphuric acid factories and just one TV tube producer. For efficient production of turbo-generators, at least some output must be exported.

Estimating cost functions

Estimating a cost function requires that a precise equation be fitted to the general function

$$C = f(Q)$$

As with estimating a demand function, the specification and estimation of a cost function necessitates that a number of problems be overcome.

The first difficulty is to determine whether a short-run or long-run cost curve is to be estimated. The answer to this question will depend on the purpose to which the cost function is to be put. Operating decisions, such as deciding the immediate price and output combination, will require that the short-run average cost be estimated. Since fixed costs, by definition, will not be affected by the short-term decision, their estimation can play no part in that decision. On the other hand, longer term decisions such as investment in new product development or the introduction of new capital equipment will require a comparison of long-run costs and benefits, and hence the long-run average cost must be estimated.

Whatever the period to be covered, one immediate problem is the choice of functional form. The usual procedure is to use regression to fit some linear, or intrinsically linear, function to observations on cost and output. However, the estimation of a linear function will generally preclude the sort of cost curves described in this chapter.

For example, suppose the cost function

$$C = a + bQ$$

is estimated by linear regression, to find the coefficients a and b. Estimation of the simple straight line makes implicit assumptions about the nature of average and marginal cost. Given the particular cost function, marginal and average cost can be determined directly:

if $C = a + bQ$

$$MC = \frac{\delta C}{\delta Q} = b$$

$$AC = \frac{a + bQ}{Q} = \frac{a}{Q} + b$$

Hence estimating a straight line cost function implicitly assumes that marginal cost is constant, and that as output expands, average cost will tend towards marginal cost. Whether average cost is greater or less than marginal cost will depend on the sign of the estimated coefficient $\hat{a}$.

Since our theoretical expectations are that marginal cost is increasing and average cost is U-shaped, economists often estimate the quadratic cost function

$$C = a + bQ + cQ^2$$

or even the cubic function

$$C = a + bQ - cQ^2 + dQ^3$$

The corresponding marginal and average cost curves are illustrated in Figure 7.6. The estimation of either function requires procedures more complex than linear regression.

(i) $C = a + bQ + cQ^2$

    $MC = b + 2cQ$

    $AC = \dfrac{a}{Q} + b + cQ$

(ii) $C = a + bQ - cQ^2 + dQ^3$

    $MC = b - 2cQ + 3dQ^2$

    $AC = \dfrac{a}{Q} + b - cQ + dQ^2$

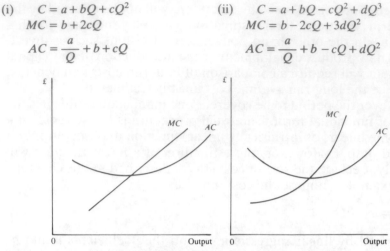

Figure 7.6   Marginal and average cost functions

Alongside the difficulties associated with functional form are those associated with data collection. Since the purpose of cost estimation is decision-making, the cost function to be estimated should be *future* cost as a function of output. Recent or even current costs may or may not be a realistic guide to the future. Moreover, the concept of cost of relevance to decision-making is opportunity cost, which may bear little systematic relation to cost information provided from company accounts (the usual source of cost data). As we saw earlier, accounting information requires careful interpretation to be of decision use.

Another basic problem is that estimating the cost–output relationship implicitly assumes that all differences in cost are entirely attributable to differences in output. This qualification applies whether we are considering different costs for the same firm over time, or looking at a cross-section of firms at the same time. In the former case, differences in costs may be attributable to differences in production methods, levels of plant, the product mix and inflation levels. In addition to these problems, cross-sectional cost differences may be the result of differences in accounting procedures or levels of efficiency.

Then there are special data problems depending on whether the estimated cost function is short or long run. With a short-run cost function, fixed costs need to be separated from variable costs, a distinction that is not always easy to make. For example, machine maintenance costs may be a function of both time and machine use. Maintenance costs due to the passage of time are fixed costs, whereas maintenance costs due to use are a variable cost. Also, the estimation of short-run costs assumes that the scale of production remains the same. In practice, changes in scale may be continuous rather than discrete.

The estimation of a long-run average cost curve also requires specific assumptions to be made. In particular, changes in cost due to scale need to be separated from changes in cost due to technology. Once more, changes in technology are likely to be continuous rather than discrete. Moreover, in the long run output is unlikely to be homogenous, so that changes in cost due to product mix changes may be difficult to separate from changes in cost due only to output changes.

Empirical evidence

Because of the difficulties outlined, academic studies of short-run costs are rare. Two major studies were carried out some time ago by Dean[5] and Johnson[6]. Both authors found that in general, short run marginal costs were reasonably constant, with short-run average costs falling slightly as output expanded. Neither study found the U-shaped average cost curves described by textbooks. However, their evidence is *not* inconsistent with the textbook model. The fact that they found SRAC to be falling over observed output ranges may only show that managers were careful to keep output below the level at which average cost may start to rise.

Empirical studies of the long-run average cost curve are considerably more common. Walters[7] surveyed early studies with the general conclusion that long-run average cost generally declined as output expanded. Salvatore examined more recent American experience, with the conclusions outlined in Table 7.5.

Table 7.5   **LRAC of small firms as a % of LRAC of large firms**

Industry	%
Hospitals	129
Electric power	112
Local airlines	100
Railroads	100
Trucking	95

Source: D. Salvatore (1986) *Microeconomics: Theory and Applications* (New York: Macmillan), p. 251.

According to Table 7.5, large hospitals and power stations have a significant cost advantage over smaller units. In the provision of local air and rail communications, costs are the same for small and large firms, whilst small trucking companies have a cost advantage over larger hauliers. In India, Gupta[8] found that long-run average cost curves were linear in six industries, U-shaped in five industries and L-shaped in eighteen industries. The major British study of the extent of economies of scale was by Pratten,[9] who found that long-run average costs were generally L-shaped implying that cost advantages disappeared at very large scale.

Summary and conclusions

The examination of costs for decision-making purposes relies heavily on the notion of opportunity costs. However, some revision and adjustment of accounting costs are necessary before these can be used to approximate opportunity costs.

The level of costs is determined by a number of variables including the different dimensions of output, input prices, and the state of technology. The economic theory of costs relates cost to the rate of output. In the short term, unit costs depend upon the productivity of the variable factor, whilst long-run average cost is influenced by the nature of returns to scale. Cost estimation is difficult but essential for rational decision-making, since every decision involves the evaluation of the expected cost/benefit ratio corresponding to different actions.

Application 7

Size and efficiency in the building society industry[10]

In the United Kingdom, building societies are the major suppliers of personal housing finance. Building societies receive deposits from individuals and make long-term loans secured by property assets. During the 1970s the larger building societies grew rapidly, often by merger, so that between 1970 and 1978 the number of building societies fell by a third, whilst total assets grew by more than two and a half times. This merger boom was often justified by the 'desire for rationalisation', so it became relevant to examine whether larger building societies were in fact more efficient than smaller ones.

However, the measurement of efficiency in the building society industry is a far from simple matter. Building societies use a variety of inputs and provide a range of mortgage outputs. Moreover, building societies are legally non-profit making bodies, eliminating the possibility of using profitability as a measure of efficiency. However, one measure of efficiency that can be used is the management expense ratio (ME), defined as management expenses divided by total assets. The primary asset of building societies is mortgage loans, although supplemented by the societies' property and equipment. Hence, a society's own assets value can be used as a measure of output.

Hill and Gough extracted the management expense ratio and total asset size from the 1976 accounts of 241 building societies, representing over 93 per cent of total industry assets. From this data two functions were estimated, with results shown below (with MTA representing mean total assets).

$$ME = 1.036 - 0.0000630 \, MTA$$

$$R^2 = 0.0035$$

and $$ME = 0.9538 + 0.0674/MTA$$

$$R^2 = 0.3487$$

The first equation explained less than four-thousandths of the variation in the management expense ratio whilst the second equation explained a third of that variation. The second equation showed that the management expense ratio declined with total assets, but at a decreasing rate. Hence there was some support for the hypothesis that efficiency increased with society size, but with the qualification that efficiency gains tailed off as society size increased.

Nevertheless, in an industry dominated by the larger societies, attaching equal weight to observations from 241 societies may give a distorted picture of the industry position. Accordingly, the equations were re-estimated for the largest 15, 25 and 40 societies, representing 73, 81 and 86 per cent of total industry assets, using data for 1978.

Societies	$ME = \alpha + \beta\,MTA$	$ME = \alpha + \beta/MTA$
1–15	$1.094 - 0.0000386$ $R^2 = 0.6286$	$0.9004 + 134.06$ $R^2 = 0.5894$
1–25	$1.077 - 0.0000338$ $R^2 = 0.1157$	$1.007 + 11.92$ $R^2 = 0.0145$
1–40	$1.079 - 0.0000340$ $R^2 = 0.0663$	$1.033 + 3.257$ $R^2 = 0.0043$

These results show that the management expense ratio declined with firm size, but the relationship weakened considerably as smaller societies were included. Since the vast majority of mergers occurred between smaller societies, efficiency gains from merger could not be relied upon.

Note that if C is cost and x output, estimating the equation

$$\frac{C}{x} = a + bx$$

implies that the total cost function is quadratic, since

$$C = ax + bx^2$$

However, estimating the reciprocal function

$$\frac{C}{x} = a + \frac{b}{x}$$

implies that the total cost function is linear, since

$$C = ax + b.$$

CHAPTER 8

The competitive environment

Contents

Introduction

Whilst demand and cost information are crucial to the firm's decision-making process, the extent and nature of competition define the external environment in which the firm operates. An understanding of this competitive environment will enable cost and demand analysis to be put together to determine an economic theory of the firm, which can offer significant insights into the decision-making process. Each and every business decision must be made in the light of anticipations about competitors' actions and reactions. The extent of competition influences the nature of both cost and demand conditions. Moreover, the competitive environment defines the discretion that the firm's managers have over pricing, marketing, input purchase and other decisions. An understanding of that decision environment is essential for both describing the limitations of market behaviour, and analysing the opportunities available in the market. The competitive environment is not stable, but rather is continuously changing. The relationship of the firm to its environment is both reactive and proactive – reactive in that the firm must respond to changes in that environment, and proactive in that the firm, by a judicious choice of policies, may influence that environment in ways that can increase the market opportunities available.

The purpose of this chapter is to examine the dimensions of competition that define the firm's market environment, and consider the impact of each dimension on the firm's decisions. The economic theory of the firm describes a series of various competitive market conditions referred to as market structures. Each structure will be examined in turn, and the decision implications of that structure considered. Finally, this chapter will examine the measurement of competition, and conclude by examining some empirical evidence and competition policies.

It is first necessary to consider what we mean by a firm, and why the form of business organisation that we call a firm exists at all. Consider the large-scale production of motor cars. It is at least theoretically possible that an individual could build motor cars, by buying in components and assembling. Such a producer of 'hand-built' cars would need to have considerable facilities and experience, and the product is bound to be expensive. Suppose, however, that demand was high. The producer would rapidly discover his capacity constraints and probably start to take on staff to perform specialist functions. It is again theoretically possible that the services of such people could be hired on a contract or self-employed basis. As the business expanded the initial producer would have to spend more and more time coordinating the activities of his self-employed assistants. Moreover, each assistant would have a specific contract and confine effort to the terms of that contract. Thus, despite the possibilities of subcontracting, there are advantages in organising production in some other form. A business firm is a form of organisation that achieves internal coordination without the use of a price mechanism. Hence, resources are directed within the firm on the basis of management authority, rather than by the workings of some internal market. The firm as an organisation can then avoid *transaction costs*, such as the costs of locating and contracting specialist services, and enjoy the synergy effects of team efforts.

As the business firm developed as the dominant production organisation, the legal structure of society changed to accommodate the business firm. Most firms of any size are now separately identifiable legal entities, often with limited liability (meaning that the firm as a legal entity, rather than the owners or managers of the firm, is responsible for its debts). As firms grew, so did the extent of competition between them.

In a general sense, competition is the availability of substitutes for the firm's products. Ultimately, all products are substitutes in the competition for consumer income. In a more restricted sense, the definition of competition comes down to a definition of products or industries. Although houses and motor cars may compete for consumers' incomes, they are not normally regarded as direct substitutes. Within the product group of motor cars, the small hatchback does not compete directly with the large luxury saloon, despite being use-substitutes in the ability to transport people. When economists consider an industry or market or even product group, they are contemplating a group of close substitutes. An industry can then be defined as a group of closely competing substitutes, relying on some natural break in the chain of substitutes to limit the size of the industry. For example, the plastic bucket will compete with a metal bucket in a much more direct sense than with a wheelbarrow, despite the latter's ability to hold water.

One solution to the problem of product definition is to use the concept of cross-price elasticity. Recall that cross-price elasticity was defined as

$$\varepsilon ab = \frac{\delta Da}{\delta Pb} \cdot \frac{Pb}{Da}$$

And if $\varepsilon ab > 0$, then a and b are substitutes. This does not solve the problem entirely, since we have seen that ultimately the cross-price elasticity between houses and motor cars will be positive. However, even if positive, that cross-price elasticity is not likely to be large. Thus the definition of a product range or industry has been reduced to defining products as direct substitutes whenever the cross-price elasticity is both positive and substantial (without worrying too much about how substantial).

The dimensions of competition

The dimensions of competition are the elements of market structure, of which three can be readily identified:

  (i)   The number and size distribution of firms.
 (ii)   The freedom of entry.
(iii)   The extent of product differentiation.

Each of these elements will determine how the firm interacts with its competitors in the market. Each determines the *market power* of the firm, or the ability of the firm to set price and output in the market. The lower the amount of competition then the greater the market power of the firm and in general the higher the price the consumer must pay for the product. The greater the amount and extent of competition, then the more alternatives the consumer will have and the greater the power of the consumer to influence price and quantity. Thus the market structure of an industry defines the distribution of power between buyer and seller.

(i)   The number and size distribution of firms

The larger the number of firms in an industry, then, other things being equal, the larger the number of available substitutes and the weaker the market power of each firm. However, note that the size distribution of sellers is also important. In Britain, there are a number of sellers of coal, but because British Coal is many times larger than the rest of the industry put together, it is British Coal which is the dominant influence on the price of coal.

(ii)   The freedom of entry

The freedom of entry into a market is an important determinant of competition. As we shall see, the firm that can effectively restrict the entry of others, usually through some cost or technical advantage, can effectively determine the price and quantity in that market. The freedom to exit a market may also be important in influencing the extent of competition elsewhere in the economy, as firms respond to the market opportunities available.

(iii)   Product differentiation

Product differentiation is the ability to distinguish products through some real or imagined quality which reduces the elasticity of demand, and hence confers the power to set a price higher than that of rivals and not lose all sales to these rivals. The greater the extent of product differentiation, then the weaker the force of competition.

Moreover, product differentiation may offer a substantial barrier to the entry of new firms.

In addition to these three main elements of competition there are three others which may confer market power in particular circumstances.

(iv)   The flow of information

Competition can only be effective when consumers are aware of the availability of alternatives. Any restrictions on that flow of information may give local advantage to one particular firm.

(v)   Buyer concentration

The number and size distribution of potential purchasers may affect the extent of competition. Returning to the coal industry, the dominant position of British Coal as purchaser of coal extraction machinery severely reduces the market power of machinery producers.

(vi)   Integration and diversification

The degree of integration refers to the extent to which the various processes involved in the transformation of input into output are under the control of a single firm. Diversification refers to the extent to which a single firm is involved in different markets. Both have implications for competition in terms of the ability to control supplies and to carry over success or failure from one market into another.

Various combinations of these elements of competition give rise to economists' classification of market structure ranging from the one extreme of perfect competition to the other extreme of monopoly. Although these forms of market structure are presented discretely, it is important to recognise that, in the words of Robinson,[1] 'The truth is that there is a continuous graduation between competition and monopoly, just as there is between light and darkness, or between health and sickness.'

Forms of market structure

Perfect competition

The necessary characteristics of perfect competition are:

(a) large number of small buyers and sellers;
(b) freedom of entry and exit;
(c) product homogeneity (i.e. no product differentiation);
(d) perfect information for both buyers and sellers.

In these circumstances, each firm will be a *price-taker* and can have no individual influence on the market. Each firm can sell as much as it wants at the given market price. Any firm charging a price higher than the market price will sell nothing, since the product is homogeneous and there are many alternative sellers known to the consumer. The demand curve faced by each firm will be perfectly elastic (with infinite elasticity), and therefore marginal revenue will equal price.

Short- and long-run equilibrium in perfect competition

Each firm will profit maximise by setting output at the point where marginal revenue equals marginal cost. In the short run, a firm will profit if the market price exceeds average cost (Figure 8.1). In the

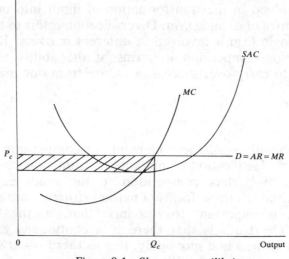

Figure 8.1   Short-run equilibrium

long run excess profits will entice the entry of other firms, forcing down the individual demand curve (as the market is shared between a larger number of firms), and completely eliminating any economic profit (surplus over opportunity costs) (Figure 8.2). Note that the cost curves of the firm are economic costs, including the opportunity cost of capital employed. The opportunity cost of capital is defined as the best return available elsewhere, so that in the long run economic profit rates will be equalised at zero if all industries are competitive.

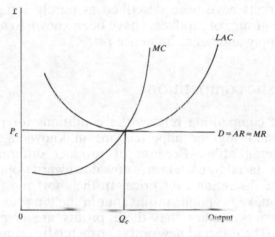

Figure 8.2   Long-run equilibrium

The long-run equilibrium position has several important characteristics which have resulted in perfect competition being seen as an idealised standard for competition. First, in long-run equilibrium price is equal to marginal costs, implying that the value of the product to the consumer is exactly equal to the resource cost of the product to the firm. Secondly, given a U-shaped long-run average cost curve, equilibrium with no economic profit must occur at the lowest point on the long-run average cost curve, implying that the product has a resource cost as low as possible.

From a decision point of view, perfect competition is of little interest. The only decision the manager has to make is the level of output, which must be where marginal cost equals marginal revenue, or a loss will be made and the firm goes out of business. Secondly, the manager has no discretion over objectives – profits must be maximised or the firm goes out of business. At the same time, profit is an elusive goal – it is the very pursuit of profit which means that profit cannot exist in the long run.

Finally, the perfectly competitive situation as described can have
no real-life counterpart. The restrictive nature of the assumptions
ensures that perfect competition has not, will not, and cannot exist.
The role of perfect competition lies in setting a standard, so that real
competitive situations can be described in terms of their departure
from perfect competition.

A closely related form of competition is *pure competition*, which
retains the major assumptions of many small suppliers, freedom of
entry and product homogeneity without the informational perfec-
tion demanded by perfect competition. Some commodity and
financial markets have been described as purely competitive, but
even in these groups of producers have been known to act in concert
to restrict supply and hence influence price.

Monopolistic competition

Monopolistic competition relaxes the conditions for perfect competition by allowing for imperfections in knowledge and some
product differentiation. Because of product differentiation the
demand curve faced by each firm is now downward sloping, allowing
the firm some discretion over price. In the short run (Figure 8.3),
the firm can make economic profits, but in the long run the absence
of entry barriers implies that these profits are competed away
(Figure 8.4). The effect of new entry, attracted by economic profits,
is to force the demand curve downwards until those profits no longer
exist.

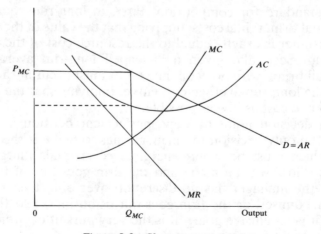

Figure 8.3   Short-run equilibrium

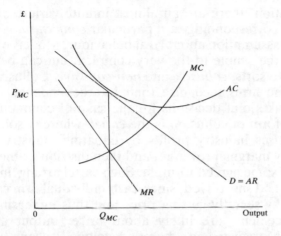

Figure 8.4 Long-run equilibrium

Note that since the demand curve slopes down, marginal revenue lies below the demand curve. In the long run, equilibrium occurs when the demand curve is tangential to the long-run average cost curve.

Because output is not at the minimum point on the average cost curve, each firm is left with *excess capacity*. This has led some economists to conclude that some production inefficiency (in terms of higher than minimum average costs) is a necessary price to pay for the product variety implied by product differentiation.

Oligopoly

Oligopoly is a form of market structure where sellers are few in number, and each is of such size that a change in price or output will have an immediate and appreciable effect on the other firms. It is the form of market structure most prevalent in the modern economy, and yet the market structure on which the economist can draw fewest and weakest conclusions. This is not a weakness, but a strength of economic theory, since the variety of possible actions and reactions in a situation of oligopoly is so large that no single theory can be expected to cover all situations. The basic problem for the oligopolist is uncertainty – before taking any action, the oligopolist will have to consider the potential reactions of competitors, since his actions will have an effect on them, and their reactions in turn will have an impact on his own performance.

In this situation, there are an almost infinite variety of possible theories, each corresponding to a particular *conjectural variation* in terms of some assumption about rival behaviour. Models of oligopoly range from the simple to the very complex, but can be basically divided into two sorts, *collusive* and *non-collusive*. Collusive models assume that the firms recognise their interdependence and come together to make joint decisions for the sake of common interest. The strongest form of collusion is the *cartel*, whereby some central agency maximises industry profits by equating industry marginal cost to industry marginal revenue, and then distributes these profits on the basis of some agreed formula. Such cartel arrangements tend to be unstable and short-lived, since each individual firm can gain in the short run by secretly cutting price and thus increasing market share. Disagreements are likely about price, output and profit distribution. Moreover, in many developed economies such arrangements are illegal, and hence more likely to be implicit rather than explicit.

Non-collusive oligopoly models assume that firms take decisions independently, but that each firm makes particular assumptions about the anticipated behaviour of rivals. The most common textbook model of oligopoly is the *Kinked Demand Curve* (but note the comments of Stigler[2]). The Kinked Demand model assumes that each oligopolist will expect the worst possible reaction from competitors. If the oligopolist increases price, the worst that can happen is that rivals don't follow, so that the price increaser suffers a large fall in market share (i.e. demand is elastic). If he decreases price, the worst that can happen is that rivals do follow, so that the price cutter has little increase in market share (i.e. demand is inelastic). In these circumstances the oligopolist faces the kinked demand curve illustrated in Figure 8.5, with the kink occurring at the current price. Then it is an unwise oligopolist who will initiate a price change, implying that prices will tend to be stable over time. Note that this is a theory of price stability, with no indication of how price came to be equal to *P* in the first place.

Monopoly

Monopoly is the other extreme of the competitive scale to perfect competition – a situation where the firm is the sole producer of a product, so that the output of that firm *is* the output of the industry. For the monopoly to persist there must be high barriers to the entry of new firms, who would otherwise be attracted by the possibility of

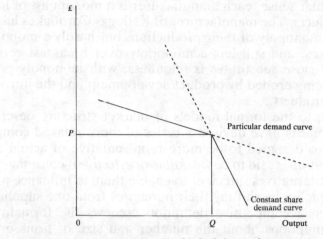

Figure 8.5   The kinked demand curve

profits. Because of these entry barriers, the long- and short-run equilibrium positions are equivalent (Figure 8.6). The monopolist charges price *Pm* for output *Qm*, and makes a persistent profit equal to the shaded area.

The conclusions from the monopoly model are excess capacity and excess profits. Like perfect competition, monopoly is unlikely to exist in a pure form. The ingenuity of self-interest knows no bounds when profitable opportunities exist, and barriers to entry are quickly breached unless reinforced by government protection. In the case of state monopolies, behaviour is unlikely to be as described by the monopoly model.

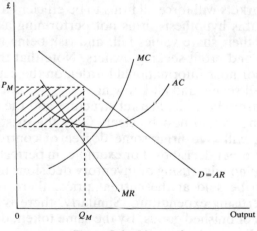

Figure 8.6   Monopoly

In a particular sense, each manufacturer is a monopolist of his or her own products. The manufacturer of Kelloggs Cornflakes has, by definition, a monopoly of their production, but hardly a monopoly over cornflakes, and still less a monopoly over breakfast cereals. The chain of close substitutes is relentless, with monopoly power continually being eroded by product development and the introduction of new products.

In addition to the formal models of market structure described above, economists have devised a series of more relaxed competitive definitions designed to be more representative of actual markets. Competition is said to be *workable* or *effective* if consumers are offered real alternatives sufficient to enable them to influence price, quantity or quality by shifting their purchases from one supplier to another. Such a competitive definition eschews the formality of concrete assumptions about the number and size of firms or the existence or otherwise of product differentiation, and concentrates upon the essential competitive attribute of consumer choice. The test of workable competition is the availability of genuine alternatives for consumers.

The theory of *contestable* markets relates most generally to situations of natural monopoly, whereby the cost structure of the industry suggests efficient production would be by a single seller. In such a situation, the market is contestable, despite its cost structure, if there is freedom of entry and exit. If the natural monopolist charges an excess price, profitable entry is possible. The threat of potential entry is sufficient to force the existing firm to be efficient and keep prices down.

The *efficient markets hypothesis* suggests that the market structure of a particular industry is unimportant, since the competitive nature of financial markets will force all firms to be efficient and profitable. According to this hypothesis firms not performing as well as they could will see their share values fall, and risk being taken over by more efficient and profit-seeking owners. Note that this hypothesis imposes an enormous informational burden on the capital markets, who must be all-seeing and all-knowing.

The relationship between market structure and the discretion for decision-making should now be clear. Only the existence of some market power will give firms some degree of control over price, marketing and other decisions. For example, in perfect competition, managers have no advertising or inventory decisions to make. Since all output can be sold at the current price, there is no point in incurring advertising expenditure. Similarly, there is little point in holding stocks of finished goods. By the same token, discretion over objectives implies market power as a necessary precondition. In the absence of market power, firms need to profit-maximise in order to survive.

The measurement of competition

Given the general nature of competition, it is not surprising that there exist many possible ways of trying to measure competition. Some of these measures refer to the various dimensions of competition listed above. Others attempt to go directly to the heart of competition by examining the degree of substitution between products, i.e. the availability of real choices to the consumer.

The degree of substitution

Since substitution is defined, from a demand point of view, in terms of the cross-price elasticity of demand, this is an obvious measure of competition (and indirectly of product differentiation). The problem is that there are many substitute goods (strictly defined as having a positive cross-price elasticity of demand) that we would not ordinarily consider as being in competition. The example used earlier was houses and motor cars. Rather there is a chain of close substitutes, and an industry is defined by natural breaks in this chain of substitution. From an empirical point of view, given sufficient data, cross-price elasticities could be measured and then ranked in order of magnitude. The problem then is to draw some line around what can be considered as close substitutes. We can shift, but not solve, the problem by defining an industry as a group of products having positive and *significant* cross-price elasticities of demand.

Even then we may not have measured what we mean by competition. It may be equally relevant to examine the degree of substitution from the supply, rather than the demand side. Competition is then the existence of other producers, able to switch easily into the production of close demand substitutes in response to profitability signals. Needham[3] gives the example of left- and right-handed golf clubs. From the consumer's point of view, these are clearly not substitutes, unless the golfer is ambidextrous! From the producer's point of view, competition may be intense, since excess profits in the supply of left-handed clubs would surely attract the attention of producers of right-handed clubs.

Just as substitution in demand can be measured by the cross-price elasticity of demand, substitution in supply can be measured by the cross-price elasticity of supply, where

$$\varepsilon ab = \frac{\% \; \Delta \; \text{quantity supplied of } A}{\% \; \Delta \; \text{price of } B}$$

However, measuring competition in this way will suffer from exactly the same problem as before – that of drawing a line between significant and insignificant cross-price elasticities of supply.

The definition of an industry actually used in much empirical work relies upon the notion of substitutability of supply in terms of the similarity of production processes, categorised into some Standard Industrial Classification (SIC). In the UK, SIC divides output into twenty-seven major industrial groups or orders. For example, order 1 is Agriculture, Forestry and Fishing. The classification continues by further and further subdivisions, e.g.:

Order 1,   Agriculture, Forestry and Fishing

divided into

001   Agriculture and Horticulture
002   Forestry
003   Fishing

Each subgroup is then further subdivided, finally ending with so-called Three Digit Industries. Hence one subgroup of Agriculture and Horticulture is Livestock, divided into Dairy, Poultry etc. The anomalies and eccentricities of the Standard Industrial Classifications are widely recognised with, for example, scarves, suspenders and artificial flowers being grouped together in industry code 4494 on the UK classification,[4] but the SICs are probably the best formal industry definitions for data collection that are achievable.

Direct measurement of the elements of competition

An alternative approach is to attempt to measure directly some element of competition, or dimension of competition.

(i)   THE NUMBER AND SIZE DISTRIBUTION OF FIRMS

Counting the number of firms in an industry is relatively easy, once the industry has been defined. However, on its own, this information says little about competition. Of more importance may be the relative size of firms. For example, even if two industries each have ten firms, the strength of competition will be vastly different if in the first industry one firm supplies 80 per cent of industry output (each of the rest supplying 20 per cent), whilst the second industry has ten equal sized firms.

One measure used to overcome this problem is the *n firm concentration ratio*, defined as

$$CRn = \frac{\text{size of the largest } n \text{ firms}}{\text{total industry size}}$$

Then, for example, in 1977 the five largest bread producers in the UK produced 81 per cent of total bread output, giving $CR5 = 81$ per cent.

The difficulties with using a concentration ratio are:

(i)   choosing n, the number of firms,
(ii)   choosing a measure of size,
(iii)   interpreting the results.

The usual answer to the first problem is to choose four, five or six as the number of largest firms, but the choice is essentially arbitrary. The measure of size adopted may be sales, output, assets or employment, depending on the problem being studied and the availability of data. The interpretation of results is more problematic, since competition may be more affected by the relative size distribution of the n largest firms than by the disparity between these and other firms.

(ii)   THE FREEDOM OF ENTRY

Barriers to entry are all the reasons why an existing firm may enjoy a competitive advantage over new entrants. Barriers may be physical (the control over some scarce input) or economic (product differentiation, economies of scale). The earliest empirical work was by Joe Bain,[5] who set the standard for later studies to emulate. Bain classified industries into four groups, according to the ease of entry:

(a)   *Easy Entry* – no competitor, actual or potential, has any significant cost advantage.
(b)   *Ineffectively Impeded Entry* – cost advantages exist, and may be used to earn profits at prices which still deter entry. However, the long-run gains of restricting entry by limiting price are insufficient to outweigh current profits forgone by limiting price.
(c)   *Effectively Impeded Entry* – cost and demand conditions are such that it is worthwhile limiting price and sacrificing short-run profits to prevent entry for long-run gain.

(d) *Blockaded Entry* – the short-run profit maximising price is not high enough to entice entry anyway.

Only classification (c) involves not maximising short-run profits, and instead adopting a policy designed to restrict entry.

(iii) PRODUCT DIFFERENTIATION

Product differentiation refers to the degree by which consumers see products as imperfect substitutes for each other. One obvious possible measure is the cross-price elasticity of demand, but this is subject to all the limitations noted above.

An alternative approach is to look at the factors which give rise to product differentiation. Product differentiation is clearly advantageous to the seller, and we can expect the seller to devote resources to try to distinguish their products in the minds of potential buyers. The primary instruments available to the firm to distinguish their products are research expenditure into product improvements and advertising expenditure.

However, research expenditure is not always undertaken with the sole objective of product differentiation. Research and development on production improvements needs to be distinguished from expenditure on product development. Moreover, not all research expenditure in product development is successful, either in creating new improved products or in reinforcing product differentiation.

A more profitable approach may be to look at advertising expenditure. By definition, advertising cannot exist in a perfectly competitive situation, although this does not imply that advertising expenditure is inversely proportional to the degree of competition. The oligopolist, for example, may have more incentive to advertise than the monopolist.

Empirical evidence

Given the difficulties of defining competition, and the even greater difficulties of attempting to measure it, it should not be surprising that a wealth of often contradictory evidence exists about the degree of competition. This selection will examine just a small sample of some evidence.

Competition in the UK

Table 8.1 lists the five-firm concentration ratios for some product groups in the UK in 1963 and 1977. In most cases the degree of concentration has increased substantially, implying a possible weakening of competition. Note, however, that the table says nothing about the extent of competition *between* the largest firms, and measures only the proportion of UK output produced by the largest five firms. Hence the table takes no account of competition from abroad, which may be particularly important for some product groups. For example, the 98 per cent concentration ratio in motor car output needs to be considered in the context of substantial import penetration in the UK car market.

Table 8.1 Five-firm concentration ratios in selected product groups (CR5)

Product	1963 %	1977 %
Beer	50.5	62.2
Biscuits	65.5	79.7
Bread	71.4	81.2
Cars	91.2	98.4
Cotton cloth	19.3	46.1
Flour	51.0	85.7
Pharmaceuticals	53.9	63.2
Refrigerators	71.9	98.8
Washing machines	85.2	96.2

Source: A. Griffiths and S. Wall (1984) *Applied Economics* (London: Longman), p. 98.

Competition in the US

In 1982, W. G. Sheperd published some surprising evidence for the US, using the concept of effective competition. He defined effective competition as an industry sector with a four-firm concentration ratio below 40 per cent, with unstable market shares, low entry barriers and low profit rates, and then measured the proportion of each sector that was effectively competitive (Table 8.2).

Note that this definition of effective competition relies on very broad industry definitions. To say that 80 per cent of US manufacturing industry was effectively competitive on this definition does not imply that no single manufacturer has a monopoly of a particular product line.

Table 8.2   Effective competition in the US, 1980

Sector	% of sector that was effectively competitive
Agriculture, forestry and fishing	86.4
Manufacturing	80.2
Transport and public utilities	39.1
Wholesale and retail trade	93.4
Services	77.9

Source: M. Chacholiades (1986) *Microeconomics* (New York: Macmillan).

Barriers to entry

Recall that Bain's investigation categorised industries into four groups, according to the ease of entry. Of the twenty industries examined by Bain,[6] ten were classified as easy entry, four as ineffectively impeded entry, six as effectively impeded entry and none as blockaded entry. However, Bain only considered the possibility of entry by completely new firms. In a world of industrial conglomerates, entry may be considerably easier for firms well established in other industries, and with considerable financial, technical and managerial resources.

Advertising

Table 8.3 lists the advertising expenditures of the UK's top ten advertisers in 1982. The largest advertiser, Procter and Gamble, has an enormous product range, mainly in personal and household

Table 8.3   Advertising expenditure of the UK's ten largest advertisers

Company	1982 advertising expenditure £m
Procter and Gamble	45.8
Mars	27.5
Imperial Tobacco	26.1
Cadbury	26.0
Kelloggs	24.6
Rowntree Mackintosh	21.8
General Foods	20.1
Electricity Council	19.6
Pedigree Petfoods	18.2
Nestle	17.3

Source: A. Griffiths and S. Wall (1984) *Applied Economics* (London: Longman), p. 100

cleaning materials. Such massive expenditure may not only reinforce product differentiation, but may also create a substantial entry
barrier for new competition.

It is not surprising that the companies listed are all major
producers of non-durable consumer products, since these are the
very goods most amenable to product differentiation.

Measuring the impact of market power is even more difficult than
proving its existence. Nevertheless, there is a body of evidence
(including the application at the end of this chapter) to show that
market concentration, entry barriers and extensive advertising all
increase the profitability of firms and increase the likelihood of
long-run survival. For example, Singh[7] showed that the probability
of takeover was inversely related to firm size rather than any other
measured dimension.

Competition policy

The foundation of public policy towards competition is the theoretical and empirical evidence that the exercise of market power leads
to a loss in public welfare as a result of high prices, restricted output
and possible inefficiency. From a managerial or decision-making
perspective, public competition policy acts as a constraint on the
exercise and acquisition of market power.

In the United States, the presumption of competition policy has
been directed against the acquisition of market power, with a
substantial body of statutory and case law providing a significant
amount of interference and restriction on the workings of the
market. In the United Kingdom, public policy has been much more
pragmatic, with a greater willingness to examine the costs and
benefits of particular situations before making particular policy
prescriptions.

Government policy towards competition in Britain is a combination of legal statute and the government's persuasive powers. The
exercise of persuasive power ranges from ministerial advice to
discretionary financial support for particular actions. The legislative
framework for competition policy has developed since 1948, with
Table 8.4 listing the major Acts of Parliament since then, together
with their effects. There have also been a number of minor Acts
dealing with particular restrictive practices such as the abolition of
resale price maintenance in 1964 and the enforcement of statutory
ballots preceding industrial action by employees in the early 1980s.

Table 8.4   Competition policy in the UK

Year	Act	Effect
1948	*Monopoly and Restrictive Practices Act* – Set up a government commission to examine monopoly situations referred to it by the Board of Trade. Defined a monopoly as one firm supplying more than one-third of a market.	
1956	*Restrictive Trade Practices Act* – required the registration and investigation of all restrictive practices by a Restrictive Trade Practices Court.	
1965	*Monopolies and Mergers Act* – allowed the investigation of proposed mergers where the merged firm would supply more than one-third of a market or where acquired assets exceeded £5m (later increased to £15m).	
1973	*Fair Trading Act* – redefined a monopoly as a firm with a market share in excess of 25%. Monopolies Commission required to take account of pricing, innovation and freedom of entry.	
1980	*Competition Act* – gave the Director-General of Fair Trading power to investigate any 'anti-competitive practice' of individual firms.	

The effects of legislation have been much more widespread than the number of cases actually investigated. For example, the power to investigate mergers has affected many more merger proposals than the relatively few actually considered under the Acts. The widespread powers of investigation given to the Director-General of Fair Trading under the 1980 Competition Act can be expected to have a similarly greater influence than the number of actual investigations would suggest.

The other arm of government policy towards monopoly in the UK has been that of nationalisation. Prior to 1979, these powers had been used to bring natural monopolies under direct state ownership, so that behaviour could be directed by central government, operating through the chairmen of nationalised industries. Since 1979, the British government has developed a privatisation policy towards nationalised industries, returning some of these industries to private control and reducing the extent of government influence.

Summary and conclusions

The economic analysis of competition and market structure examines the way that the business organisation reacts with its competitive environment. The form of that market structure has important implications for the conduct and performance of individual firms.

The actual concept of competition proved to be difficult to define, resting as it does on the availability of purchase choices to the consumer, and the power of individual firms to set prices and/or outputs. The major determinants of competition were seen to be the size distribution of firms, the degree of product differentiation and barriers to the entry of new firms.

The economic theory of the firm has evolved various models of market structure, which are useful as reference points to the behaviour of individual markets. The more general concepts of workable or effective competition may be of more practical value in establishing the degree of competition. The measurement of market power was complicated by the difficulties of defining an industry or market. The cross-price elasticity of demand, the concentration ratio and the height of barriers to entry were each found to say something about the degree of competition, although no single index of market power exists. A sample of empirical evidence was considered, showing that competition had weakened in the UK and grown stronger in the USA, but that each conclusion depended on the partial measure of competition adopted.

Finally, competition policy in the UK was described, as it has developed since the Second World War. The emphasis of UK competition is on setting guidelines and using persuasion rather than the full force and majesty of British law.

Application 8

Late entry and competitive survival: the case of synthetic fibres[8]

Introduction

The economic analysis of market structure draws together elements of demand and cost analysis into a theory of the firm that relates the firm's performance to the behaviour of its competitors. In doing so, the analysis of market structure produces a number of testable hypotheses about the timing of entry and the chances of competitive survival. This application will examine those hypotheses in relation to one particular industry: the market for synthetic fibres in Western Europe.

The background

The market development of three main synthetic fibres – acrylic, nylon and polyester – occurred after the end of the Second World War, and experienced rapid growth until around 1973. Table A8.1 shows the growth of output in Western Europe, and illustrates the product life-cycle, with slow initial growth followed by rapid expansion, and finally tailing off as the market approached maturity (corresponding to the logistic demand function in Figure 5.10). Rapid growth was largely at the expense of natural fibres. After 1973, growth tailed-off as a result of rising costs (due to the oil crisis), increasing imports of finished textiles and the change in tastes back towards natural fibres.

The Western European synthetic fibre industry has several special characteristics. Until the mid-1960s, the Western European market was subdivided along national boundaries, with these divisions

Table A8.1 Output levels in the Western European synthetic fibre industry (thousand tonnes)

Year	Acrylic	Nylon	Polyester
1955		55	
1960	21	130	51
1965	125	313	151
1970	399	599	458
1973	651	813	826
1975	540	630	682
1980	732	647	762

Source: R. W. Shaw and S. A. Shaw (1984) 'Late Entry, Market Shares and Competitive Survival: The Case of Synthetic Fibres', *Management and Decision Economics*, vol. 15, no. 2, p. 74.

reinforced by patents and tariffs. However, in the mid-1960s, patents had mainly expired and the development of the European Economic Community drastically reduced tariff barriers. Secondly, as a part of the chemical industry, synthetic fibres are relatively research intensive, and substantial development expenditure is necessary for product and production improvements. Finally, despite physical and chemical similarities, synthetic fibres cover a multiplicity of separate products, ranging from tyre cord to carpets and clothing.

Economic analysis

Given the technological nature of the industry, the cost structure of production can be expected to correspond to a learning curve, with unit costs falling in proportion to accumulated experience. Thus the late entrant can be expected to have a substantial cost disadvantage, allowing existing firms to charge a limit price exceeding the perfectly competitive price. In addition, the life-cycle of the product implies that entry is more likely to be successful if it occurs during the growth phase, again bestowing an advantage on the early entrant.

New entry may succeed if the new entrant can introduce superior production processes, and/or identify a specialised segment of the market. However, a profitable submarket is more likely to be identified during the growth stage of the product cycle, conferring yet another competitive advantage on the early entrant.

The conclusion drawn from this analysis is that the early entrant is likely to enjoy a competitive advantage over the late-comer. This hypothesis can be tested in a number of ways. One way would be to examine the relationship between market share and profitability.

Table A8.2

(i) Nylon

Early entrant (producing by 1953)

Firm	Share of capacity 1975	1980	Survival end 1981
ICI	19.0	21.0	√
Rhone Poulenc	16.5	17.5	√
AKZO	18.0	16.0	√
Snia Viscosa	9.5	11.0	√
Bayer	6.0	5.0	√
Montefibre	5.5	4.5	√

Late entrant

Firm	Entry date	Share of capacity 1975	1980	Survival end 1981
DuPont	1968	6.0	6.5	√
Courtaulds	1965	5.5	4.0	Withdrawing
ANIC	1965	1.5	2.5	√
Fabelta	1960	0.5	1.0	?
Monsato	1966	4.0		Withdrawn

(ii) Acrylics

Early entrant (producing by 1953)

Firm	Share of capacity 1975	1980	Survival end 1981
Courtaulds	20.0	18.0	√
Bayer	14.5	13.5	√
Montefibre	12.5	12.0	√
Monsato	8.0	8.0	√
Hoeschst	9.5	7.5	√
Rhone Poulenc	6.5	3.5	Withdrawing

Late entrant

Firm	Entry date	Share of capacity 1975	1980	Survival end 1981
AKZO	1967	4.5	6.0	√
ANIC	1964	5.5	10.5	√
DuPont	1962	7.5	4.0	Withdrawing
Fabelta	1960	3.0	3.0	Withdrawing
SIR	1968	1.0	3.0	Withdrawing
Snia Viscosa	1961	5.0	6.0	√

(iii) Polyesters

Early entrant (producing by 1957)

Firm	Share of capacity 1975	1980	Survival end 1981
AKZO	22.0	23.0	√
Hoeschst	22.0	20.0	√
ICI	14.0	14.0	√
Rhone Poulenc	13.5	14.0	√
Montefibre	6.0	4.0	√

Late entrant

Firm	Entry date	Share of capacity 1975	1980	Survival end 1981
DuPont	1967	6.5	7.5	√
ANIC	1968	3.0	5.0	√
Snia Viscosa	1966	2.5	2.5	√
SIR	1968	2.0	2.0	Withdrawing
Courtaulds	1971	1.5	2.0	√
Bayer	1966	4.5	0.5	Withdrawing

Source: R. W. Shaw and S. A. Shaw (1984) 'Late Entry, Market-Shares and Economic Survival', pp. 75–7.

Since the early entrant is likely to have a high market share, a positive correlation between market share and profitability is an indication of relative competitive strength. Another method would be to examine the stability of market share. If the late entrant has no competitive disadvantage, market shares can be expected to be unstable over time, since the late entrant has an equal chance of growth. If, however, the early entrant can establish and maintain a high market share, this indicates some advantage over the late entrant. The ultimate test of competitive advantage is the ability to survive in a stagnant or declining market. If the total market declines, it is the high cost firms who can be expected to be the first casualties. This is the approach adopted by Shaw and Shaw, who examined the relationship between date of entry and survival over the critical years 1975–80, with the results shown in Table A8.2.

Of the firms withdrawing from a segment of the synthetic fibre market, only one was an early entrant. Of the surviving late entrants one firm DuPont (represented in each market) had massive experience in the US market, offsetting any learning–curve effects.

Conclusions

Early entrants in the synthetic fibre industry generally managed to maintain their market share leads in the later stages of the product cycle. Late entrants usually failed to establish a significant market share (with the exception of DuPont), and risked a much higher chance of failure. Finally, in the market depression of the late 1970s, late entrants with characteristically small market shares were particularly vulnerable. Shaw and Shaw conclude with the contention that 'in a rapidly growing product area, the most successful strategy is to achieve and hold a dominant market position'.

Pricing decisions

Contents

Introduction

Pricing is a decision area which draws together contributions from the theories of demand, cost and market structure. The pricing decision has been the major focus of economic theory in the analysis of resource allocation, but its position in managerial economics is more limited. In the analysis of business decision-making, pricing is just one element in a comprehensive competitive strategy. Moreover, the pricing decision is a *means* to an end, and not the end in itself, so that decisions about price must be considered in the context of overall business objectives. As we shall see, price is a strategic as well as an operational variable, so that pricing decisions can have a profound effect on future as well as present performance. Because of this time dimension, pricing objectives need to be carefully defined. For example, setting a low current price may be an optimal decision if the consequent establishment of a dominant market position leads to long-run profits sufficient to outweigh any short-run profit sacrifice.

The purpose of this chapter is to derive a pricing policy, in the form of some general pricing rules, which can be used to govern pricing behaviour. In doing so, we shall consider pricing only from the seller's viewpoint, which means leaving the implications of pricing behaviour from the consumer's or society's point of view to that body of theory known as welfare economics.

Merely to consider the determination of a pricing policy is to assume that the seller has some discretion over price, i.e. that the market situation is not perfectly competitive. For in a perfectly competitive market there is no pricing decision to make, since the firm must take the price determined by the market. Hence the primary influence on pricing discretion is the competitive environment. The theories of market structure outlined in the previous chapter will be an important guide in the analysis of pricing decisions, but with the important proviso that actual market situations don't fit neatly into the compartments defined by the theory of market structures. This chapter will consider pricing strategies in a variety of market situations, but where the market is defined by the product rather than the number and size of firms. This inevitably leads to some overlap between market structures as previously defined, but captures the dynamic nature of pricing strategy in terms of product market development. The chapter will conclude by considering some pricing practices, but first it is useful to develop a general model of economic pricing

A general pricing model

Assume that the firm seeks to maximise profits. This is achieved when marginal cost is equal to marginal revenue. Total costs for the firm is the product of average cost (AC) and output (Q), whilst total revenue is the product of price (P) and output.

$$TC = AC \times Q$$

$$TR = P \times Q$$

Then $MC = \dfrac{dTC}{dQ} = AC + Q \cdot \dfrac{dAC}{dQ}$

and $MR = \dfrac{dTR}{dQ} = P + Q \cdot \dfrac{dP}{dQ}$

To maximise profit, $MR = MC$

$$P + Q \cdot \dfrac{dP}{dQ} = AC + Q \cdot \dfrac{dAC}{dQ}$$

Therefore, $P = AC + Q\left(\dfrac{dAC}{dQ} - \dfrac{dP}{dQ}\right)$

The profit maximising price then depends on both cost and demand conditions, with AC and dAC/dQ determined by costs, and Q, dP/dQ determined by demand. The implications of any change in cost or demand conditions can be derived by comparative static analysis (i.e. comparing the pre and post change situations), and are summarised in Table 9.1. Thus an increase in variable cost leads to an increase in price and a fall in the profit margin.

Table 9.1   The consequence of change on price and profit margins

Change	Price	Profit margin $P - AC$
1. Increase in Demand (D curve moves right)	+	?(+)
2. Demand less elastic (D curve steeper)	+	+
3. Rise in fixed cost	0	−
4. Rise in variable cost	+	−
(bracketed value if AC constant)		

As an analysis of change the general pricing model is simple and generally unambiguous. However, at best the model can only indicate the direction rather than the size of change. Moreover, the model imposes strict informational requirements. Few firms know their cost (let alone demand) conditions with the precision required. The model takes no account of any uncertainty over rivals' reactions, and ignores the time dimension of competition.

Monopoly and entry

The natural starting point for an analysis of situations of pricing discretion is the monopoly model outlined in the previous chapter. It is necessary to exercise some caution though in the definition of products and markets. The monopoly may be long run, where product distinctiveness is maintained over some long period, or short run, where the product is soon copied and monopoly power eroded. However, the monopolist may well be able to sustain that position by the adoption of a moderate pricing policy which will deter entry, but only at the cost of losing the major advantage of a monopoly position – the power to achieve high economic profits.

The economic model of monopoly pricing is shown in Figure 9.1. To maximise profits, the firm equates marginal cost and marginal revenue, resulting in the monopoly price *Pm* and output *Qm*. The abnormal profits generated (shaded area) persist because of some barrier to the entry of new competition.

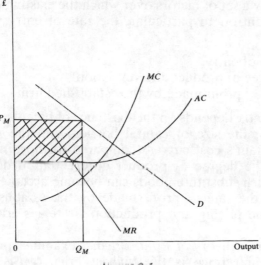

Figure 9.1

As an analytical tool, the model is useful, but suffers from some serious practical limitations:

(1) Information

To achieve the profit maximising price and output requires precise information about cost and demand conditions.

(2) Time

The model is static and takes no account of the effects of behaviour on future profits (because of the assumption of insurmountable entry barriers).

In practice the monopoly is likely to be *transitory* rather than permanent, with high profit acting as a powerful incentive for competitors to overcome the entry barriers. Then the informational requirements of the monopolist are compounded by the need to estimate the possible future costs of potential entrants. A new entrant may have higher or lower costs than the established firm, depending on the opportunities offered by new technology, the scale of entry and the existence or absence of any consumer loyalty to the established producer.

The rate of entry into the market is an economic variable determined by a set of factors over which the existing producer may have some control. In particular, the rate of entry will be determined by:

(a)   the ease of entry;
(b)   the degree of product differentiation;
(c)   the rate of profit made by the established firm.

The ease of entry depends on the existence of patents, the control of scarce inputs, the size of capital barriers and the nature of the potential entrant's cost curves (compared to those of the existing producer). The degree of product differentiation determines the ease with which substitute goods can become accepted by consumers. Finally, the rate of profit made by the established firm will depend on the pricing and production strategies adopted by that firm.

The economic theory of *Limit Pricing*[1] examines pricing to deter entry. The limit price is the highest price consistent with not attracting new entry. One useful limit-pricing model is that developed by Modigliani[2] on the behavioural assumption that the potential entrant expects the established firm to maintain its pre-entry output level after entry occurs. The model is demonstrated in Figure 9.2, assuming a downward sloping industry demand curve and asymptomatic L-shaped long-run average cost curve.

On the assumption that the established firm maintains its output, only that part of the industry demand curve to the right of the existing price output combination is available to the new entrant. Since the limit price is the highest price consistent with no part of that residual demand curve being profitable to the entrant, the limit price can be found by sliding the long-run average cost curve to the right until no part lies inside the industry demand curve ($LRAC^1$). This is equivalent to moving the origin from 0 to 0^1, resulting in the limit price of P_L (and output $0\,0^1$) for the existing firm. At the limit price P_L, the average cost curve for the entrant is $LRAC^1$ and no profit is possible. Thus, the established firm can maintain the profit shown by the shaded area without attracting entry. The limit price then depends upon:

(i)   the relative cost conditions of the potential entrant and

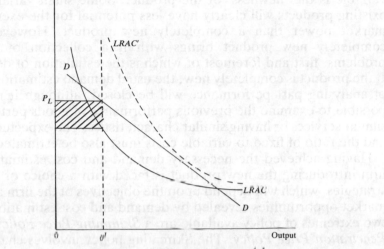

Figure 9.2   The limit-pricing model

existing producer. If the entrant can achieve average costs lower than $LRAC^1$, profits will be possible after entry.

(ii)   the elasticity of demand. The lower the elasticity of demand (the more steep the demand curve), the higher the limit price.

(iii)   the extent of economies of scale. The steeper the long-run average cost curve, the higher the limit price (and the greater the cost disadvantage of entering at less than optimal scale).

(iv)   the output (and price) reaction of the established firm. If the potential entrant expects the existing firm to increase output (lower price) after entry, entry will be deterred. Alternatively, entry will be made easier by the expectation that the existing firm will reduce output to accommodate the entrant.

Pricing new products

One useful application of the monopoly and entry situation is the pricing of new products. By definition, the introduction of a new product creates a monopoly, whose duration depends on a list of strategic variables inside and outside the firm's control. The basic problem for the firm is to find a price and promotional mix that will maximise the long-run profit from the new product. One important variable is the 'newness' of the product. Some small variation on existing products will clearly have less potential for the exercise of market power than a completely new product. However, the completely new product brings with it a collection of special problems, first and foremost of which is the estimation of demand. If the product is completely new, the usual demand estimation route of analysing past performance will be closed, although it may be possible to examine the previous performance of goods performing similar services or having similar characteristics. The expected costs, and the ratio of fixed to variable costs must also be estimated.

Having achieved the necessary demand and cost estimates, the firm introducing the new product is faced with a choice of pricing strategies, which will depend upon the objectives of the firm and the market opportunities revealed by demand and cost estimation. The two extremes of policy available are a *Skimming Price Policy* and a *Penetration Price Policy*. The Skimming policy involves charging a high initial price, recovering development costs quickly and making large profits that attract entry. The Penetration policy implies charging a low price to deter entry, so that a smaller profit is made over a longer period. One solution to that choice is to estimate the discounted net present value of profits from each strategy, and choose the option to maximise this. However, this again implies a level of information which is unlikely to be attained, since projected profits will depend on the anticipated behaviour of future competitors. Moreover, the choice of a discount rate for net present value calculations could be crucial, with a higher discount rate favouring the Skimming policy.

A more useful alternative approach may be to examine the cost and demand characteristics that favour each approach, and then compare the anticipated market situation with each set of characteristics.

The Skimming policy is useful for new products when:

(i)   demand is more elastic in the short run than the long run because of novelty.

(ii) each consumer only purchases the good once. Then setting a high initial price will attract high income/low price elasticity customers. The price can then be lowered for the next income group, etc. Such an approach 'skims the cream off' each market segment, maximising revenue.

(iii) the firm has cash flow problems, and thus needs a high return quickly.

(iv) the firm is a 'snatcher' and intends to leave the industry after a short period of high profits.

One obvious example of a Skimming policy is in publishing, whereby the new novel is sold first in hardback at high prices, then to a book club at a lower price, and finally in paperback at low price.
The Penetration price policy is likely to be successful if:

(i)   the short-run price elasticity of demand is high. By charging a low price, the first entrant is able to establish a market, creating brand loyalty and a high barrier to entry.

(ii) economies of scale are significant. By entering at a large scale the first firm can both enjoy low average costs and impose a cost penalty on any small scale subsequent entrant.

(iii) the firm is a 'sticker' and intends to remain in the industry long term.

One example of a penetration policy is the introduction of the Amstrad Word Processor, at a price substantially lower than any competitor. This brought 'serious' computing applications within the reach of a vast market untouched by previous producers. By producing and selling in large numbers, Amstrad were able to take advantage of substantial scale economies, and created a vast and profitable market for software and peripherals.

Figure 9.3 illustrates the time profiles of revenue corresponding to each strategy. The Skimming policy builds up revenue quickly, but revenue then falls as competitors enter. The Penetration policy takes longer to generate revenue, but revenue persists over a longer period.

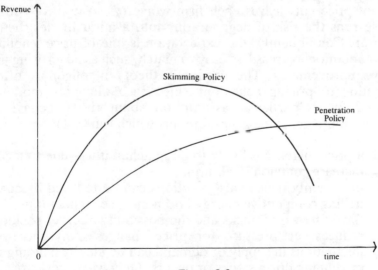

Figure 9.3

Ultimately the choice of a pricing strategy for the new product depends on the elasticity of demand, the nature of costs (own and potential entrants) and the firm's rate of time preference for profits. Note finally that the policies are not mutually exclusive – it may be advantageous to start with a skimming policy and then switch to a penetration policy when new entry looks likely.

Pricing established products

Pricing for established products generally implies pricing in an oligopolistic market, where the actions of each firm have an effect on the performance and behaviour of competitors. The market may be a homogeneous oligopoly, where the rivals' products are similar, or a differentiated oligopoly, whereby price differentials may persist but competition is sufficiently strong to ensure rivals pay close attention to each other's behaviour. The previous chapter demonstrated the growing importance and prevalence of oligopolistic markets in national terms, which is likely to understate the extent of oligopoly in local markets. Furthermore, both competitive and monopoly markets have a tendency towards oligopoly over time as competitors search for product differentiation and entrants encroach into monopoly territory.

The general characteristic of oligopoly markets is an aversion to price-cutting. Each firm may expect any price cut to be met promptly so that market share may not increase, and a general round of price cuts leaves each firm worse off. Any price-cutting exercise runs the risk of degenerating into a mutually destructive price war. Consequently, the expectation is one of price stability, with competition in areas less easy to match, such as advertising and quality improvements. The economic theory of oligopoly offers little guide to pricing behaviour since each oligopoly model is restricted by its particular assumption about rivals' behaviour. However, there are some general points which can be made:

(i)   a price increase is likely to be matched if it is due to a cost increase common to all firms.
(ii) uncertainty over rivals' reactions can be reduced by channelling competitive energy into non-price competition.
(iii) the existence of stocks and the possibility of order backlogs reduces the pressure for price changes. Any short-run fluctuations in supply or demand can be met by building up or running down stocks or orders. Only when stocks rise to

levels expensive to hold or fall to levels which may fail to meet demand, need a price change be contemplated.

(iv) Price uncertainty can be reduced or eliminated by the formation of collusive agreements, though these may be unstable because individual firms' interests may clash with group interests.

One variable that may be important in the determination of a pricing strategy for established products is the position of that good in the product life-cycle. The concept of a product life-cycle was introduced in Application 8, with Figure 9.4 reproducing the product life-cycle for man-made fibres.

In the initial growth phase, both the market share and total market size grow rapidly, possibly prompted by a penetration price strategy. As the market reaches maturity, growth tails off. The high market share/high quality product can often maintain a high price on the basis of established reputation. Heavy promotional and product development expenditure may be incurred to maintain this market position. Production cost may be relatively low because of scale economies. Finally, the total market declines, because of changing tastes or innovations elsewhere. The judicious firm will channel previously generated resources into a search for alternative markets, leaving the declining market to be met by declining production facilities.

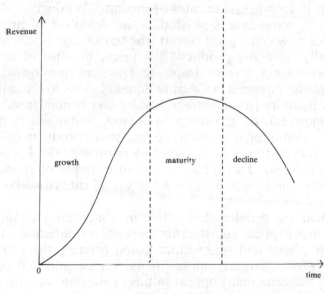

Figure 9.4

Pricing strategies

So far we have examined pricing strategies in relation to competition (both actual and potential) and product maturity. However, there are a variety of market situations that call for subtlety in the pricing approach, carefully considering how price reacts with other product dimensions, and how customers may respond to various pricing attributes. For example, most companies sell product lines, rather than single products. The formal analysis of multiproduct pricing will be considered later, but for the moment we can note that an optimal pricing strategy for the product range involves explicit recognition of the demand and production interrelationships between the various products in that product range. For example, a new car model is not a single product, but a range of cars varying in performance and comfort. Then one common product line pricing strategy is to price the basic model low, attracting customers to the showrooms, who can then be enticed to purchase more refined versions at premium prices. A related problem is that of pricing optional extras and spare parts. Since these are *complements* to the initial product, a low price/low profit margin strategy for the initial product may create a captive market for high price/high profit margin spare parts. Most razor manufacturers are happy to sell razors at low prices (perhaps even below average cost), since this creates a captive market for replacement blades. The policy cannot be carried to extremes, however, since a reputation for high spare part prices is detrimental to sales of the initial product.

Moreover, some care is needed in the definition of prices. The actual price at which a good is sold (the transaction price) may vary substantially from the product's list price, because of discounts, trade-in allowances, finance deals, etc. Discounts may be offered for cash or prompt payment (reflecting liquidity gains to the seller), for buying in quantity (to encourage loyalty and benefit from scale or stock economies), or according to season. Some sellers may use price as a promotional weapon, selling some products below unit cost to attract customers who then buy normally priced products as well (loss leaders). January sales are an example of special-event pricing, attracting customers in what would otherwise be a quiet period.

One recurrent problem for sellers in a modern economy is the need to make price adjustments because of inflation. Inflation pushes up labour and other input costs, offering the prospect of squeezed profit margins unless prices can be adjusted upwards. However, there are many opportunities to alleviate adverse customer reactions by disguising price rises. Some examples are:

Escalator clauses Where there is a time-lag between order and delivery, the quoted price may contain some adjustment factor allowing the seller to pass on any subsequent cost increases.

Reduction of discounts The company eliminates any special offers or discounts to bring transaction prices into line with list prices.

Quality changes Profit margins are restored by reducing quality, size or services offered. Charges may be introduced for previously free services or extras.

One common strategy is to introduce a new list price alongside some special offer such as a discount or extra quantity (125 grammes for the price of 100!). The special offer can then be quietly dropped at some future date, once customers have got used to the new list price.

Price discrimination

Price discrimination is the practice of selling the same product to different customers at different prices, where the difference in price is unrelated to any difference in costs. Price discrimination can add to the revenue of the firm (and hence profits) if

— the markets for the products are separable, and
— the price elasticity of demand is different in different markets.

The separability of markets is essential if low-price customers are not to resell to high-price ones. Markets may be separated geographically, or through time, or by selling a non-transferable product. For example, a hairdressing firm may charge lower prices at the out-of-town branch than in the city centre, or offer cheaper haircuts at some off-peak time (Tuesday mornings!) or offer a reduced price to students or pensioners. However, the first two practices may not be price discriminative if costs are lower out of town, or at off-peak periods (because of spare capacity). The leakage between markets may depend on the price difference, especially if market separation is due to inertia or price ignorance.

The basic profitability requirement for price discrimination is a difference in demand price elasticities. The firm facing different markets for the same product will profit maximise by setting marginal revenue equal to marginal cost in each. This implies that price will be lower in the more elastic market.

Suppose a firm sells the same good in two markets x and y, whilst the good has a common and constant average cost (c). Then total profit to the firm will be π, where

$$\pi = PxQx + PyQy - C(Qx + Qy)$$

To maximise profit, differentiate π with respect to Qx, Qy, and set each partial derivative equal to zero.

$$\frac{\delta\pi}{\delta Qx} = Px + Qx \cdot \frac{\delta Px}{\delta Qx} + Qy \cdot \frac{\delta Py}{\delta Qx} - C = 0$$

$$\frac{\delta\pi}{\delta Qy} = Py + Qy \cdot \frac{\delta Py}{\delta Qy} + Qx \cdot \frac{\delta Px}{\delta Qy} - C = 0$$

Since the markets are separate, demand in each market will be unrelated to price in the other, so that $\delta Py/\delta Qx$, $\delta Px/\delta Qy = 0$

So $$Px + Qx \cdot \frac{\delta Px}{\delta Qx} - C = 0 = Py + Qy \cdot \frac{\delta Py}{\delta Qy} - C$$

and $$Px + Qx \cdot \frac{\delta Px}{\delta Qx} = Py + Qy \cdot \frac{\delta Py}{\delta Qy}$$

By multiplying the top and bottom of each second term by the relevant price, the demand elasticities can be introduced,

i.e. $$Px + Px \cdot \frac{Qx}{Px} \cdot \frac{\delta Px}{\delta Qx} = Py + Py \cdot \frac{Qy}{Py} \cdot \frac{\delta Py}{\delta Qy}$$

So $$Px\left(1 + \frac{1}{\varepsilon x}\right) = Py\left(1 + \frac{1}{\varepsilon y}\right)$$

$$\frac{Px}{Py} = \frac{1 + (1/\varepsilon y)}{1 + (1/\varepsilon x)}$$

where εx is the price elasticity of demand for x and εy is the price elasticity of demand for y.

The optimal price differential will depend on the relative demand elasticities. If the price elasticity of x exceeds that of y, the price of x will be set lower than that of y.

The same result can be achieved graphically. Suppose the demand curves corresponding to the markets x and y are as illustrated in Figure 9.5. Corresponding to each demand curve will be a marginal revenue curve lying below it (MRx and MRy). The total market demand can be found by the horizontal summation of the demand curves, to give market demand curve ΣD. Similarly, the total marginal revenue curve can be found by adding together the individual marginal revenue curves (to get ΣMR). If the marginal cost curve for the common product is shown by the line MC, profit will be maximised in the absence of price discrimination by producing output Z at price P. However, if the markets can be separated, revenue can be increased by equating *each* individual marginal revenue with marginal cost. Total industry output remains at Z, giving the marginal cost shown by the line AB. Equating individual marginal revenue with this marginal cost results in output Qx in market x, and QY in market y. Price is determined in each market by tracing back the price corresponding to that output level to each individual demand curve. Thus the price in market x is Px, and in market y is Py.

Price discrimination may be used to accomplish other objectives as well as increasing revenue. For example, the off-peak low pricing strategy for electricity may reduce demand fluctuations during the day, and hence reduce production costs. Offering free banking to students (even if overdrawn) may capture the future banking custom of potential high-earners. Finally, price discrimination may accomplish social objectives, for example, improving the mobility of pensioners through the use of discount qualifying bus passes. Whether offering discounts to students is a social or profit motivated action is a matter of debate!

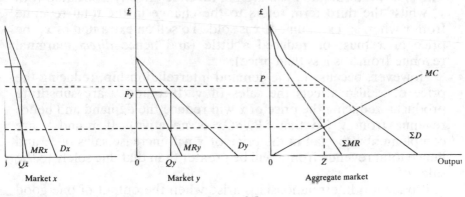

Figure 9.5

Multiproduct pricing

If the firm had perfect information, the addition of extra products would cause few pricing problems, since overall profit would be maximised by equating the marginal cost and marginal revenue of each product. However, the addition of multiple products adds considerably to the informational complexity of pricing decisions, because of the possibility of demand and production interrelationships.

Demand interrelationships arise because of competition or complementarity *within* the product range. If products are substitutes or complements, a price change for one good will affect the demand, and hence revenue, of the others. Optimal pricing requires that this interrelationship be explicitly accounted for in the pricing process.[3]

Suppose the firm produces two goods, x and y, where the price of one affects the demand for the other, i.e.

$$Qx = f(Px, Py) \qquad Qy = g(Py, Px)$$

Then total revenue will be the sum of revenues from each product, i.e.

$$TR = PxQx + PyQy$$

The marginal revenue from product x is found by differentiating total revenue with respect to Qx,

$$\text{i.e. } MRx = Px + Qx \cdot \frac{\delta Px}{\delta Qx} + Qy \cdot \frac{\delta Py}{\delta Qx}$$

The first two terms are the marginal revenue directly associated with x, whilst the third term refers to the change in the total revenue from y when an extra unit of x is sold. To sell an extra unit of x, the price of x must be reduced a little (and hence *direct* marginal revenue from x is less than price).

However, because of the demand interrelationship, reducing the price of x also affects the sales of y. If x and y are substitute products, reducing the price of x will reduce the demand and hence revenue from y (so that $\delta Py/\delta Qx$ is negative). If x and y are complements, the fall in the price of x will increase sales of y, and hence total revenue from x will be greater than that due solely to the sales of x.

Production interrelationships arise when the output of one good affects the output of the other. Once more the products may be complements or substitutes on the supply side, depending on whether increased output of one results in increased or decreased output of the other. For example, increasing the output of petrol will increase the output of fuel oil, since both are produced from crude oil in more or less fixed proportions. However, increasing the output of men's shoes may reduce the output of ladies' shoes, since scarce shoe-making equipment may be tied up. Once again, the conceptual difficulty is in identifying the separate marginal costs due to each product, for equating with marginal revenue. The allocation of joint costs between separable products is a topic worthy of its own chapter if not book! Suffice to say that often the only sensible solution is to equate the total marginal cost with the total marginal revenue.

Transfer pricing

The large multiproduct, multinational firm is often decentralised by being split into semi-autonomous divisions, each responsible for its own price and output decisions and profit performance. Indeed, economists now talk about an international division of labour, with components being produced in different countries according to cost conditions and assembly in some other country. Such decentralisation brings with it its own resource allocation problems, one aspect of which is the pricing of products transferred between divisions. The transfer pricing problem is then one of determining the transfer price which maximises the overall profit for the company. For example, one division may be able to increase its own profits by raising the transfer price, at the cost of profits made by the receiving division.

The general answer to the transfer pricing problem is that the transferred product should be priced at marginal cost. There are a variety of possible situations, depending on the existence and competitive nature of any external market for the transferred product, as well as the nature of the market for the final good. We shall consider only the simplest case of a perfectively competitive market for the transferred good and an imperfect market for the final good, although the analysis can be extended for a variety of market forms.[4]

Suppose that Division I produces good T, which can be sold on a perfectly competitive external market at price Pt, or transferred to Division II to be used in the production of good F, for which there is an imperfect external market. Assume one unit of T is needed to produce one unit of F. The situation is illustrated in Figure 9.6. Division I faces a perfectly elastic demand curve for good T (and therefore $AR_T = MR_T$), and an upward sloping marginal cost curve MC_T. Division II faces a downward sloping demand curve for $F(DF)$ and consequently a marginal revenue curve inside this.

There will be costs of producing F, irrespective of the transfer price. Let the marginal cost of producing F, before the transfer price is paid, be MC_F.

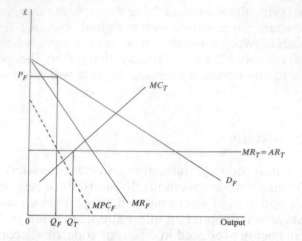

Figure 9.6   Transfer pricing: perfectly competitive market for transferred good

Then a new curve can be found by subtracting these production costs of F (independent of the transfer price) from the marginal revenue of F, showing the marginal profit contribution of F before the transfer price is paid, $MPC_F = MR_F - MC_F$.

The profit maximising output of F occurs where the marginal revenue from F is equal to the marginal total cost of F, i.e. where $MR_F = MPC_F + P_T$.

Let the transfer price be P_T. Optimal production of F is where

$$MR_F - MC_F = MPC_F = P_T$$

i.e. $MR_F = P_T + MC_F$

This is at output level Q_F, with a final product price of P_F.

The optimal production of T requires $MC_T = MR_T$. Division I therefore produces Q_T, and sells at price P_T. Overall profit is higher than at any other transfer price.

Note that as drawn, Division I is producing more of good T than is needed in the production of F. Because of the competitive external market, the surplus $Q_T - Q_F$ can be sold externally at price P_T. If the optimal solution had meant Division I producing less than required by Division II, any shortage could be made up by purchase on the external market at P_T.

When divisions are located in countries with different tax structures, transfer pricing can be used to redistribute profits between countries to minimise overall tax liability. For example, if country A has a high profits tax relative to country B, the transfer price could be set artificially low in country A, so that profits are realised in country B. Such arrangements are generally illegal under free trade regulations but extremely difficult to monitor, particularly if the market for the transferred good is either uncompetitive or absent.

Empirical pricing evidence

Despite the dominance of pricing in the history of economic thought, and a large number of empirical investigations into pricing practice, there remain many unresolved issues in pricing practice, and considerable difficulty in trying to relate pricing behaviour to price theory.[5]

There are a number of reasons for these difficulties:

— inferring what firms *are* doing about price from what they *say* they are doing or even what they *appear* to be doing may be impossible.

— different market situations or levels of management experience and ability may give rise to entirely different pricing procedures.

— price is just one element in competitive strategy and may not be particularly important when compared to product development, advertising, etc.

— the price of a product may be ambiguous, subject to discount or service qualifications, or even to negotiation for large buyers.

— factors determining the price level and those that determine price adjustments may be different.

— pricing in a world of uncertainty, with time lags, stocks and order backlogs, booms and recessions may be very different from pricing in a world of certainty and perfect information.

— pricing objectives may vary, from survival, through maintaining or increasing market share to growth or profit maximisation. Pricing for short-term survival, where the intention is to keep production flowing and cover variable costs, will differ substantially from pricing to maximise long-run profit.

Average cost or cost-plus pricing

The most famous study of pricing was by Hall and Hitch[6] in 1939. They interviewed managers of thirty-eight firms in manufacturing, retail and construction. They found that firms did not use marginalist principles, did not seek to maximise profits, and operated in oligopolistic markets. Out of the thirty-eight firms, thirty claimed to set price on the basis of some mark up over unit costs (usually 10 per cent). Numerous later studies in the UK and other countries have confirmed the widespread prevalence of average cost pricing. This involves some variation of the formula:

P = Average variable cost + some margin for overheads (fixed costs) + profit margin

Firms differ widely in the degree of sophistication attached to this formula, from the inclusion of only the most easily identifiable costs (labour plus raw materials) to complex models for allocating joint and overhead costs.[7] Different firms use one or more methods of obtaining cost figures, such as current actual costs, unit costs over a period, expected average costs or standard unit costs expressed as average costs over some planned or normal output level.

The implication of average cost pricing is that only supply side considerations are important. This is particularly true if the profit margin to be added to unit costs is either arbitrary or traditional. In Hall and Hitch's study, 40 per cent of firms using average cost pricing claimed that margins were fixed by convention, whilst the rest allowed some variation in margins according to demand or competitive conditions.

In response to average cost pricing, economists were quick to point out that the practice may be compatible with the marginalist profit maximising model *if* the added on profit margin varies according to the elasticity of demand.

Recall from the general pricing model above,

$$P = AC + Q\left(\frac{dAC}{dQ} - \frac{dP}{dQ}\right), \text{ to maximise profit}$$

If average cost is approximately constant, $dAC/dQ = 0$, and

$$P = AC - Q \cdot \left(\frac{dP}{dQ}\right)$$

The second term can be expressed in elasticity form,

$$P = AC - P\left(\frac{Q}{P} \cdot \frac{dP}{dQ}\right)$$

$$= AC - P\frac{1}{\varepsilon}, \text{ where } \varepsilon = \text{price elasticity of demand.}$$

Rearranging, $P + P\dfrac{(1)}{\varepsilon} = AC$

i.e. $P = \dfrac{AC}{1 + 1/\varepsilon}$

By manipulation,

$$P = AC - \dfrac{AC}{\varepsilon + 1}$$

Profit maximisation then implies adding a margin to average cost (since $\varepsilon < -1$ for a profit maximiser, so $\varepsilon + 1 < 0$ and $-AC/(\varepsilon + 1) > 0$).

However, for average cost pricing to be compatible with profit maximisation, the profit margin added on must vary inversely with demand elasticity. Empirical studies of pricing lend little support to this hypothesis and suggest strongly that margins are determined largely by rule of thumb. In general, average cost pricing ignores demand, and the crucial effect of price upon sales in particular. The cost figures used most often reflect what information is available, and bears little relation to opportunity cost. The conclusion is inevitable that average cost pricing is incompatible with optimality.

The fact remains that average cost pricing is widely used and some explanation must be offered for its continued practice in the face of well-known deficiencies. The most obvious point is that average cost pricing is convenient and simple, particularly for new products, and that the addition of a fair or reasonable profit margin may be an accurate reflection of the firm's objectives. Average cost pricing may be safe and reliable, particularly if competitors price in the same way. The practice is an easy way of inflation pricing, since prices rise automatically in line with costs.

Finally, the practice of average cost pricing may well reflect the impracticability of applying marginal analysis in a world of incomplete information. Moreover, if the profit margin is systematically revised in the light of sales and market opportunities, the price may eventually adjust to something reasonably approximating optimality.

Summary and conclusions

Pricing is just one decision area in the development of a comprehensive competitive strategy. In setting a price for a product, the influence of price upon sales, and the effects of various sale quantities upon costs, need to be carefully considered. Pricing policy cannot be divorced from objectives, and in particular the firm's time preference for profits. Pricing decisions bear a crucial relationship to the entry decisions of potential competitors, so that a judicious pricing policy can define the stream of future, as well as current profits. Pricing to deter entry involves taking account of the elasticity of demand and the relative cost conditions of potential entrants. Pricing a new product implies locating a strategy somewhere on the scale between a Skimming Price Policy and a Penetration Price Policy. Pricing established products generally means oligopolistic pricing and the explicit recognition of likely competitor actions and reactions. A strategy for product-line pricing, or the multiproduct firm can only be formulated once production or demand interdependencies are taken into account. Price discrimination offers the opportunity to increase revenue by pricing in each separable market according to demand elasticity.

Empirical pricing evidence reveals a substantial gap between theory and practice, with many firms adopting the simple policy of average cost pricing. This practice *may* be compatible with profit maximisation, but appears more likely to be chosen for reasons of simplicity and competitive safety.

Application 9

The Sunshine Car Company: pricing demand related products

When a firm produces two products that are demand related, Manes, Shoumaker and Silhan[8] show that optimal pricing occurs when:

$$\frac{\delta\pi}{\delta Px} = Qx + Px\left(\frac{\delta Qx}{\delta Px}\right) + Py\left(\frac{\delta Qy}{\delta Px}\right) - Cx\left(\frac{\delta Qx}{\delta Px}\right) - Cy\left(\frac{\delta Qy}{\delta Px}\right) = 0 \quad (1)$$

and

$$\frac{\delta\pi}{\delta Py} = Qy + Py\left(\frac{\delta Qy}{\delta Py}\right) + Px\left(\frac{\delta Qx}{\delta Py}\right) - Cy\left(\frac{\delta Qy}{\delta Py}\right) - Cx\left(\frac{\delta Qx}{\delta Py}\right) = 0 \quad (2)$$

where Px, Py, Qx, Qy are the prices and quantities of x and y, and Cx, Cy are the (constant) average costs. Despite the apparent complexity, these two equations are relatively easy to apply *if* the demand functions are known.

The Sunshine Car Company produces two versions of a particular car, a family saloon (*a*) and a functional estate (*b*). The average variable costs of each are constant at 3 and 4 units respectively (possibly thousands of pounds). The company estimates the demand functions for the cars to be:

$$Qa = 10 - Pa$$
$$Qb = 16 - 2Pb$$

Profit is maximised in each market by equating marginal revenue to marginal cost. Since average variable cost is constant in each market, marginal cost must equal average variable cost. Marginal revenue can be found by expressing price in terms of quantity, multiplying by quantity and then differentiating, i.e.

229

$$Pa = 10 - Qa$$

$$TRa = Qa \cdot Pa = 10Qa - Qa^2$$

$$MRa = \frac{\delta TRa}{\delta Qa} = 10 - 2Qa$$

$$Pb = 8 - \frac{Qb}{2}$$

$$TRb = 8Qb - \frac{Qb^2}{2}$$

$$MRb = \frac{\delta TRb}{\delta Qb} = 8 - Qb$$

Setting each marginal revenue equal to marginal cost, price and output can be found in each market.

$$\text{If} \quad MCa = MRa$$
$$10 - 2Qa = 3$$
$$Qa = 3.5$$
$$MCb = MRb$$
$$8 - Qb = 4$$
$$Qb = 4$$

substituting back into the respective price equations,

$$Pa = 10 - 3.5 = 6.5$$
$$Pb = 8 - \frac{Qb}{2} = 6$$

Note that because the demand curve for estates is more elastic than that for saloons, the estate is sold at a lower price than the saloon, despite being more expensive to produce.

The marketing director of the Sunshine Car Company notices that when the price of saloons increases, the demand for estates rises and vice versa, i.e. that the products are demand substitutes. When the demand estimates are reworked to allow for this relationship, the following estimates result:

$$Qa = 10 - Pa + 0.2Pb$$

$$Qb = 16 - 2Pb + 0.5Pa$$

The marketing director is concerned that the cars should be priced to take this demand relationship into account. She quickly calculates that at $Pa = 6.5$ and $Pb = 6$, sales of the cars will be 4.7 and 7.25 respectively, resulting in a total profit of 30.95 (check her calculations!).

Being an avid reader of economic journals, she is familiar with equations (1) and (2) above. Applying these to the new demand estimates gives:

$$Qa + Pa(-1) + Pb(0.5) - 3(-1) - 4(0.5) = 0 \tag{3}$$

or $Qa = Pa - 0.5(Pb) - 1$ (4)

and $Qb + Pb(-2) + Pa(0.2) - 4(-2) - 3(0.2) = 0$ (5)

or $Qb = 2Pb - 0.2(Pa) - 7.4$ (6)

Equations (4) and (6) can be solved by using the estimated demand functions, i.e.

$$Qa = Pa - 0.5(Pb) - 1 = 10 - Pa + 0.2(Pb)$$

$$2Pa = 11 + 0.7(Pb) \tag{7}$$

and $Qb = 2Pb - 0.2(Pa) - 7.4 = 16 - 2Pb + 0.5Pa$

$$4Pb = 23.4 + 0.7(Pa) \tag{8}$$

from (7), $Pa = 5.5 + 0.35(Pb)$

substituting into (8)

$$4Pb = 23.4 + 0.7(5.5 + 0.35(Pb))$$

$$4Pb = 23.4 + 3.85 + 0.245Pb$$

$$3.755(Pb) = 26.85$$

$$Pb = 7.15$$

and $\quad Pa = 5.5 + 0.35(7.15)$

$$Pa = 8.025$$

The quantities sold at these prices can be found from the respective demand curves,

$$Qb = 5.7125, \quad Qa = 3.405$$

The total profit from these price–output combinations is

$$\pi = 7.15(5.7125) - 4(5.7125) + 8.025(3.405) - 3(3.405)$$
$$= \underline{38.51}$$

By taking explicit account of the demand interrelationships, profit has been increased from 30.95 to 38.51, an increase of more than 24 per cent! Note that the cross-price elasticity of demand for *a* with respect to the price of *b* is:

$$\varepsilon ab = \frac{Pb}{Qa} \cdot \left(\frac{\delta Qa}{\delta Pb}\right)$$

$$= \frac{7.15}{3.405}(0.2) = \underline{0.42}$$

whilst $ba = \dfrac{Pa}{Qb}\left(\dfrac{\delta Qb}{\delta Pa}\right)$

$$= \frac{8.025}{5.7125}(0.5) = \underline{0.70}$$

A 10 per cent increase in the price of estates would increase the demand for saloons by 4 per cent, whilst a 10 per cent increase in saloon prices would increase estate demand by 7 per cent. The saloon customer is more likely to switch to the estate in response to a saloon price increase than conversely.

CHAPTER 10

Marketing decisions

Contents

'Marketing is the primary management function which organises and directs ... business activities in converting consumers purchasing power into effective demand for a specific product or service ... so as to achieve company set profit or other objectives.'

L. W. Rodgers, 1965[1]

Introduction

According to this definition, the purpose of marketing is to translate the buying ability of consumers into sales of the firm's products. Marketing decisions are concerned with the allocation of resources to this effort, and the effective utilisation of these resources. In practice, marketing decisions encompass decisions about market segmentation, product quality and design, the choice of distribution

233

channels, corporate image-building, advertising budgets, sales promotions, etc. – that is, all the firm's decisions which can be expected to have an impact upon present and future sales. In this sense, marketing decisions cannot be divorced from the output, price and competitive strategy decisions discussed in previous chapters. Thus marketing decisions, like all business decisions, need to be considered within the overall context of company strategy and objectives.

In recent years, the focus of attention from business, politicians and academics has shifted towards the marketing effort, partly as a result of the search for new market opportunities, and partly as a consequence of growing awareness of the absolute size of marketing expenditure. Table 10.1 lists a recent estimate of marketing expenditure in 1983, when direct marketing expense totalled more than £10 billion in Britain, or around 3 per cent of total national income.

Table 10.1 Marketing expenditure in UK, 1983

	£m
Media expenditure	3580
Sales promotion	4000
Sales personnel	2350
Market research	130
Total	£10 060m

Source: N. Piercy (1986) *Marketing Budgeting* (London: Croom-Helm), p. 20.

Taken together with Table 8.3, listing advertising expenditure by company, Table 10.1 shows that marketing expenditure is significant in both absolute and company terms. Moreover, each table probably understates the importance of the marketing effort by including only direct expenditure on marketing. Indirect expenditure, such as internal market research or extra costs involved in building prestigious office blocks, etc., may well be larger than any direct marketing expenditure.

We shall adopt the economist convention of considering marketing decisions in terms of the advertising decision. This is not to deny the importance of other marketing decisions, but rather to suggest that the decision-making process for each marketing decision is sufficiently similar to that for the advertising decision to allow the same approach to be adopted. Like other decisions, the search for an optimal allocation of advertising resources involves the comparison of costs and benefits of advertising.

The economic analysis of advertising

The purpose of advertising is to increase sales revenue by shifting the demand curve outwards, allowing more to be sold at the same price, the same quantity to be sold at a higher price, or some combination of the two (depending on the relative slopes of demand and supply curves). Like any demand influencing variable, the effects of advertising can be measured by the elasticity of demand with respect to advertising, or

$$\varepsilon a = \frac{\delta D}{\delta A} \cdot \frac{A}{D}$$

Note that before advertising elasticity can be measured, the units of advertising must be defined. The definition used will depend entirely on the problem under consideration. For example, the effectiveness of further newspaper advertising could be measured in terms of the advertising elasticity with respect to newspaper adverts of a given size and type. More commonly, in dealing with the overall advertising budget, the advertising elasticity with respect to advertising expenditure will be the relevant measure.

The size of the advertising elasticity is determined principally by the nature of the product and in particular the opportunity for product differentiation. Thus toothpaste is amenable to advertising, since perceived differences can be emphasised, whilst nuts and bolts are not. In economic terms, advertising can have two effects, depending on the nature of the advert and the market structure of the industry – a *market expansion* effect and a *market redistribution* effect. An advertisement claiming that 'soap is good for you' will have a market expansion effect by shifting the *industry* demand curve, whilst an advert claiming 'soap X will make your skin softer' has a market redistribution effect by shifting the demand curve for soap X at the expense of other soaps. In a monopolistic industry, only the market expansion effect is important, whilst oligopolistic advertising is designed to redistribute consumer demand towards a particular producer. Oligopolistic advertising, even if the market redistribution effects are cancelled by competitors' adverts, may be profitable if it creates a barrier to the entry of new firms.

The search for an optimal advertising budget is a recurring management problem. According to Lord Leverhume: 'Probably half of every advertising appropriation is wasted, but nobody knows which half.'[2] The point being made is that the effect of a particular advert is notoriously difficult to measure, since changes in demand over time due to that advert need to be separated from changes in demand occurring simultaneously for other reasons.

The obvious theoretical solution to the advertising budget is to maximise profit by equating the marginal cost of the last advert to its marginal revenue. This is theoretically correct, but not particularly helpful, since the informational requirements of this approach are so difficult to meet. Besides, an advertising induced shift in demand affects both output (and hence production cost), and price (and hence revenue). Separating out these simultaneous changes is a difficult task operationally.

The aggregate approach

One solution to this dilemma is to analyse the effects of advertising in terms of total revenue and total cost, thus recognising the revenue and cost implications of any advertising change.

Assume that the impact of advertising is to shift the total revenue curve upwards, but by decreasing amounts for successive units of advertising (i.e. the most effective adverts are undertaken first). Then there will be total revenue curves corresponding to different amounts of advertising (TR, TRa_1, and TRa_2 corresponding to zero, a_1 and a_2 units of advertising respectively).

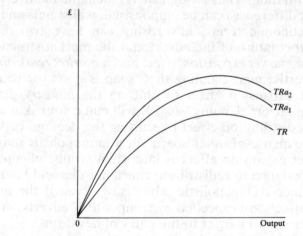

Figure 10.1   Advertising and total revenue

From an expenditure point of view, advertising is an addition to total cost which will shift the total production cost curve upwards by an amount corresponding to the associated expenditure on advertising. Thus Figure 10.2 shows the total cost curves corresponding to zero, a_1 and a_2 amounts of advertising.

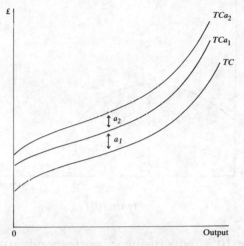

Figure 10.2   Advertising and total cost

Putting together Figures 10.1 and 10.2 enables the profit maximising price and output combination to be derived for any level of advertising (Figure 10.3). In the absence of advertising, profit is maximised by producing output level Q, with a resulting profit of $ab(TR-TC)$. With the amount of advertising a_1, profit is maximised at output Q_1, giving profit level cd. Finally, with advertising level a_2, profit is maximised at output Q_2, leaving profit $ef(TRa_2 - TCa_2)$.

Given Figure 10.3, the absolute amount of profit can now be measured against the amount of advertising (Figure 10.4). Maximising overall profit is then the simple matter of choosing the highest profit point on this diagram (advertising a_1 and profit cd).

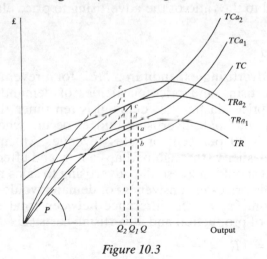

Figure 10.3

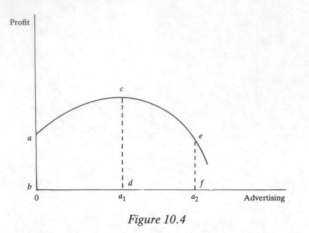

Figure 10.4

From Figure 10.3, advertising a_1 corresponds to optimal output Q_1 and optimal price P_1 (since price is the slope of the line from the origin to the total revenue curve). The optimal price, output and advertising quantity have then each been determined simultaneously. Note that this approach is exactly equivalent to the marginalist approach since advertising is profitable if it increases total revenue more than it increases total costs.

The Dorfman–Steiner model

The Dorfman–Steiner model uses first principles to establish that the optimal advertising budget occurs when the advertising to sales ratio is equal to the ratio of the advertising to price elasticity, or

$$\frac{A}{TR} = \frac{\varepsilon a}{\varepsilon p}$$

where A is advertising expenditure, TR is total revenue, and εa, εp are the advertising and price elasticities of demand respectively. Then if the price elasticity of demand is ten times the advertising elasticity, the optimal advertising budget occurs when advertising expenditure is 10 per cent of sales revenue. An increase in the advertising elasticity (through perhaps a new and effective advertising gimmick) should increase the advertising to sales ratio whilst an increase in the price-responsiveness of demand would decrease it.

Define profit (π) as the difference between total revenue (TR) and the sum of production and advertising costs ($C+A$).

Then $\pi = TR - C - A$

Now let demand be a function of price and advertising, whilst production costs are a function of quantity.

i.e. $\pi = P \cdot Q(P, A) - C(Q) - A$

To maximise profit, differentiate with respect to advertising and price, set equal to zero and solve, i.e.

$$\frac{\delta\pi}{\delta A} = P \cdot \frac{\delta Q}{\delta A} - \frac{\delta C}{\delta Q} \cdot \frac{\delta Q}{\delta A} - 1 = 0 \tag{1}$$

and $$\frac{\delta\pi}{\delta P} = P \cdot \frac{\delta Q}{\delta P} + Q - \frac{\delta C}{\delta Q} \cdot \frac{\delta Q}{\delta P} = 0 \tag{2}$$

from (1), with $\delta C/\delta Q = $ marginal cost (MC),

$$\frac{\delta Q}{\delta A}(P - MC) = 1$$

Now multiply both sides by A/PQ, and translate into elasticity terms,

$$\frac{\delta Q}{\delta A} \cdot \frac{A}{Q} \frac{(P-MC)}{P} = \frac{A}{PQ}$$

$$\varepsilon a \frac{(P-MC)}{P} = \frac{A}{PQ} \tag{3}$$

Then advertising elasticity, times the price-marginal cost margin over price, is equal to the ratio of advertising expenditure to sales revenue.

Now multiply equation (2) throughout by P/Q

$$P \cdot \frac{P}{Q} \cdot \frac{\delta Q}{\delta P} + Q \cdot \frac{P}{Q} - \frac{\delta C}{\delta Q} \cdot \frac{P}{Q} \frac{(\delta Q)}{(\delta P)} = 0$$

Recall that $\varepsilon p = -(P/Q) \cdot (\delta Q/\delta P)$ defines price elasticity of demand,

So, $P(-\varepsilon p) + P - MC(-\varepsilon p) = 0$

or $(-\varepsilon p)(P - MC) = -P$

So, $\dfrac{P-MC}{P} = \dfrac{1}{\varepsilon p}$

Substituting into (3)

$$\frac{\varepsilon a}{\varepsilon p} = \frac{A}{PQ}$$

The Dorfman–Steiner model has been extended to include quality, style and variety considerations.[3] However, like all implicitly marginalist approaches, the Dorfman–Steiner model has been criticised for assuming that the effects of advertising on sales can be measured and for ignoring the dynamic time effects of advertising, both in terms of sales response and the changing costs of advertising over time. Nevertheless, Piercy[4] defends the marginalistic approach as providing an analytic framework for understanding the advertising decision, rather than acting as a decision tool for budget determination.

Recognition of the dynamic nature of the response to advertising has led to two parallel developments in the economic analysis of advertising – the investment approach and the informational approach.

The dynamic response to advertising

In practice, current advertising has a 'carry-over' effect on future sales. A current television advertising campaign may create a brand image in the minds of consumers that is reflected in future buying behaviour. Subsequent adverts may reinforce or amend this brand image. Thus an advert now will have an effect on revenue that is spread over subsequent periods. Figure 10.5 shows three possibili-

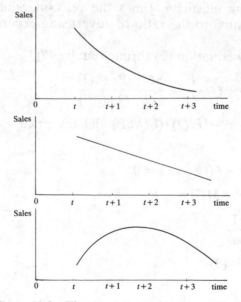

Figure 10.5   The response to advertising over time

ties, with the effect of advertising over time declining rapidly, declining at a constant rate, and first increasing and then declining. The time sales response to a particular advert depends on the natures of the product and the advert.

An advertising campaign spread over several periods may have a cumulative effect on sales, as each advert reinforces the image created by previous adverts.

Advertising as investment

Recognition of the time response to advertising has led to advertising expenditure being appraised like any other investment good, i.e. in terms of a return on capital invested. Thus instead of treating advertising expenditure as a current cost, advertising may be analysed as an addition to current assets and evaluated in terms of a rate of return on those assets to be compared to the opportunity cost of capital, or the rate of return obtainable by investing elsewhere.

Then if current advertising expenditure Ao yields a stream of returns into the future $r_1, r_2 \ldots$, advertising should be undertaken until the net discounted present value of the last advertisement is zero, or until

$$\Sigma \frac{ri}{(1+d)^i} - Ao = 0$$

where d is the discount rate or opportunity cost of capital.

By treating advertising expenditure as a current cost rather than an addition to assets, firms will underestimate the value of their assets and therefore overstate the profit rate on present assets.

Advertising as information[5]

This view of advertising expenditure sees advertising as providing valuable information to consumers about the nature of a product and the identity of sellers, thereby reducing the search and transaction costs of consumers. Advertising is needed because the information available to consumers is incomplete – the nature of products and the identities of buyers and sellers are continuously changing. Then advertising affects the proportion of potential buyers who are aware of a particular product and seller.

Suppose that in the first period, the firm purchases a units of advertising, consequently informing some fraction f of potential buyers.

i.e. $f = g(a)$

The fraction of buyers informed by advertising is a function of the quantity of advertising.

$$\frac{df}{da} > 0, \frac{d^2f}{da^2} < 0$$

Increases in the quantity of advertising increase the informed proportion of potential buyers, but at a decreasing rate.

Let the total number of potential buyers (size of the market) be N.

Then a adverts inform fN potential customers. Of the potential buyers informed by the adverts, some lose that information (forget), and some leave the market.

Let b equal the proportion of informed buyers losing that information between periods.

Then of the fN buyers informed in the first period,

$(1 - b)fN$

are still informed at the start of the second period. Now the firm undertakes second period advertising. For $(1 - b)fN$ potential buyers, second period advertising is unnecessary. However, the second period advertising reaches some of the potential buyers not informed by the first adverts $((1 - f)N)$, and reinforms some who were informed but had forgotten (bfN).

By the end of the second period, λN potential buyers have been informed, where

$$\lambda N = (1 - b)fN \quad + \quad f(bfN \quad\quad + \quad (1 - f)n)$$

[informed from 1st period]   [reinformed]   [newly informed]

which simplifies to:

$$\lambda N = fN(1 + (1 - b)(1 - f))$$

If advertising is continued for k periods,
$$\lambda N = fN(1 + (1 - b)(1 - f) + (1 - b)^2(1 - f)^2 + \ldots$$
$$+ (1 - b)^{k-1}(1 - f)^{k-1}$$

If advertising continues indefinitely[6] ($k \to \infty$),

$$\lambda N = \frac{fN}{1 - (1 - f)(1 - b)}$$

or $\quad \lambda = \dfrac{f}{1-(1-f)(1-b)}$

Thus the number of informed buyers is fN after the first period, and approaches λN eventually.

The situation is represented graphically in Figure 10.6.

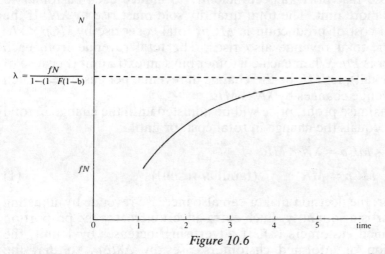

Figure 10.6

For example, if a continuous advertising campaign reaches 30 per cent of potential buyers each period, and 10 per cent of these informed lose that information between periods, the proportion eventually informed will be

$$\lambda = \frac{0.3}{1-(0.7)(0.9)} = 0.81 = 81\%$$

The proportion of informed buyers depends only on f and b. An increase in the retention rate of advertising $(1-b)$ increases the proportion of informed buyers. Therefore, advertisers are continually striving to make adverts more memorable.

Profit maximisation

If the price of the product is P, total sales Q, the costs of production TCp, and the price and quantity of advertising are Pa and a respectively, total profit will be

$$\pi = PQ - TCp - Pa \cdot a$$

Assume that every potential customer informed by the advertiser buys from him. Then total sales will be the product of the number of informed customers (λN) and the quantity purchased by each (q).

Then $\pi = (\lambda Nq)P - TCp - Pa \cdot a$

Increasing the proportion of informed customers will increase revenue. However, given a downward sloping demand curve, each customer will buy less (q falls) when the price increases. Therefore, price, output and advertising must be determined simultaneously.

Suppose that price falls sufficiently to induce each customer to buy one more unit. The total quantity sold must rise by λN. If the marginal cost of production is MCp, total costs rise by $MCp \times \lambda N$. However, total revenue also rises. The total revenue from each customer is Pq. When each customer buys an extra unit (because of the price fall), let MR be the change in revenue per customer. Then total revenue changes by $\lambda N \times MR$.

To maximise profit, price will be adjusted until the change in total revenue equals the change in total cost, or until

$$\lambda N \times MCp = \lambda N \times MR$$

$$MCp = MR \qquad \text{(familiar result!)} \qquad (1)$$

However, the decision-maker can also increase revenue by adjusting the advertising quantity. Each extra advert increases the proportion of informed customers (λ). If advertising increases by 1 unit, the proportion of informed customers rises by $\Delta\lambda/\Delta a$, so that the quantity of sales rises by

$$Nq\frac{(\Delta\lambda)}{(\Delta a)}$$

since each informed customer buys q.

However, in order to buy this extra unit of advertising, the firm must spend Pa. Dividing the price of the advert by the increase in sales as a result of the advert gives the expenditure necessary to increase sales by one unit through advertising, or the marginal cost of increasing sales through advertising,

$$= \frac{Pa}{Nq(\Delta\lambda/\Delta a)}$$

By the sale of this extra unit through advertising, the producer makes extra profit equal to the difference between the price of the product and the cost of producing an extra unit ($P - MCp$). Profit is then maximised by equating the marginal cost of selling the extra unit through advertising to the marginal benefit gained, or

$$P - MCp = \frac{Pa}{Nq(\Delta\lambda/\Delta a)} \qquad (2)$$

Together with equation (1), equation (2) gives the necessary conditions for profit maximisation. Equation (2) can be analysed by plotting both sides of the equation against the quantity of advertising (Figure 10.7).

As advertising increases, the marginal cost of production rises, so that the marginal benefit of the advertising induced extra sale $(P - MCp)$ falls. Moreover, as advertising increases, the effectiveness of the last advertisement falls $(\Delta\lambda/\Delta a\downarrow)$. Then the marginal cost of inducing an extra sale by advertising rises, even if the price of the advert, the size of the market and the amount bought by each customer each stay constant.

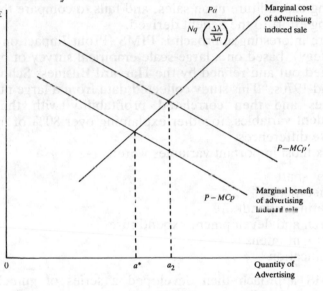

Figure 10.7

Figure 10.7 can be used to analyse the effect of exogenous changes on the optimal quantity of advertising.

For example:

(1)   Suppose that new production technology reduces the marginal cost of production. Then $P - MCp$ shifts to $P - MCp'$, and the optimal amount of advertising increases to $a2$.

(2)   A rise in the cost of advertising (Pa) shifts the marginal cost of advertising induced sales curve to the right and decreases the optimal quantity of advertising.

(3)   An increase in the total market size (N), the amount bought by each customer (q) or the effectiveness of advertising $(\Delta\lambda/\Delta a)$, reduces the marginal cost of advertising induced sales and increases the optimal quantity of advertising.

Other budgeting approaches

A variety of other budgeting approaches have been offered for the marketing allocation problem. The *Objective and Task* approach involves defining some marketing objectives, estimating the costs necessary to achieve these targets and then summing those costs to find the marketing budget. Such an approach owes as little to optimality as the *Judgemental* approach of adopting some marketing rule of thumb by basing the marketing budget on a given proportion of sales, or parity with competitors, or some notion of affordability. Each of these fails to take explicit account of the impact of marketing expenditure upon sales, and fails to compare the cost of marketing effort to the benefit derived.

A more interesting approach is PIMS (Profit Impact on Marketing Strategy), based on a large-scale empirical survey of profitability, carried out and refined by the Harvard Business School in the 1960s and 1970s.[7] This study collected data from a large number of companies and then correlated profitability with thirty-seven independent variables, together explaining over 80% of individual profit rate differences.

The six most important variables were:

— market share
— product quality
— marketing expenditure
— research and development expenditure
— investment intensity
— diversification

The PIMS approach then developed a series of guidelines for improving profitability in particular circumstances, arguing that the survey results represent pooled experience as a prescriptive guide for decision-making.

Finally, Piercy[8] argues that the marketing budget is not the result of an optimisation procedure but the product of a political conflict between marketing and other interests inside the firm, in line with the arguments expressed by Cyert and March, and discussed in Chapter 3.

Empirical evidence[9]

The analysis developed in this chapter suggests that advertising expenditure by the firm will be a function of the company's objectives, the nature of the product, the level of price and output and the extent of competition. Empirical attempts to relate advertising expenditure to these variables run into an immediate problem of two-way causation, in that advertising both affects revenue and is affected by revenue. Allied to the problem of predicting a current and future sales response to advertising expenditure, it is little wonder that advertising practices seem to be characterised by non-optimising policies such as per cent of sales, all-you-can-afford competitive parity and objectives and task methods.

Consequently, most empirical evidence has been directed at the consequences of advertising, rather than the determination of advertising budgets. Studies of the economic impact of advertising can be divided into three broad areas.

(1) Advertising and competition

The economic analysis relating advertising and competition is ambiguous. On the one hand, advertising may encourage market concentration by rewarding successful advertisers with increased market shares. Conversely market concentration may encourage high advertising as oligopolistics seek to compete in non-price ways. In addition, oligopolistic advertising may be a deterrent to new entry. Thus advertising expenditure may be expected to increase with market concentration.

Mann and others[10] studied fourteen narrowly defined industries to find a high degree of correlation between advertising as a proportion of sales and concentration ratios, implying that advertising as a proportion of sales increases with the concentration ratio. Greer[11] found that the advertising to sales ratio increased up to medium concentration levels, and then fell as the concentration ratio increased further. He suggested that beyond medium concentration, increases led to oligopolistic collusion, resulting in mutually reduced levels of advertising as a proportion of sales.

(2) Advertising and prices

Once more the economic relationship is unclear. If advertising does act as information, then by increasing the level of consumer awareness, higher advertising may increase the price elasticity of demand. On the other hand, one of the reasons why advertising is undertaken is to increase demand and reduce price elasticity (through product differentiation), enabling firms to increase price.

The growth of non-advertised, low price unbranded products, at the expense of high price advertised brands, supports a positive association between advertising and price levels. However, the higher prices of branded goods may reflect a saving in search costs to the consumer. Then own-brands may simply have benefited from the market expansion effects of brand advertising.

(3)   Advertising and profitability

Advertising may increase profitability by increasing demand, by creating brand loyalty, and by acting as a barrier to entry (by forcing a new entrant to incur high selling costs, particularly if there are economies of scale in advertising). However, circularity must again be avoided. Do large advertisers make high profits or is it the profitable firms which advertise most? Moreover, we saw earlier that the treatment of advertising as a current expense, rather than a capital outlay, may lead to the overstatement of profit rates.

Summary and conclusions

Marketing decisions are concerned with all the activities of the firm which attempt to influence consumer purchasing behaviour. Prominent amongst these activities is the advertising decision. By 1983, marketing expenditure exceeded 3 per cent of British total national income.

The purpose of advertising is to increase revenue, and the effects of advertising can be analysed in terms of the advertising elasticity of demand. The nature of the product is the dominant influence on advertising elasticity, with the opportunity for product differentiation being the basic guide to advertising effectiveness. Advertising influences demand via the market expansion and market redistribution effects, depending on the nature of the advert and the market structure of the industry.

The determination of an optimal advertising budget rests on the comparison of the costs and benefits of advertising. However, by affecting demand, advertising also influences output and price, and the cost and revenue implications must be taken into account. One simple method of doing this is the aggregate approach, looking at total cost and revenue approaches. The Dorfman–Steiner model analyses the advertising decision in terms of price and advertising demand elasticities, to show that the profit maximising advertising to revenue ratio is equal to the ratio of advertising to price elasticity. One interpretation of this is that the advertising to revenue ratio should be set equal to the elasticity of price with respect to advertising.

The effects of advertising are not instantaneous but occur over time. Recognition of this has led to advertising expenditure being treated as a capital expense, and as the provision of valuable consumer information that builds up over time. The optimal advertising budget can be determined by equating the marginal cost of an extra unit sold through advertising to the marginal benefit of that sale, with useful comparative static predictions. However, empirical investigation of the actual decision processes used to determine advertising expenditure reveal a range of non-optimising approaches, reflecting both the nature of company objectives and the difficulties of effectively measuring the sales response to advertising. There is some evidence that high advertising to sales rates are associated with high levels of market concentration, higher prices and higher profit rates, although the direction of causation is less than certain.

Application 10

Nigel Piercy: UWIST

Worldwide Computer Corporation

WCC[12] is a long-established computer manufacturer based in the UK, but operating worldwide. In view of its size and the diversity of its customers, WCC is organised into a number of 'business centres', each of which is concerned with a single area of business – either a customer-type, a geographic area, or a specialised product application.

One of these business centres is concerned with meeting the specialised needs of a single customer – International Telecommunications Ltd (ITL). The customer concerned is one of the largest international organisations in the world, based in the international telecommunications business.

The 1985 sales turnover of this WCC business centre was £30m representing approximately 14 per cent of the market (i.e. ITL's expenditure in the UK on computer products and services).

The business centre did not have any formal budget in 1985 for advertising or sales promotion, but the operating expenses of the business centre amounted to approximately £1m. This figure includes the costs of sales personnel in contact with various parts of the customer organisation, in-house service personnel providing a pre- and post-sales service and advisory function, and a small amount of expenditure on sales literature and public relations events (e.g. Wimbledon tickets, golf matches, theatre outings, and the like) to facilitate contacts with the customer.

The marketing activities of the business centre were organised around sales teams, each specialising in a different computer type or set of applications. In addition, there was one executive responsible for organising sales promotions for all the sales teams.

The business centre was, in 1985, for the first time carrying out a formal marketing planning process, which involved the senior management team in devising a five-year plan.

The underlying goal of the planning exercise was to develop the business centre into a £100m turnover business by 1990. Although this involved more than tripling the size of the WCC business centre, this represented only 25 per cent of the estimated 1990 market (i.e. the UK spend). Although the planning gap facing the WCC managers seemed considerable, a laborious process of defining user segments in the market was carried out. This changed the picture dramatically from one of a single customer whose need was for computers, to a number of user-oriented segments with different needs, which could be met with different combinations of products and services. Examples of these segments were:

Operations needed to use computers for telecommunications control to carry out ITL's own market-place activities.

Customer services needed to upgrade the systems used to cope with customer queries, the scheduling of repair services, the billing of users, and so on.

Management needed information systems to plan and control the strategy of ITL in the market-place.

In fact, there were some six major user-oriented segments in ITL which were distinct in: the customer needs to be met; the types of products and services required; the locations and constitution of the key decision-making units and influencers. As a consequence it was possible to define various targets for information and persuasion at a variety of locations in ITL, and to plan very distinct mixes of activities to attack each segment.

The starting point was the 1986 position where sales to ITL were £30m, divided between hardware (40 per cent), software (40 per cent) and services (20 per cent). The company's estimates of the gross margins, i.e. cost of goods sold before the operating expenses of the business centre (marketing costs) were: hardware 20 per cent, software 50 per cent, services 60 per cent. The current business centre operating expenses were £1m in 1986.

The plan formulated involved a large increase in the personal selling effort, and sales promotion and advertising targeted at the chosen market segments. The out-turn in 1991 was estimated sales (at 1985 prices) of £100m, divided between hardware (10 per cent), software (40 per cent) and services (50 per cent) and gross margins

are assumed constant. However, to achieve this result requires that
the marketing spend should increase from £1m to £6m in 1991.

The problem facing the business centre managers is how this
'bottom' budget requirement can be justified to senior management,
i.e. can a sixfold increase on the marketing budget be justified to
grow the business from £30m to £100m sales turnover?

Inventory decisions

Contents

Introduction

Inventories are the physical stocks held by the firm, and may include raw materials, components, spare parts, work in progress and finished goods. Inventories appear on the company balance sheet as a current asset, and may form a substantial proportion of the value of the firm. From a managerial perspective, large stock-holdings may prove to be more of a liability than an asset, with the high costs of carrying stock being a primary reason for many business failures.

Until recently, the management of inventories was often seen as an administrative rather than strategic or operational task, with inventory decisions based on rules of thumb or custom and practice. However, developments in management science, together with a growing awareness of the costs of stock, have led to recognition of the need for a carefully considered inventory policy in efficiently managed firms. The basic principle of inventory policy is that there are economic costs involved in holding too many stocks, and economic costs of holding too few. The determination of an optimum inventory level involves a balancing that minimises the overall sum of costs.

Reasons for holding stocks

The simplest motive for holding stock is speculation, based on the expectation that the value of stock will rise over time by more than the economic costs of holding that stock. Speculation is normally thought of in terms of rare paintings, foreign currency, company shares, etc., but from a national economic point of view the appreciation of stock held by firms is far more significant. In a period of inflation, stock appreciation may be the most profitable aspect of company performance.

A more common motive for holding stock is to enable the rate of output to be kept constant. This may involve holding stocks of raw materials or unfinished goods to ensure that production is not interrupted by shortages, or it may involve adjusting stocks of finished goods whenever output differs from sales, to enable output to be kept on an optimum level from a production cost point of view. The first decision (precautionary holdings) depends on the estimated probability distribution of future shortages and the costs of interrupting production. If delivery of a particular component is frequently disrupted, planning for continuous production will necessitate holding large stocks of that component. Normally, these precautionary stock holdings per unit of output decrease as output increases and represent a real economy of scale.

The decision to hold stocks as an adjustment mechanism for occasions when output differs from sales is more complicated. Generally, stocks of the finished good may be held whenever output differs from sales, if the cost of holding stock is less than the cost of adjusting to this discrepancy by changing either output or some other economic variable (such as price or marketing effort). We saw in Chapter 7 that there may be considerable costs in adjusting output *per se* in the short run, whilst Chapter 8 showed that companies may be reluctant to change price in particular market situations. Then allowing the level of stocks to rise or fall whenever output does not equal sales may provide an alternative safe and inexpensive adjustment mechanism. Clearly, this policy cannot be taken to extremes. If the level of product inventory falls to very low levels, the possibility of not being able to meet profitable sales increases. Similarly, given that holding stocks is expensive, rapidly rising stocks may impose a considerable cost burden on the firm, leading to a search for other adjustment mechanisms.

The final motive for holding stock is demand uncertainty. Indeed, if demand was perfectly predictable and the costs of changing output low, there would be little point in holding stocks of finished goods, since production would simply be scheduled to meet predicted changes in demand. In practice the demand for most goods is erratic, varying in some manner that may be predicted only with uncertainty. Then in any given period it is possible that demand for the product will exceed output. Stocks must be held to reduce the possibility of forgoing profitable sales opportunities. The optimum stock level will then depend on the probability distribution of demand, the costs of holding stock and the estimated cost of shortages. The shortage cost is determined by the reactions of potential customers to any shortages. If demand is postponeable, or if customers have a strong preference for that good, it may be possible to take *back orders* for the good, so that profitable sales are not missed. Alternatively, there may be substitute products easily available, so that unsatisfied purchasers buy elsewhere (and may continue to do so in future). This is the *lost-sales* case, and the higher the potential profit forgone then the greater the optimum level of stock.

The costs of stock

The costs of inventories include the purchase cost of stock, any order costs, the costs of holding stock and the shortage costs of insufficient stock.

The purchase cost of stock is normally the product of the quantity of stock and purchase price per unit, although any quantity discounts must be taken into account (and may increase the optimum stock level).

Order costs include not only the actual cost of placing an order but also the costs of processing that order and any delivery or receiving costs. In general, order costs are assumed to be fixed, so that total order costs depend only on the number of orders placed. The situation is analogous to that of a firm which can produce many different items on a particular machine. Each time the product of the machine is varied, a set-up cost is incurred. To reduce total set-up costs, the production run for each item can be increased but this results in higher average stock levels. In the same way, placing large orders reduces the number of orders and thus total order costs, but increases the average inventory level.

Holding costs are the expenses incurred by storing stock. These will be the sum of real and opportunity costs. Real costs are the actual expenses on insurance storage, maintenance and warehousing. Probably more important but difficult to measure are the opportunity costs due to the fact that capital tied up in stock could have been invested elsewhere, so that opportunity cost is at least the market rate of interest. In addition, if the physical resources used in storing stock have alternative uses (such as the redeployment of staff or the profitable storage of other items), the benefit forgone must be added to the opportunity cost of capital. The holding cost of stock depends on the value of stock held and for how long. Generally, the cost of holding stock per unit is assumed constant, so that total holding costs are proportional to the average value of stock held over a period.

As we have seen, a shortage cost of stock is incurred wherever demand for a particular item exceeds available supply (current output plus inventory), and depends on the reactions of unfulfilled customers. In the back order case, the shortage cost may simply be the cost of placing an additional order, although even then shortage costs may increase with the time between order and receipt, as customer loyalty becomes stretched with the length of wait. Alternatively, the shortage cost may be the cost of emergency procurement, for example, obtaining the item from an external supplier or initiating a special production run. If the failure to supply immediately leads to a lost sale, the shortage cost is equal to the profit forgone (and may be higher if the customer shops elsewhere in future). In general, the shortage cost is assumed to be proportional to the excess of demand over supply which is equivalent to assuming that the shortage cost per unit is constant.

In the determination of an optimal inventory policy, each of the above costs may be important. However, note that only those costs affected by the choice of policy should be considered when determining that policy. For instance, the purchase cost of stock is important only in so far as it affects inventory policy. If a given quantity of an item will be purchased over a period, irrespective of the policy adopted, total purchase costs will be irrelevant to the choice of policy. In the same way, if the decision-maker is paid the same salary independent of the number of decisions made, the costs of his involvement in the inventory decision are irrelevant to that decision.

Inventory policy

An inventory policy is a set of decision-rules that can be applied to inventory decisions over time. From an operational perspective, the two inventory decisions to be made are:

(i)   how much of an item to order;
(ii) when to order that item.

Obviously, the two decisions are not independent. To meet a given annual requirement, the optimal strategy may be to order a small quantity frequently or a large quantity infrequently. There are two basic inventory systems that can be used to meet this annual requirement. Under a Fixed Order Level (FOL) system, a predetermined quantity is ordered whenever stock falls to a particular level (the reorder level). With a Fixed Interval Order Level (FIOL) system, or periodic review system, stock is ordered at fixed points in time to bring the level of inventory up to a required amount. Both systems are illustrated in Figure 11.1.

As drawn, both systems assume that the replenishment rate is infinite (all the order is filled at the same time), and that the lead time is zero (orders are filled at the moment placed). Both of these

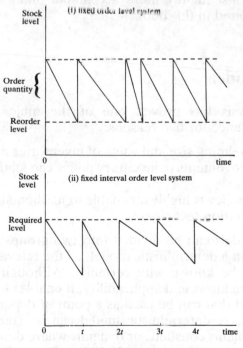

Figure 11.1   Inventory systems

assumptions are unrealistic, since orders take time to be filled, and replenishment may occur in batches. The effect of relaxing these assumptions will be examined later.

The FOL system requires continuous monitoring of stock levels, placing an order for a fixed amount whenever the reorder level is reached. In practice, monitoring may be simplified by a *two-bin* system. Stock is divided into two groups and an order placed when the first becomes empty. For example, a bookseller may place a coloured card in a stack of books: when the card becomes visible, an order is placed.

Under the FIOL system, continuous monitoring is avoided, and irregular sized orders are placed at regular intervals (whereas the FOL system involves regular sized orders at irregular intervals). Obviously the FIOL system reduces the cost of administering stock but may increase its average level, since stock must be large to preclude the possibility that demand will exceed the stock level over the fixed interval. Reducing that fixed interval reduces both this possibility and the average stock level, but at higher ordering costs. Consequently, the FOL system is usually preferred, since the chance of incurring shortage costs is lower. The FOL system is also more amenable to the concept of optimisation as a business strategy, and consequently more acceptable under the analytical approach advocated in this book.

Inventory models

Inventory analysis has proved one of the major successes of management science for two reasons:

— the overwhelming size and value of inventories mean that even minor improvements in inventory policy can lead to substantial savings;
— inventory policy is highly amenable to mathematical modelling and optimisation techniques.

Inventory models can be divided into two groups: deterministic and stochastic. In a deterministic model, all the relevant parameters are assumed to be known with certainty. Although this robs the model of some richness and applicability, it enables basic principles to be established that can be used as a point of departure for more realistic models. A deterministic model can be static, where the demand rate remains constant, or dynamic where demand is known to change over time. Stochastic models take explicit account of uncertainty, usually by specifying parameters in terms of some probability distribution. Such models may be stationary or non-stationary, depending on whether those probability distributions change over time.

Taha[1] provides the following diagrammatic representation of inventory models and emphasises that the level of complexity increases with the introduction of uncertainty (Figure 11.2).

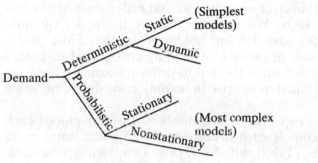

Figure 11.2 Types of inventory model

A final reason for the success of inventory policy is the results of sensitivity analysis. Sensitivity analysis assesses the effects of parameter estimation error on solution reliability. In general, the optimum strategy is fairly insensitive to the parameter estimates, implying that even imperfect information can lead to a considerable improvement through the introduction of inventory analysis. For example, Lowenthal[2] shows that a 28 per cent relative error in estimating the value of a parameter in the simplest inventory model leads to a relative cost of prediction error of less than 1 per cent.

A deterministic inventory model

Suppose that a firm knows with certainty that annual demand for a particular item will be D units at a uniform rate, so that, for example, $D/52$ units will be demanded each week. The problem for the firm is to determine the optimal level of inventories to meet that known demand. Under the FIOL system, the order level is determined simply by the duration of the fixed interval. If the interval is one month, $D/12$ should be ordered, assuming instant replenishment. Much more interesting is the FOL system, where the problem is to determine the optimal order quantity (known as the Economic Order Quantity or EOQ).

If demand is known and replenishment instantaneous, the firm can avoid shortages by reordering whenever stock equals zero. Then shortage costs will be irrelevant.

The objective is to minimise total annual inventory costs. Assume ordering costs (per order) are known and constant. Then the problem is to balance the cost of ordering against the cost of holding stock so that total costs are minimised. The firm could order small amounts frequently, so that average inventory levels and therefore holding costs will be low, but order costs will be high. Alternatively, the firm could order in large amounts, so that order costs will be low and holding costs high. We can see that as the order quantity increases, total order costs fall but holding costs rise. Since inventory costs are the sum of order plus holding costs, total inventory costs will be minimised when the fall in ordering costs by ordering an extra unit is just equal to the rise in holding costs due to ordering that extra unit.

Let q be the order quantity. The number of orders placed each year will then be D/q. If each order costs £r to place, total order costs over the year (TOC) will be £rD/q. Graphically, the relationship between total order costs and order quantity will describe a rectangular hyperbola.[3] Define the marginal order cost (MOC) as the change in order costs due to a unit increase in order quantity.

$$\text{Then } TOC = \frac{rD}{q}$$

$$\text{and } MOC = \frac{\delta TOC}{\delta q} = \frac{-rD}{q^2}$$

As the order quantity increases, order costs will fall at a decreasing rate.

If the order quantity is q and orders are placed after stock has fallen uniformly to zero, the average level of stock will be $q/2$. Assume that the purchase cost of stock is constant at £c per unit. Then the average value of stock will be £$cq/2$. Let the cost of holding stock be a constant proportion of the value of that stock, say h. Then total holding costs (THC) will be £$hcq/2$, and the cost of holding stock will increase directly with the order quantity. Marginal holding cost (MHC) will be $hc/2$. If total holding costs were plotted against order quantity, this curve would be an upward sloping straight line with a slope of $hc/2$.

We saw earlier that total inventory costs will be minimised when the fall in order costs, as order quantity increases one unit, just equals the rise in holding cost. This position defines the economic order quantity q^*. If more than q^* is ordered, holding costs rise by more than order costs fall, and conversely for orders less than q^*.

The parameters of the deterministic model

D = Annual Demand
q = order quantity
r = cost/order
h = holding cost/unit
c = purchase cost/unit

To find the economic order quantity, equate the fall in order costs to the rise in holding costs as one more unit is ordered, i.e.

$$-MOC = -MHC$$

Then $\dfrac{rD}{q^2} = \dfrac{hc}{2}$

$$q^2 hc = 2rD$$

$$q^2 = \frac{2rD}{hc}$$

at the optimum,[4] $q^* = \sqrt{\dfrac{2rD}{hc}}$

This is the basic equation of inventory analysis, and is often called the *Wilson lot size formula* in honour of an early proponent. One of the fascinations of inventory analysis is that this expression, or ones very like it, keep recurring as the assumptions are relaxed.

Digression – positive lead times

Since we have assumed orders are filled immediately, there is no need for order placement until stock falls to zero. The situation is illustrated in Figure 11.3. At time t_1 the stock level is q^*, which falls uniformly to zero at t_2, when another order is placed for q^*. Now relax the assumption of instantaneous replenishment, and assume a positive lead time between order placement and stock arrival. If this lead time is known, the problem is unaltered. Since demand is uniform, all that is necessary is to calculate demand over the lead time, and reorder whenever stock falls to this level. Then at time of delivery, stock will have fallen to zero. Assume the lead time is $t_2 - t'$. Then the order is placed at t' when stocks have fallen to q', and the new order arrives at the moment stock falls to zero.

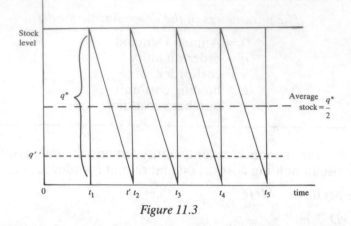

Figure 11.3

If the lead time is unknown or uncertain, the situation is considerably complicated. The optimal inventory policy will depend upon the probability distribution of lead times, and a deterministic model is inadequate. Sufficient stock must be kept over the variable lead time interval to meet expected demand, plus an allowance for demand to be higher than expected.

An algebraic formulation

It is useful to consider an alternative derivation of the economic order quantity, by explicitly defining a total cost function which can be minimised by differentiation.

Total cost is the sum of three components:

(i)   stock purchase cost, equal to annual demand times purchase price, Dc.
(ii)   total order costs, equal to rD/q
(iii)   total holding costs, $hcq/2$.

$$T = Dc + \frac{rD}{q} + \frac{hcq}{2}$$

Note that purchase cost is independent of order quantity. The second and third parts are the *acquisition* cost of stock.

T is minimised by differentiating with respect to the decision variable (q), setting to zero and solving, checking for a minimum through the second order condition.

$$\frac{\delta T}{\delta q} = \frac{-rD}{q^2} + \frac{hc}{2}$$

If $\dfrac{\delta T}{\delta q} = 0, \dfrac{rD}{q^2} = \dfrac{hc}{2}$

$$q^* = \sqrt{\dfrac{2rD}{hc}}$$

Now $\dfrac{\delta^2 T}{\delta q^2} = \dfrac{2rD}{q^3}$

which is greater than zero if q is positive, showing that a minimum has been achieved.

Now substitute q^* back into the formula for total cost, to find the minimum total cost T^*, i.e.

$$T^* = Dc + \dfrac{rD}{\sqrt{2rD/hc}} + \dfrac{hc}{2}\sqrt{\dfrac{2rD}{hc}}$$

which simplifies to:

$$T^* = Dc + \sqrt{2rDhc}$$

The minimum total cost is the sum of stock purchase cost and the second term, called the *Minimum Acquisition Cost* (MAC).

Sensitivity analysis

So far, the analysis has led to an expression for the economic order quantity to minimise total cost, and an expression for that total minimum cost. It is now relevant to enquire how the economic order quantity changes as the parameters change, and how total cost changes if an amount different from the economic order quantity is ordered. Thus the sensitivity of the model can be determined, which may be relevant in applications where information is incomplete or uncertain.

The economic order quantity is

$$q^* = \sqrt{\dfrac{2rD}{hc}}$$

The economic order quantity will increase with order costs (r) or annual demand (D), and decrease with holding costs (h) and the purchase cost of stock (c). Moreover, the extent of any change can be identified. The economic order quantity will increase with the square root of order costs or demand, which implies that the increase in order quantity will be less than proportional to the increase in order costs or demand. If order costs doubled, the optimal order quantity would increase by a proportion of $\sqrt{2}$ or 1.414. If demand trebled, the economic order quantity would increase by a factor of $\sqrt{3}$ or 1.732. The economic order quantity is also inversely proportional to the square root of holding cost or unit purchase price. If the purchase price quadrupled, the economic order quantity would fall by a half. The sensitivity of the economic order quantity is illustrated in Figure 11.4.

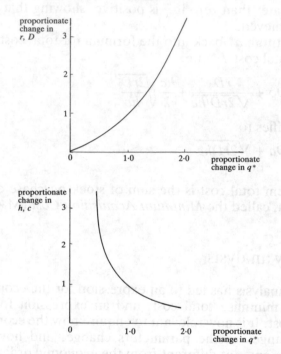

Figure 11.4   The sensitivity of the economic order quantity

The significance of this analysis lies in the disproportionate relationship between the economic order quantity and the parameters. This implies that any rule of thumb inventory policy, such as keeping the stock value of different items the same, or keeping so many weeks supply in stock, is extremely unlikely to be close to optimal, and suggests that a serious analysis of inventory policy is likely to lead to a substantial reduction in costs.

The effect on cost of ordering a quantity differing from the economic order quantity can now be analysed. Recall that total cost (T) is

$$T = Dc + \frac{rD}{q} + \frac{hcq}{2}$$

and is minimised when $q = \sqrt{\dfrac{2rD}{hc}}$

Suppose that for some reason a quantity k times the economic order quantity is ordered. Appendix 11A shows that the associated increase in costs will be

$$\frac{(k-1)^2}{2k}\sqrt{2rDhc}$$

or $(k-1)^2/2k$ times the minimum acquisition cost. This is illustrated in Figure 11.5, and shows that total cost is less sensitive to absolute increases in the order quantity than to absolute decreases. Thus if we are uncertain about the actual economic order quantity, it is probably cheaper to overestimate than to underestimate.

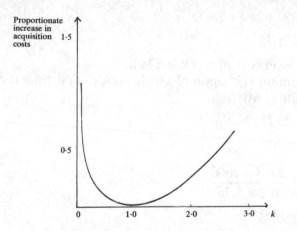

Figure 11.5   Sensitivity of costs to changes in order quantity

The deterministic model – an example

A supermarket sells, at a uniform rate, 2600 cases of beans each year. Each case costs the supermarket £5.75 from a wholesaler who also charges £5 for each delivery. The wholesaler guarantees delivery the same day the order is placed. The supermarket owner has all her working capital, borrowed from a local bank at an interest rate of 15 per cent, tied up in stock. The storage and maintenance of stock is estimated to cost 5 per cent of average stock value.

The owner wishes to review her present policy of ordering fifty cases each week and establish an inventory policy to minimise annual cost.

From this information the parameters of the problem can be established. Annual demand (D) is 2600 units. Order costs (r) are the £5 delivery charge (regarding the cost of a telephoned order as negligible). The cost per unit purchased is £5.75, and holding cost is 15 per cent interest charge plus 5 per cent maintenance cost (so $h = .15 + .05 = .20$).

The equation for total cost is:

$$T = Dc + \frac{rD}{q} + \frac{hcq}{2}$$

Under the present policy, $q = 50$, so total cost is

$$2600 \times 5.75 + \frac{5 \times 2600}{50} + \frac{0.2 \times 5.75 \times 50}{2}$$

$$= 14\,950 + 260 + 28.75$$

$$= 15\,238.75$$

The acquisition cost of stock is £288.75.

To determine the optimal stock policy, first find the economic order quantity, where

$$q^* = \sqrt{\frac{2rD}{hc}}$$

$$= \sqrt{\frac{2 \times 5 \times 2600}{0.2 \times 5.75}}$$

$$= 150.35$$

$$= 150 \text{ cases}$$

This implies placing an order every three weeks, with a new total cost given by the formula

$$T^* = Dc + \sqrt{2rDhc}$$

$$= 14\,950 + \sqrt{2 \times 5 \times 2600 \times 0.2 \times 5.75}$$

$$= 14\,950 + 172.92$$

$$= \underline{£15\,122.92}$$

Note that the Minimum Acquisition Cost is £172.92, a saving of £115.83 each year.

Now suppose that the wholesaler, wishing to take advantage of discounts offered by the manufacturer, offers a discount of 2 per cent for orders placed in lots of 600 cases. Is the discount worth accepting to the supermarket owner?

To determine the answer the owner must compare the savings in purchase cost to the increased inventory cost of ordering in large lots. The initial purchase cost was £14 950. A discount of 2 per cent then offers a saving of $14\,950 \times 0.02 = £299$. Ordering in large lots will increase holding costs, but with some saving in order costs.

Recall that if k times the economic order quantity was ordered, the increase in inventory costs would be:

$$\frac{(k-1)^2}{2k} \times MAC$$

Now 600 cases is four times the economic order quantity, and the minimum acquisition cost is £172.92. Then ordering in lots of 600 cases would increase acquisition costs by:

$$\frac{(4-1)^2}{2 \times 4} \times 172.92$$

$$= £194.54$$

Then taking advantage of the discount would lead to a net saving of $299 - 194.54 = £104.46$. Note that this assumes that ordering in large lots will have no effect on the relevant parameters. If, for example, such an increase in stock necessitated extra expenditure on storage space, this extra cost must be compared to the net savings above.

The deterministic model can be extended to take account of situations when stock is received as a flow over time (rather than assuming instantaneous replenishment). This corresponds closely to the situation where the inventory holder is the producer of the good, and illustrates the analogous relationship between set-up costs and order costs. Such an extension is considered in Appendix 11B, with results that closely parallel the economic order quantity model.

Stochastic inventory models

So far, we have proceeded on the assumption that demand was known with certainty, a hypothetical situation, but one which may be a useful approximation in many cases. For example, a supermarket manager in a large town may find that although daily demand by a particular family is highly variable, aggregate demand (demand over all families) over a period of time may fluctuate only slightly around some mean. Then the use of an economic order quantity model may be appropriate.

In other situations, it may be necessary to take explicit account of demand uncertainty. For example, the demand for new cars at a particular dealer may vary with the time of year, the state of local economic well-being, and a host of many different factors, so that average monthly demand varies considerably. The method adopted to take account of uncertainty depends upon the situation and in particular the amount of information available. We shall examine several models, but first some general remarks can be made.

Earlier we noted that if the lead time (interval between order placement and receipt) was known and demand was uniform, the economic order quantity model could be easily adjusted to take this into account. The solution was to specify a reorder level equal to the lead time demand, secure in the knowledge that by the time stock fell to zero, the order would be received. In practice, the lead time is uncertain – hence so is lead time demand. However, if daily demand is itself uncertain, the possible variation in lead time demand may be considerably increased. For example, if daily demand is 10 units and the lead time is 5 days, lead time demand is 50 units. If daily demand varies between 8 and 12 units, lead time demand is between 40 and 60 units. If, however, the lead time itself can vary from 4 to 6 days, lead time demand could vary from 32 to 72 units.

If the lead time is positive, the inventory problem is to determine both the optimal order quantity and the reorder level. If the lead time is uncertain, the optimal policy is likely to involve a reorder level greater than average lead time demand, to allow for the possibility that lead time demand exceeds the average. The difference between average lead time demand and the reorder level is the *safety* or *buffer* stock. The higher the buffer, the less likely that lead time demand will exceed the amount of good available. However, carrying stock involves a cost, so that finding the optimal buffer stock involves balancing the gains by reducing the possibility of shortages with the costs of holding extra stock. This balance is affected by the shortage cost of stock, which may be itself uncertain.

Then one possibility is to calculate a customer *service-level* corresponding to different levels of stock. The service-level is defined as the probability that over a given period the firm will be able to meet demand. Obviously the higher the level of safety stock, the greater the service-level. It is then a subjective matter to choose a service-level corresponding to the needs of customers and the objectives of the firm. The choice may be made on the basis of historical practice or the behaviour of competitors.

The usual approach to inventory analysis in the face of uncertainty is to estimate a probability distribution for lead time demand, and then maximise the expected profit (or minimise expected cost). We shall examine three models for uncertain inventory decisions, presented discretely. However, the range is continuous rather than discrete, with the choice of model depending on the circumstances of a particular problem.

The simple decision theory approach

The newsboy problem considered[5] in Chapter 4 is actually an inventory problem under conditions of uncertainty. The newsboy had to decide how many copies of the 'Daily Gossip' to stock tomorrow, and made that decision by estimating likely demand and then maximising expected profit. This involved examining the conditional profit corresponding to different combinations of act (stock) and event (sales), and then weighting each outcome by the probability of its occurrence. The model was then extended to consider opportunity losses, and expected profit replaced by expected utility.

The simple decision theory approach is logical, consistent and provides useful answers on the basis of estimated probabilities. However, the analysis quickly becomes unwieldy as the number of possible alternatives increases. For example, if there were twenty possible stock actions, and thirty possible states of demand, the pay-off matrix would consist of $20 \times 30 = 600$ elements, and the calculation of expected profit for each action becomes extremely tedious. It is then simpler to perform the analysis in marginal terms.

The marginal approach

Assume the decision-maker can assess the probability that D units will be demanded. Each unit sold results in a profit of £S, so that £S is the opportunity cost per unit of failing to meet demand. Each unit purchased has a cost of £C, so £C is the cost per unit of ordering too many. These three variables are then the parameters of the model, and are sufficient to enable an optimal stock policy to be calculated.

Assume the decision-maker is risk-neutral, and therefore tries to maximise expected profit. We seek the expected profit from the nth unit purchased. If this is greater than zero, this unit will be added to stock, if less than zero stock is too large. Therefore, the optimal stock occurs when the nth unit has an expected profit at least equal to zero.

The expected profit from the nth unit will equal the profit from selling that unit times the probability that unit is sold (i.e. the probability at least n units are demanded), minus the cost of not selling that unit minus the probability it remains unsold (i.e. the probability that less than n units will be demanded),[6] i.e.

$$E\,(\pi \text{ from } n\text{th unit}) = S \times P(D \geqslant n) - C \times P(D < n).$$

If the expected profit from the last unit at least equals zero,

$$S \times P(D \geqslant n) - C \times P(D < n) \geqslant 0$$

Now $P(D \geqslant n)$ and $P(D < n)$ are mutually exclusive and exhaustive (one must occur) so that

$$P(D \geqslant n) + P(D < n) = 1$$

or $\quad P(D \geqslant n) = 1 - P(D < n)$

Substituting:

$$S \times (1 - P(D < n)) - C \times P(D < n) \geqslant 0$$

$$S - S \times P(D < n) + C \times P(D < n) \geqslant 0$$

$$S \geqslant (S + C) \times P(D < n)$$

$$\frac{S}{S + C} \geqslant P(D < n)$$

or $\quad P(D < n) \leqslant \dfrac{S}{S + C}$

To maximise expected profit, n units of the item should be stocked so that the probability demand is less than n is no greater than the critical ratio $S/(S + C)$.

This sounds rather complicated but is easy to use in practice. Recall that our newsboy bought the 'Daily Gossip' for 15p and sold it for 25p. Then the profit from each sale (S) equals 10p, whilst stocking too many involves an extra cost of 15p per unsold unit ($C = 15$). From Chapter 4, the probability distribution of demand was:

Table 11.1

	Demand	Probability	$P(D < n)$
$n =$	20	0.25	0
	30	0.50	0.25
	40	0.25	0.75
	50	0	1.0

The probability distribution (first two columns) is first converted into a cumulative probability distribution (column 3). Note that the probability demand is less than 20 is zero, as is the probability demand equals 50.

The optimal stock is given by the formula

$$P(D<n) \geqslant \frac{S}{S+C}$$

if $S = 10, C = 15$

$$P(D<n) \geqslant \frac{10}{25} = 0.4$$

Reading down Table 11.1, this occurs when 30 units are stocked. If n was greater than 30, the probability demand was less than n would exceed the critical ratio, and therefore additions to stock would add more to expected costs than to expected revenue.

The newsboy problem was much simplified, and hardly justified the application of a marginal approach. The real value of this approach can be seen with more realistic and complex problems, when a greater number of alternatives must be considered.

Suppose that each day a particular florist assembles flowers into an ornate arrangement. He estimates the direct costs of each arrangement at 55p, whilst the arrangements are sold for £2.00 each. Then profit per sale (S) is £1.45. Because of the perishable nature of the flowers, any unit unsold at the end of the day is worthless (and therefore $C = 0.55$). By keeping a careful check on past demand, this is expected to follow a Poisson[7] distribution with a mean of 12 units.

The problem for the florist is to determine the number of units to be made each day to maximise expected profit. The probability distribution for a Poisson distribution with a mean of 12 can be found from Statistical Tables[8] and is shown in Table 11.2.

From Table 11.2, there are twenty-two levels of demand that have a positive probability. Hence a pay-off matrix allowing each possible act (making between 3 and 24 units) and demand would have $22 \times 22 = 484$ elements!

It is far simpler to use the rule that n should be stocked so that the probability demand is less than n is no greater than the critical ratio $S/(S+C)$. In this example, $S = 1.45$ and $C = 0.55$, so that

$$\frac{S}{S+C} = \frac{1.45}{1.45+0.55} = 0.725$$

Reading from Table 11.2, 14 units is the largest stock with a

Table 11.2 Poisson distribution with mean of 12

n	P(D = n)	P(D < n)	n	P(D = n)	P(D < n)
0	0.000	0.000	13	0.106	0.576
1	0.000	0.000	14	0.091	0.682
2	0.000	0.000	15	0.072	0.773
3	0.002	0.000	16	0.054	0.845
4	0.005	0.002	17	0.038	0.899
5	0.013	0.007	18	0.026	0.937
6	0.026	0.020	19	0.016	0.963
7	0.044	0.046	20	0.010	0.979
8	0.066	0.090	21	0.006	0.989
9	0.087	0.156	22	0.003	0.995
10	0.105	0.243	23	0.001	0.998
11	0.114	0.348	24	0.001	0.999
12	0.114	0.462	25	0.000	1.000

probability that demand will be less than this that does not exceed the critical ratio (since $P(D < 14) = 0.682$). If 15 units were stocked, the probability that demand is less than 15 is 0.772, which is greater than the critical ratio. Therefore, the 15th unit would add more to expected cost than to expected revenue, and would reduce expected profit.

Service level models

So far we have assumed that ordering occurs at fixed intervals, and that stock-out costs are known. The fixed interval order assumption was facilitated by presuming that stock had a limited economic life. In practice, most goods have at least some durability, which together with order costs implies time periods between order placements that may be variable. If the good is durable, usual practice involves some review system that monitors current stock levels, with order placement whenever stock falls to the predetermined reorder level. The reorder level equals expected lead time demand plus some buffer stock to take account of lead time variability. We saw earlier that the level of buffer stock depends upon the variability of lead time demand, the costs of holding stock and the costs of any shortages. As buffer stock rises, shortage costs fall and holding costs increase. Thus the optimal buffer stock occurs when the marginal fall in shortage cost is equal to the marginal increase in holding cost. Unfortunately, this calculation may be impossible to perform since shortage costs may themselves be uncertain. The shortage cost may be less than the profit lost on a forgone sale if that sale is just postponed, or greater than this if the potential customer buys elsewhere in future.

The absence of reliable shortage cost information may lead to the adoption of a service level policy, defined as holding sufficient stock to satisfy demand on a predetermined proportion of occasions (normally 90 or 95 per cent). Recall the florist, who estimated that demand had a Poisson distribution with a mean of 12. With a cost per unit of 55p and a profit margin of £1.45, the optimal quantity was found to be 14 units. The service level associated with this policy is the probability that demand will be less than or equal to 14. If demand is discrete (as in the Poisson probability distribution), then the probability demand is less than or equal to 14 is equivalent to the probability that demand is less than 15. From Table 11.2 this is equal to 0.773. Thus stocking 14 will lead to a 77 per cent service level.

Suppose now that the florist is concerned about the 23 per cent of occasions when some demand is unsatisfied, because he feels that such customers may not return in future. This implies that he considers stock-out costs to be greater than £1.45 but may have little idea of how much greater. Then a reasonable response may be to specify a service level. If the chosen service level was 90 per cent, the resulting stock level is 16, since this leaves just a 10 per cent chance of not meeting all demand.[9] The safety stock is defined as the stock level minus average demand, so a 90 per cent service level implies a safety stock of 4 units (16 − 12). To achieve a 95 per cent service level stock must be increased to 18, whilst a service level of 99 per cent is only achieved with a stock level of 21. Note that as the level of stock increases the service level increases but at a decreasing rate. This is an important result, and implies that as the service level increases, cost increases at an increasing rate. The possibility of shortages is only precluded by stocking 24 units (twice average demand), and would be extremely expensive. Hence most commercial organisations have to compromise at some service level less than 100 per cent, and accept that there will be times when all demand cannot be met.

Summary and conclusions

Inventory decisions may have considerable operational, strategic and financial significance. Indeed many commercial organisations can be seen as inventory systems, buying in large lots for resale in smaller lots. Stocks are held for speculative, precautionary and transactional reasons, and may provide an important adjustment mechanism, allowing price and output to remain constant. However, stocks may be expensive to order, hold and maintain, particularly in terms of the capital tied up in stock – usually a non-interest bearing and illiquid asset. Inventory models offer the opportunity to minimise the cost of stock, often leading to significant savings.

The simplest inventory models are deterministic, i.e. assume that demand is known beforehand. Then an optimal inventory policy involves balancing order and holding costs. Deterministic models can be extended to allow for positive lead times and flow receipts. Moreover, the economic order quantity model was seen to be fairly insensitive to parameter estimation errors. Inventory models that allow for uncertain demand rely on the estimation of probabilities, with all the attendant problems this implies. The simplest decision theory model combines conditional outcomes with estimated probabilities to minimise expected costs (or maximise expected profits). More complex models eliminate the need for repetitive calculation by concentrating on the marginal costs and benefits from stocking an extra unit. Finally, service level models recognise that shortage costs may be unknown, and settle for an inventory policy that can meet demand on a predetermined proportion of occasions.

Appendix 11A

The effect on acquisition costs of ordering non-optimal amounts

Recall that:

$$T = Dc + \frac{rD}{q} + \frac{hcq}{2}$$

If kq^* ordered, new total cost ($T1$) will be

$$T1 = Dc + \frac{rD}{kq^*} + \frac{hckq^*}{2}$$

As $q^* = \sqrt{\frac{2rD}{hc}}$

$$T1 = Dc + \frac{1}{k} \cdot \frac{rD}{\sqrt{2rD/hc}} + k \cdot \frac{hc}{2} \cdot \sqrt{\frac{2rD}{hc}}$$

$$= Dc + \frac{1}{k} \sqrt{\frac{rDhc}{2}} + k \sqrt{\frac{2}{rDhc}}$$

$$T1 = Dc + \left(\frac{1}{k} + k\right) \sqrt{\frac{rDhc}{2}} \tag{1}$$

Note if $k = 1$, the economic order quantity is ordered, and

$$T1 = Dc + \sqrt{2rDhc},$$

or purchase cost plus the minimum acquisition cost.

From equation (1), the acquisition cost will be the same when $k = 2$ or when $k = \frac{1}{2}$. Doubling or halving the order quantity will have the same effect on costs.

If k times q^* is ordered, the increase in costs can be calculated by subtracting the minimum total cost (T^*) from the new total cost ($T1$).

Now $T^* = Dc + \sqrt{2rDhc}$

$$T1 = Dc + \left(\frac{1}{k} + k\right)\sqrt{\frac{rDhc}{2}}$$

Then[10] $T1 - T^* = \left(\frac{1}{k} + k - 2\right)\sqrt{\frac{rDhc}{2}}$

$$= \frac{k^2 - 2k + 1}{k}\sqrt{\frac{rDhc}{2}}$$

$$= \frac{(k-1)^2}{2k}\sqrt{2rDhc}$$

or the increase in costs is $(k-1)^2/2k$ times the minimum acquisition cost.

Appendix 11B

A flow-receipts model

This model considers a situation where the stock holder is also the producer of the good. Suppose the known daily demand is d units. The good is made in batches at a rate of p units per day, with a set-up cost of £s and an average variable cost of £c per unit. Then the production cost per batch will be:

$$c(q) = s + cq$$

when production stops, stock is run down until it equals zero, when production starts again. Obviously the production rate (p) must exceed the demand rate (d), with a stock situation illustrated in Figure 11B.1. In the early part of the cycle stock is built up (at a rate of ($p-d$) per day) whilst production takes place. The maximum stock level is at the time production stops, after which stock falls gradually to zero.

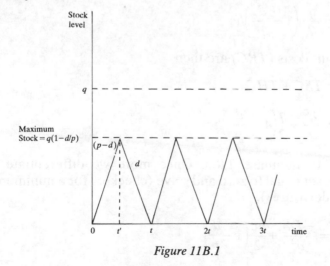

Figure 11B.1

277

The problem is to determine q, the total production run or batch size, to minimise total cost. The number of days production necessary to produce q is q/p. During the period production takes place, the amount sold will be $q/p \times d$. Maximum stock occurs at the moment production stops, and will equal the amount produced minus the amount sold.

Maximum inventory $= q - (q/p)d = q(1 - d/p)$

Average inventory $= q/2(1 - d/p)$

The total cost of producing and stocking the good will equal the total variable cost of production, plus total set-up costs, plus total holding costs.

The total variable cost of production per year, of producing to meet an annual demand of D units, will be $D \times c$. Moreover, this is the same regardless of the batch size, and therefore does not enter the batch size decision. The *relevant* cost to be minimised is the sum of set-up and holding costs, which both vary with the size of the production run.

The number of production runs per year will equal total demand D divided by the size of each batch q. Each production run incurs a set-up cost of £S, so that total set-up cost per year (TSC) will be:

$$TSC = \frac{DS}{q}$$

Total holding cost (THC) equals the holding cost (h) times the average value of inventory. If the average size of inventory is $q/2(1 - d/p)$, the average value of inventory will be $q/2(1 - d/p) \times c$,

and $THC = \dfrac{q}{2}\left(1 - \dfrac{d}{p}\right)hc$

Total relevant costs (TRC) are then

$TRC = TSC + THC$

$$TRC = \frac{DS}{q} + \frac{q}{2}\left(1 - \frac{d}{p}\right)hc$$

We seek q to minimise TRC. Once more we differentiate with respect to q, set equal to zero and solve (checking for a minimum via the second derivative).

$$\frac{\delta TRC}{\delta q} = \frac{-DS}{q^2} + \frac{hc}{2}\left(1 - \frac{d}{p}\right)$$

If $\quad \dfrac{\delta TRC}{\delta q} = 0, \dfrac{DS}{q^2} = \dfrac{hc}{2}\left(1 - \dfrac{d}{p}\right)$

$$q^2 hc\left(1 - \dfrac{d}{p}\right) = 2DS$$

Therefore[11] $\quad q^* = \sqrt{\dfrac{2DS}{hc(1 - d/p)}}$

Note the similarity to the economic order quantity formula. The differences are that order costs are replaced by set-up costs, and we now take account of the daily production and demand rates. Since p is less than d, the denominator is smaller than in the block receipt case, and therefore the optimal quantity is larger. This makes intuitive sense, since as the order arrives over time some of it is used up.

Maintaining the text example of the supermarket owner, suppose that instead of buying beans from the wholesaler the owner packages her own brand using a small workroom at the back of the store. The machine cans beans at a rate of twenty cases per day. Each time the machine is used for a new production run, it is overhauled at a cost of £5. Each case of beans produced uses inputs valued at £5.75. Once more annual demand is for 2600 cases, and holding costs are 20 per cent. Moreover, the supermarket is open five days per week, or 260 days each year, so that the daily demand rate is ten cases. Then the parameters of this problem are:

$D = 2600$	$S = 5$
$c = 5.75$	$d = 10$/day
$h = 0.2$	$p = 20$/day

Now $q^* = \sqrt{\dfrac{2 \times 2600 \times 5}{0.2 \times 5.75 \times (1 - 10/20)}}$

$\qquad = \sqrt{\dfrac{26000}{0.575}}$

$\qquad = 213$ cases.

The optimal production schedule is then to produce 213 cases (over $213/20 = 10.65$ days), wait for stock to fall to zero (after 21.3 days) and then start again.

Average stock level will be

$$\frac{q}{2}\left(1-\frac{d}{p}\right)=\frac{213}{2}\times\left(1-\frac{10}{20}\right)$$

$$= 53.25 \text{ cases}$$

and total relevant costs are:

$$\frac{DS}{q}+\frac{q}{2}\left(1-\frac{d}{p}\right)hc = \frac{2600\times5}{213}+\frac{213}{2}\times\left(1-\frac{10}{20}\right)\times0.20\times5.75$$

$$= £122.26,$$

which is the smallest possible.

Application 11

Reading electricity meters[12]

In Britain, the Central Electricity Generating Board (CEGB) supplies electricity to some 15 million domestic consumers. Each consumer effectively receives electricity on credit, since consumption is metered with the consumer being sent an electricity bill after the meter has been read. Consequently, there is an interest cost to the CEGB which could be reduced by more frequent meter reading and billing At the same time, meter reading consumes resources. Increasing the meter reading frequency would reduce the interest cost of the sum outstanding to the CEGB, but would increase meter reading costs.

This is then an inventory problem, and total cost to the CEGB can be minimised by equating the marginal saving in interest costs from more frequent reading to the marginal cost of that extra reading. Present policy is for the 15 million domestic meters to be read quarterly by some 6000 meter readers, each costing on average £6000 per year. Then the total reading cost of quarterly readings is £36 million. Each meter could be read twice each year at presumably half present reading costs. Column 2 in Table A11.1 shows how total reading cost varies with reading frequency.

Table A11.1   The cost of reading electricity meters

Frequency/year	Reading costs £m	Interest costs £m	Total cost
1	9	324	333
2	18	162	180
4	36	81	117
8	72	40.5	112.5

Suppose that each domestic consumer uses on average £432 worth of electricity each year. If each meter was read once each year, the average sum outstanding to the electricity board would be £432/2. Reading meters q times per year results in an average sum outstanding of £432/q – hence quarterly readings imply an average sum outstanding of £54 (the average quarterly bill is £108, with the sum outstanding rising from zero to £108 over the quarter – hence averaging £54).

The total interest cost of present policy is then £54 times the number of households times the rate of interest. If the number of households is 15 million, and the rate of interest is 10 per cent, the annual interest cost of present policy is $54 \times 15 \times 0.10 = $ £81 million. Column 3 of Table A11.1 lists the interest cost of different meter reading frequencies, whilst column 4 sums interest and reading costs. From the table, reading meters eight times each year would save £4.5 million compared to present policy.

In order to determine an optimal policy and consider the effects of parameter changes, it is helpful to generalise. Suppose that q is the frequency of meter readings per year, x is average annual consumption, n is the number of domestic consumers, r is the rate of interest and c is cost of reading all meters once.

If each meter is read q times per year, total reading costs (TRC) with be $c \times q$. The average sum outstanding is $x/2q$, so that total interest costs (TIC are $xnr/2q$. Since total cost is the sum of reading plus interest costs,

$$T = TRC + TIC$$

$$= cq + \frac{xnr}{2q}$$

Marginal reading cost is $MRC = \dfrac{\delta TRC}{\delta q} = c$

whilst marginal interest cost is $MIC = \dfrac{\delta TIC}{\delta q} = \dfrac{-xnr}{2q^2}$

As the frequency of readings increases, total reading costs increase but total interest costs fall. Equating the marginal cost of an extra reading to the marginal savings in interest costs,

$$MRC = -MIC$$

$$c = \frac{xnr}{2q^2}$$

$$2q^2c = xnr$$

$$q = \sqrt{\frac{xnr}{2c}}$$

Note the similarity to the economic order quantity. Using the parameter values above:

$$x = 432, n = 15, r = 0.10, c = 9$$

$$q = \sqrt{\frac{432 \times 15 \times 0.10}{2 \times 9}}$$

$$= 6$$

Hence to minimise total costs, meters should be read six times per year (or every other month). Total costs would then be:

$$T = 9 \times 6 + \frac{432 \times 15 \times 0.10}{2 \times 6}$$

$$= £108 \text{ million,}$$

saving £9 million on present quarterly readings policy.

Note that an increase in average consumption, the number of consumers or the rate of interest would increase the optimal reading frequency (but by less than proportionately), whilst a rise in meter reading costs would reduce reading frequency.

CHAPTER 12.

Employment and labour management decisions

Contents

Introduction

In Chapter 6 we saw that the profit maximising firm will choose the particular input combination that minimises the cost of output, determined by the productivity of inputs and their relative prices. Later chapters have considered the relationship of the firm to its competitive environment in terms of output, price and marketing decisions. It is now time to take a step back, and examine the competitive environment surrounding input purchase decisions, and in particular the special problems and opportunities encountered in the employment and deployment of labour.

Labour management decisions warrant particular attention for a variety of reasons. First and foremost the management of labour is the management of people, with all the complexity, variety and rewards that this implies. Secondly, direct and indirect labour costs form a substantial proportion of the total costs of any business organisation. Typically, some 70 per cent of total costs are attributable to labour. Thirdly, labour differs from other inputs in that the owner of the input (receiver of the input price) must accompany the use of that input. This implies that the seller of labour has an immediate interest in the circumstances and conditions under which that labour is used. Finally, the productivity of labour is itself a variable depending not only on the use of other inputs but also on working conditions, the amount and quality of training and education and the form of payment system adopted.

This chapter will proceed by presenting the traditional microeconomic analysis of the employment decision, which will then be widened to include other dimensions of labour services. The chapter will then consider other aspects of labour management including variables affecting the productivity of labour such as investment in training and the provision of fringe benefits. The recruitment and deployment of labour will also be examined.

All labour management decisions must be taken within the context of an institutional and legal framework provided by custom and practice, legislation and the existence of employee groupings. The chapter will thus conclude with an examination of this framework and the resulting constraints which restrict the decision-making abilities of both employers and employees.

Employment decisions

The demand for labour, like that of any other factor of production is a *derived demand*, i.e. the demand for labour is derived from the demand for the final product that labour can help to make. Chapter 6 (Production) examined the determination of the optimal input combination to produce a given output, and concluded that this occurred when the ratio of factor marginal products was equal to the factor price ratio. If the price of labour (wage rate) rose relative to the price of other factors, other factors would be substituted for labour.

It is now necessary to drop the assumption of a fixed output level and examine directly the determination of labour demand. This is simplified by the twin assumptions of perfect product and factor markets (so that product and factor prices are fixed), although these assumptions will be relaxed later.

A central theme of this book is that profit can be maximised by continuing any activity until marginal revenue is equal to marginal cost. Analysis of the firm's employment decision proves no exception. To examine the application of this principle to the labour market, assume that labour is the only variable input. The relationship between output and the quantity of labour is then defined by the law of diminishing returns, with Figure 12.1 below reproducing Figure 6.10 of Chapter 6, to show that labour's marginal and average products will increase, reach a maximum and then decrease.

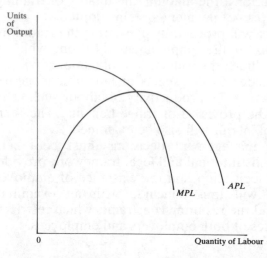

Figure 12.1   The average and marginal products of labour

Figure 12.1 shows the average and marginal products of labour in terms of physical output. Because of the assumption of a perfect product market, these can be transformed into revenue terms simply by multiplying output by price. Then the value of the marginal product (*VMP*) and the average revenue product (*ARP*) are defined as the marginal and average products multiplied by price, i.e.

$$VMP = MP \times P$$

$$ARP = AP \times P$$

where *P* is the price of output.

If the firm employs an extra unit of labour, it will gain revenue equal to the value of that unit of labour's marginal product (*VMP*). This extra revenue must be compared with the extra cost of employing that labour unit. Given a perfect factor market, the marginal cost of an extra unit of labour will be the wage rate (and is equal to the average cost of labour). The profit maximising condition for employment is then to employ labour until:

$$VMP = W, \text{ where } W \text{ is the wage rate.}$$

From Figure 12.2, if the wage rate is $W1$, $L1$ units of labour will be demanded to maximise profit. If the wage rate rose to $W2$, labour demand would fall to $L2$. Note that if the wage rate rose to $W3$, labour demand would be zero rather than $L3$, since at $W3$ the average revenue from labour (ARP) is less than the average cost of labour ($W3$) and the firm will be making a loss.

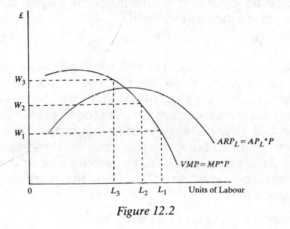

Figure 12.2

The demand curve for labour is then that part of the value of the marginal product curve which lies below the average revenue product. A change in the wage rate will cause a movement along that demand curve, whilst a change in labour productivity or output will cause a shift in the demand curve. For example, a rise in labour productivity would shift the VMP curve outwards, as would an increase in product price.

Note, however, that if all inputs are variable, an increase in the wage rate would both directly reduce the demand for labour *and* lead to the substitution of other inputs for labour. The introduction of other inputs in place of labour would increase labour productivity, shifting the labour demand curve outwards and offsetting some of the immediate fall in labour demand.

If the product market is imperfect, the demand curve for that product will slope down. Then any addition to output will necessitate a fall in product price. Hence the marginal revenue from extra output will be less than the price of that output, implying that an extra unit of labour adds less to total revenue than the value of the marginal product. The addition to revenue from the employment of an extra labour unit is then the marginal revenue product of labour ($MRPL$), where:

$$MRPL = MPL * MR < VMPL = MPL \times P$$

since $MR < P$

Given a downward sloping product demand curve, the value of the marginal product curve will have a corresponding marginal revenue product curve that lies below it (Figure 12.3). If the factor market remains perfectly competitive, the relevant employment decision rule is to increase employment until:[1]

$$MRPL = W$$

Similarly, if the factor market is imperfect, the assumption of a fixed wage rate must be abandoned. If the supply curve for labour slopes up an extra worker can only be employed by raising the wage rate, not only for the extra employee but for all previous employees. Then the cost of an extra worker (marginal factor cost = *MFC*) will exceed the wage rate. For example, suppose the firm employs ten labourers at £100 per week each. To employ an extra labourer, the wage rate must be raised to £105. Then the marginal cost of the extra labourer will be:

TC (employing 11) − TC (employing 10)

$= (11 \times 105) - (10 \times 100)$

$= 1155 - 1000$

$= £155.$

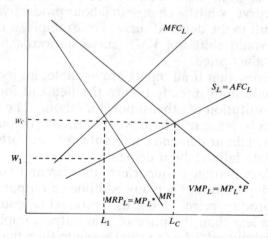

Figure 12.3   Imperfection in product and factor markets

Then the marginal factor cost is £155, considerably in excess of the wage rate.[2] Figure 12.3 illustrates a marginal factor cost curve above average factor cost (or the labour supply curve). Given the imperfect factor and product markets, the profit maximising firm will employ $L1$ at a wage of $W1$. Note that if factor and product markets had been perfectly competitive, employment would have been LC at a wage of WC – both of which are greater than the uncompetitive case.

Table 12.1 summarises the profit-maximising employment conditions according to the competitive structure of product and factor markets.

Table 12.1   Conditions for profit maximisation

| | Factor Market | |
	Perfect	Imperfect
Product Market — Perfect	$VMP = W$	$VMP = MFC$
Product Market — Imperfect	$MRP = W$	$MRP = MFC$

In the above model, the optimal *number* of people to employ has been analysed through the application of the basic marginalist principle – that any activity should be continued until the marginal benefit from that activity equals its marginal cost. As a logical prescriptive device the model is unassailable. However, in terms of its operational value, the model has a number of deficiencies, quite apart from the usual problem of estimating marginal values. The model assumes that all labour is homogeneous, i.e. that the productivity of a unit of labour is independent of the specific unit employed. In practice, of course, each employee differs in terms of skills, education, experience and commitment. These differences will, in the presence of sufficient information, give rise to differences in labour reward. Moreover, the demand for labour services has other dimensions than just the number of people employed.

Other dimensions of labour services

Recall that the demand for labour is a derived demand. Labour is purchased because of its productive services. The productivity of labour will depend on other variables as well as the quantity employed, such as the hours of work, the intensity of effort, etc. Brechling[3] analysed these other dimensions of labour by considering the level of effective labour services to produce a given output, i.e.

$$S = E \times U$$

where S is the level of labour services, E the number employed and U some index of labour utilisation such as hours worked per person, the intensity of effort, etc.

Then the number employed and the level of utilisation are substitute inputs in the production of labour services. A given level of labour services is then the product of both numbers employed and the utilisation rate. The actual choice between employment and utilisation depends upon the relative prices of each input dimension. For example, consider the distribution of labour services between the number employed and the hours worked per person. A given level of labour services could be achieved with a particular number of people each working a certain number of hours per period, or with a larger number each working fewer hours etc.

The analysis can be conducted in terms of isoquants, illustrating the possible combinations of employment and average hours to produce a given output. Because numbers employed and average hours are imperfect substitutes, each isoquant will be convex to the origin. In Figure 12.4, the isoquants Q_1 and Q_2 show combinations of hours and employment to produce these output levels.

The motivational force behind the hours/employment choice will be the desire to produce a given output at least cost. Brechling considers a payment system of a standard hourly wage rate up to 'normal' hours, with a premium rate for overtime hours. Then the isocost line, showing combinations purchasable with a fixed money sum, will be kinked at the level of normal hours (line XYZ in Figure 12.4).

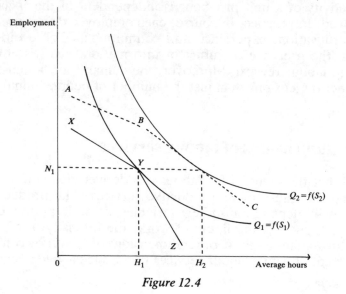

Figure 12.4

Given this payment system and the desired output level Q_1, N_1 people will be employed with the average hours per person of H_1. As drawn, the point of tangency occurs when actual hours equal normal hours (i.e. no overtime is worked). This, of course, need not be the case. With the payment system represented by curve ABC, and the desired output level Q_2, actual hours exceed normal hours and overtime will be worked. As drawn output level Q_2 will be produced with the same number of people as Q_1, but with each person working much longer hours.

The Brechling model can then be manipulated to determine the effects of changes in the model parameters, such as the marginal rate of substitution between hours and employment, the level of normal hours and the overtime premium.[4] Changes in labour productivity will change the slope of the isoquants, whilst changes in the payment system will affect the isocosts. The effect of payment changes will depend on the initial distribution of hours worked. For example, if actual hours worked are less than normal hours (so that no overtime is worked), changes in normal hours or the overtime premium can have no effect (unless normal hours are reduced below actual hours, in which case actual hours fall and employment rises). Alternatively, if overtime is worked initially (with actual hours exceeding normal hours), reductions in standard hours will increase the amount of overtime and decrease employment.

Investment in human capital

One qualification that was noted to the employment model is that labour is heterogeneous – i.e. that people have different skills and abilities reflected in different levels of productivity. Unlike most other inputs, the productivity of labour can be improved by expenditure on training and education. Given that the rewards to labour depend, at least in part, on the productivity of labour, each worker will have an incentive to increase these rewards by the acquisition of further skills and the refinement of abilities. At the same time, the firm has some incentive to spend money on improving the productivity of its workforce. The distribution of investment in human capital between employer and employee will depend on the specificity of that investment to the particular firm. For example, few firms have an incentive to provide training in general skills, such as typing, because the worker acquiring these skills will be able to realise the value of those skills by transferring employment to another firm, who in turn has an incentive *not* to spend money on training since it can 'poach' employees away from other firms. Thus we expect general skills to be financed by employee investment, whilst firm specific skills that have a value only to one firm will be financed by that firm.

In practice, of course, few skills are either firm specific or completely general. Then we can expect most skills to be financed by a combination of employee and employer contribution. Alternatively, a firm may be willing to finance general skills *if* the employee acquiring these skills can be tied to the firm for long enough for the firm to recoup its investment. Then, for example, a firm may be willing to finance an employee onto a part-time MBA programme if that employee contracts to remain with that firm for three years after graduation. Note that the firm then recoups its investment by paying that employee over the three years a salary less than the employee could receive elsewhere by transferring his newly acquired skills.

Any investment in human capital, whether by employer or employee, will be profitable if the present value of returns exceeds the cost of the investment. For the employee the benefits of the investment are the differences the investment makes to expected salaries over the working life, whilst to the employer, the benefits of the investments are the differences between expected productivity and expected salary over the returns period. Since the present value of any investment varies inversely with the interest rate, a fall in interest rates will increase the amount of investment in human capital.[5]

Other aspects of labour management

The deployment of labour, the provision of fringe benefits, expenditure on employee safety and the decision of whether to increase employment or provide more overtime can each be analysed by comparing marginal costs to marginal benefits.

Consider a bank branch that must decide the number of cashiers to provide. The fewer the number of cashiers, the lower the cost to the bank but the longer the average waiting time of customers (and the greater the probability that potential customers will take their accounts elsewhere). Then we have what is essentially an inventory problem, where the reduction in bank costs from fewer cashiers must be balanced against the probability that profitable custom will be forgone. No bank will be able to afford the cost of completely eliminating waiting time (or providing a 100 per cent service level).

The optimal number of cashiers will depend upon the average cost of cashiers, the probability distribution of demand and the expected cost of not meeting customer demand immediately (stock-outs). For example, the only bank in a small town will have less incentive to provide cashiers than will a bank branch located alongside several competitors, since the opportunity for customers to go elsewhere is much less. This logic explains both the proliferation of bank branches in financial districts (where the profitability of the average transaction is higher), and the introduction of 'hole in the wall' automatic cash-vending machines which both reduce average waiting times and increase the average profitability of expensively provided cashier transactions.

Fringe benefits are the non-salary remunerations of employees, and may include pension contributions, a company car, health insurance or a subsidised company canteen. In choosing employers the rational employee will consider *all* the benefits and costs of a particular job, so that fringe benefits are part of the full employee compensation package. Because of the structure of the income tax system, the payment of fringe benefits may be more preferable for both employer and employee than the equivalent salary payment. For example, a subsidised canteen increases the real income of employees. Suppose that an employee pays a marginal rate of tax of 30 per cent. Then paying that employee an extra £100 per year will increase her disposable income by £70 ($100 \times (1 - 0.3)$). If instead the employer spends £85 per year on providing subsidised lunches to that employee, both the employer and employee gain a net £15 per year compared to the pay rise. The higher the employee's marginal rate of tax, then the greater the potential value of fringe benefits, so that higher paid employees can also be expected to enjoy a higher proportion of fringe benefits to salary.

The analysis of employee remuneration is also helpful in the determination of optimal safety levels. If the employee must bear the cost of industrial accidents through wages forgone as a result of accidents, then wages in risky industries must be high enough to compensate. Consequently, the employer has an incentive to provide safety equipment, thereby reducing riskiness and the level of wage differentials. Similarly, if the employer must bear the cost of industrial accidents through sickness payment and industrial compensation schemes, the employer will have a direct interest in reducing the probability of accidents by spending more on safety. Specifically, safety equipment will be bought until the marginal cost of the last item is exactly equal to the marginal benefit in terms of the expected reduction in the cost of accidents.

The sum of wage costs, fringe benefits and safety equipment are not the total costs of employing labour. Labour costs also include the costs of recruitment (finding and choosing employees), the costs of training, national insurance payments, employers' contributions and the cost of providing productive working conditions to employees. Typically these fixed (or quasi-fixed) costs of labour add some 25 per cent to the direct salary costs of labour. Then, for example, firms have an interest in meeting a temporary decline in labour demand by some adjustment mechanism other than the number of people employed, given that there are transaction costs of hiring and firing labour. The cost-minimising firm has an incentive to reduce the quit rate, since any leaving employee immediately implies that recruitment and training costs have been lost.

Suppose that the firm experiences an increase in demand, so that 40 hours of extra labour are required each week. The firm has a choice between taking on one extra person to work those 40 hours or persuading 40 employees to work one hour's overtime each week. Let the cost of recruitment and training be £t, the standard wage rate equal $W1$ and the overtime wage rate be $W2$ (where $W2 > W1$). Employing the extra person will be cheaper if

$$t + 40W1 < 40W2$$

or $$t < 40(W2 - W1)$$

$$t/40 < W2 - W1$$

The cost-minimising employer will take on the extra person if the fixed costs per hour are less than the overtime premium. The other variable to be taken into account is the expected duration of the extra output demand. If demand is expected to be high for more than one week the fixed cost per hour of the extra employee will fall. On the other hand, if there are firing costs of labour, the extra demand must be expected to last for a considerable period to make the extra employment worthwhile.

Finally, whilst there are costs of recruitment to employers, there are also costs of job search to potential employees, in terms of the time, effort and money expended in acquiring information about potential employment opportunities. Because information is expensive, the optimising employee will search the job market until the marginal cost of the last search is equal to the marginal benefit. The cost-minimising manager, facing high recruitment costs, will have an incentive to reduce the costs of search by advertising for employees, or reduce the benefits of further search by offering high wages. At the same time, high wages will reduce the labour turnover rate by making alternative employment less attractive.

The institutional framework[6]

As noted earlier, labour management decisions are taken inside an institutional, legal and political framework that limits the manager's decision-making discretion, usually by protecting the employment rights of individual employees. There may be legal restrictions on the recruitment and selection of employees, the working conditions of employment and the power to terminate or suspend employment. In addition to statutory requirements, there may be 'custom and practice' restrictions built up by precedence into normal working conditions. The existence of Trade Unions or Employee Associations must be taken into account in the labour management process. On the one hand, the presence of unions may simplify the task of management by providing a channel of communication between employers and employee groups, and by providing a focus for negotiation. On the other hand, the ability of an active union to impose substantial costs on the firm may act as a constraining influence on the exercise of managerial prerogative.

Table 12.2 identifies recent major employment legislation in Britain. The Equal Pay Act of 1970 outlaws discrimination in payment on the grounds of sex, whilst the Sex Discrimination and Race Relations Acts were designed to prevent discrimination on the grounds of sex, race, origin or marital status in the recruitment, selection and employment of people. As well as making direct discrimination illegal, these Acts impose on management the necessity of developing positive policies to avoid indirect discrimination. The Contract of Employment Act ensures that all full-time employees are issued with a contract of employment setting out a job description and including details such as remuneration, holiday and sick pay entitlements, notice periods, etc.

Table 12.2 Employment legislation, UK

Equal Pay Act	1970
Contract of Employment Act	1972
Health and Safety at Work Act	1974
Employment Protection Act	1975
Sex Discrimination Act	1975
Race Relations Act	1976
Employment Protection Act (Consolidation)	1978

The Employment Protection Act of 1975, consolidated in 1978, extended the rights of employees against the summary termination of employment (unfair dismissal), ensuring that employment may only be ended for fair reason (such as the inability to perform work one was employed to do, or misconduct, or redundancy). Any employee dismissed without 'fair reason' has to resort to an Industrial Tribunal which can enforce reinstatement or award compensation. Employees made redundant are entitled to compensation under the Redundancy Payments Act (1965) according to age and length of service. Finally, the Employment Protection Acts give women the right to resume employment after pregnancy, and provide for maternity pay and leave in the weeks leading up to and following confinement.

In addition to legislation constraining the rights of employers, recent legislation has also restricted the activities of trade unions. In particular, employees now have a right *not* to join trade unions (in addition to their earlier right to do so), and unions must hold a secret ballot of members before calling for strike action.

Despite the aggregate effects of legislation, both managers and unions retain considerable power over the number, working conditions and remuneration of employees. For example, managers have been quick to respond to the Employment Protection Acts by increasing the proportion of temporary employees (not subject to the Acts). At least some of the growth of part-time employment in Britain since 1980 can be seen as a response to the 'encumbrances' of employment legislation.

We noted in Chapter 8 that firms exist to internalise transactions costs. Some forecasters[7] see the beginnings of a 'disintegration' process occurring, whereby in many cases, employment is replaced by self-employment, with future labour services provided on a contract basis by self-employed professionals. Such a form of organisation provides flexibility to both sides of the contract, as well as avoiding many of the responsibilities imposed by employment legislation.

Summary and conclusions

The employment of labour differs from the employment of other factors because labour is supplied by people who are by nature productive, thinking and creative as well as capricious, potentially inefficient and destructive. Labour management decisions are about the management of people, requiring that needs, tastes, preferences, skills and abilities are all taken into account.

The microeconomic analysis of employment decisions requires that people will be employed until the marginal factor cost of the last employee is equal to marginal revenue product of that employee. However, the employment of labour services has other dimensions than simply the number of people employed, with the optimal allocation of labour services between employment, hours and effort depending on both the relative prices and productive potential of these labour dimensions.

Unlike other inputs, labour productivity can be increased through training and education. The distribution of investment in human capital between employer and employee will depend upon both the firm specificity of that investment and the distribution of the benefits of that investment between employee and employer.

The allocation of labour time between extra employment and extra overtime, the provision of fringe benefits and the physical deployment of labour can each be analysed in terms of marginal benefits and marginal costs. Finally, labour management decisions are taken within an institutional and legal context that may considerably restrain the discretion of management. However, management has been quick to respond to legal necessity by the introduction of part-time or temporary employment, or even self-employment.

Application 12

Labour output elasticity: the South Wales engineering industry[8]

Introduction

The British recession of the early 1980s has had its most obvious effect on manufacturing employment. Between June 1979 and June 1983, over a quarter of British manufacturing jobs were lost. By the end of 1983, there were some indications that the recession was over but little evidence of any employment increase in manufacturing. Was manufacturing employment going to recover from recession, or had a more fundamental change taken place, which meant that firms were not going to respond to an increase in demand by taking on extra workers?

In order to address this question, a research team in South Wales conducted a survey of engineering firms. Amongst other questions, managing directors were asked about their employment response to an increase in demand.

The background

The theory of employment assumes that labour is a variable factor. A permanent increase in demand and hence desired output would be met by a combination of increased employment, increased labour utilisation and the increased use of other factors of production, depending on relative productivities and relative prices. If manufacturing employment was to be restored, the output elasticity with respect to labour (εL), defined as

298

$$\varepsilon L = \frac{\delta Q}{\delta L}\,\frac{L}{Q} \text{ with } Q = \text{output}, \quad L = \text{no. employed}$$

must be both positive and significant.

The survey was conducted by interviewing the managing directors of twenty-seven engineering firms in South Wales, ranging in activity from small-scale electrical assembly to large-scale forging and foundry work. Firms varied in employment size from less than 100 to more than 1000 employees, and in turnover from less than £1m per year to over £50m. Out of the 27 firms, only 3 had increased employment since 1980, with 21 firms suffering a fall in employment, in 7 firms of more than 50 per cent. On average, employment per firm had fallen 44 per cent between 1980 and 1984. The primary reason for this fall in employment was a reduction in demand, with falling employment imposing substantial financial and psychological burdens on management.

The results

In order to assess the employment potential of the industry in a period of recovery, firms were asked how they would achieve a desired increase in output of (a) 10 per cent and (b) 50 per cent.

Most firms claimed the ability to increase output by 10 per cent with little or no change in employment levels (suggesting the existence of excess capacity). The most common response in the short term would be to increase overtime levels, with some changes in either the amount of plant or the organisation of existing technology. Several firms indicated the possibility of taking on extra employees on a short-term contract basis, emphasising the widespread reluctance to incur long-term commitments to more employees in the light of recent (painful) experience.

With regard to the hypothetical 50 per cent increase in output, investing in new plant and equipment was at least as important as taking on new employees. Surpisingly, given the levels of local unemployment, several firms pointed to the existence of skill shortages as a restraining factor on potential output growth. In some cases, the reintroduction of a shift system was seen as a feasible alternative to investing in new plant and equipment.

Conclusion

Overall it was difficult to avoid the conclusion that the employment elasticity of output was very low, so that a sustained recovery from recession would bring about only a small increase in engineering employment. A general increase in demand would help considerably in maintaining existing employment levels, but was unlikely to lead to a marked fall in local employment. The survey results suggested that a fundamental change *had* taken place, possibly due to the introduction of new technology which redefined the workplace relationship between capital and labour, substantially reducing the employment potential of manufacturing industry. At the same time, the general reluctance to incur long-term employment commitments was due in part to the painful redundancy experiences of the recent past, with the importance of this factor possibly receding as time elapses. However, this application also emphasises the increasing importance of alternative working arrangements, with employers keen to achieve the flexibility implicit in temporary or part-time working.

Investment decisions

Contents

Introduction

Previous chapters have considered the shorter term operational decisions of the firm, such as price, output and advertising decisions, with the occasional look at the longer term implications of those decisions. It is now necessary to examine explicitly the longer term strategic decisions that affect the future viability of the organisation: including financing, growth and investment decisions. In doing so, the emphasis of our attention will shift from the optimal allocation of existing resources to the determination of an optimal level of current and future resources.

The primary distinction between operational and strategic decisions is in terms of the duration of the decision implications. Operational decisions affect current and near future performance so that mistakes can be quickly rectified. Strategic decisions concern the longer term performance of the firm, and are the consequence of considerable planning, in which various long-term objectives are set in the light of expectations about future demand and cost conditions.

The introduction of a longer time horizon within the decision framework brings with it two attendant problems. The first is the need to take explicit account of the time value of money, or the need to make intertemporal comparisons of money sums. As we shall see, the appropriate solution to this problem is to calculate the net present value of any future money sum, so that sum is discounted according to its position on the time horizon and the opportunity cost of money. The second problem associated with a lengthening time horizon is uncertainty about the future. Different decision alternatives chosen now will not only lead to different time profiles of future money sums, but also each alternative will have a different degree of risk associated with that time profile. Then the choice between alternatives will depend not only on the preference between alternative income streams but also on the attitude towards risk of the decision-maker. The situation is further complicated by the fact that the business risk or variability of returns associated with any project will be compounded by the financial risk corresponding to the method of financing that project. Basically, the range of decision alternatives open to the firm can be increased by considering the possibility of borrowing money now to finance alternatives. However, the adoption of external finance brings with it the possibility that returns generated by the project may be insufficient to repay the capital borrowed plus interest, thereby adding to the riskiness of the project.

Investment refers to the current outlay of money in the expectation of future gain, i.e. in anticipation of future returns being sufficient to exceed the current outlay by a margin sufficient to compensate both the risk involved and the sacrifice of the next best alternative now. At an individual level, investment refers to the sacrifice of current consumption for anticipated future gain. At the organisational level, investment is the acquisition of durable assets in the expectation of future return. Normally investment by the firm will be in physical assets – the acquisition of durable productive facilities such as land, buildings, plant and equipment but may include the acquisition of financial assets such as company shares, bank deposits, Treasury bills, etc. Financial assets may be risky (company shares) or riskless (Treasury bills), and offer the prospect of capital gains and losses (changes in share prices) as well as income.

Since investment is current expenditure in the anticipation of future return, the basic problem in investment appraisal is the comparison of anticipated returns with present outlay. The solution to this problem is discounting.

Discounting

The logic of discounting is that future money sums can be made comparable to present sums of money by finding the *present value* of that future sum. Consider a Treasury bill, promising to pay the bearer £100 in one year's time. Our purpose is to find the value of that bill now, i.e. what is the maximum amount of money we are prepared to pay to obtain that Treasury bill. Since the bill is backed by the government, it can be assumed riskless. The value of that bill depends on what else we could do with our money now, i.e. the opportunity cost of capital. Suppose that the next best alternative is to invest our present money in a bank deposit at an interest rate of 10 per cent. Then to get back £100 in one year's time, we would have to invest £x now, where

$$x(1 + 0.10) = 100$$

i.e. $x = \dfrac{100}{1.1} = £90.90p$

Thus £90.90p invested in the bank deposit will yield £100 in one year's time. If the Treasury bill costs less than this, our return will be higher by purchasing the Treasury bill than by investing in the bank. If the Treasury bill cost more than this, we would invest our money in the bank deposit. Therefore, at equilibrium, the present value of the Treasury bill must be £90.90p.

Let An be a sum of money n years into the future. Then the present value of An, denoted by P, is

$$P = \frac{An}{(1+i)^n}$$

where i is the opportunity cost of capital. Thus a sum of £100 000 in five years' time, when the opportunity cost of capital is 12 per cent, has a present value of

$$P = \frac{100\,000}{(1+0.12)^5} = \frac{100\,000}{1.7623}$$

$$= £56\,744,$$

since £56 744 can be invested now at an interest rate of 12 per cent to become £100 000 in five years' time.

The principle of discounting is that £1 now is worth more than £1 in the future, regardless of inflation, because the present £1 can be invested now to yield more than £1 in the future. Inflation confuses the picture by making present sums more valuable than future sums, independent of the investment opportunities available. To adjust the discounting procedure to take account of inflation, it is necessary to express future sums in terms of current prices and then discount by the *real* opportunity cost of capital. Expressing future sums in terms of current prices obviates the need to forecast future price changes, whilst the real opportunity cost of capital can be found by adjusting present interest rates by the current inflation rate, using the formula:

$$\text{real interest rate } r = \frac{x-y}{1+y}$$

where x is the money rate of interest and y is the current inflation rate. For example, if the nominal rate of interest is 14 per cent, whilst the inflation rate is 6 per cent, the real rate of interest[1] is

$$r = \frac{0.14-0.06}{1.06} = 7.5\%$$

The arithmetic of discounting is eased by the tabulation of *discount factors*, listing the discount factor corresponding to a particular discount rate and time period. The discount table is used by reading from it the relevant discount factor, which is then multiplied by the future money sum to find the present value of that sum. Table 13.1 lists discount factors for discount rates from 2 to 20 per cent, and for periods 1 to 20 years into the future.

Earlier we found the present value of £100 000 in five years' time at a discount rate of 12 per cent. Reading from the table, at a discount rate of 12 per cent the discount factor for five years' time is 0.567. Then £100 000 in five years' time has a present value of

$$100\,000 \times 0.567 = 56\,700,$$

the same result as before.

The net present value of any investment project can now be found by calculating the present value of the series of estimated returns, and deducting the initial cost. Suppose that an investment project cost £Io now, and yields a time stream of net returns (projected revenue minus costs) $A1 \ldots An$ in the n future periods. If the opportunity cost of capital is r per cent, the Gross Present Value (*GPV*) of the project is

$$GPV = \frac{A1}{1+r} + \frac{A2}{(1+r)^2} + \ldots \frac{An}{(1+r)^n}$$

Table 13.1   Table of discount factors

Year	2%	4%	6%	8%	10%	12%	14%	16%	18%	20%
					Discount rate					
1	0.98	0.962	0.943	0.926	0.909	0.893	0.877	0.862	0.848	0.833
2	0.961	0.925	0.89	0.857	0.826	0.797	0.77	0.743	0.718	0.694
3	0.942	0.889	0.84	0.794	0.751	0.712	0.675	0.641	0.609	0.579
4	0.924	0.855	0.792	0.735	0.683	0.636	0.592	0.552	0.516	0.482
5	0.906	0.822	0.747	0.681	0.621	0.567	0.519	0.476	0.437	0.402
6	0.888	0.79	0.705	0.63	0.565	0.507	0.456	0.41	0.37	0.335
7	0.871	0.76	0.665	0.584	0.513	0.452	0.4	0.354	0.314	0.279
8	0.854	0.731	0.627	0.54	0.467	0.404	0.351	0.305	0.266	0.233
9	0.837	0.703	0.592	0.5	0.424	0.361	0.308	0.263	0.226	0.194
10	0.82	0.676	0.558	0.463	0.386	0.322	0.27	0.227	0.191	0.162
11	0.804	0.65	0.527	0.429	0.351	0.288	0.237	0.195	0.162	0.135
12	0.789	0.625	0.497	0.397	0.319	0.257	0.208	0.169	0.137	0.112
13	0.773	0.601	0.469	0.368	0.29	0.229	0.182	0.145	0.116	0.094
14	0.758	0.578	0.442	0.341	0.263	0.205	0.16	0.125	0.099	0.078
15	0.743	0.555	0.417	0.315	0.239	0.183	0.14	0.108	0.084	0.065
16	0.728	0.534	0.394	0.292	0.218	0.163	0.123	0.093	0.071	0.054
17	0.714	0.513	0.371	0.27	0.198	0.146	0.108	0.08	0.06	0.045
18	0.7	0.494	0.35	0.25	0.18	0.13	0.095	0.069	0.051	0.038
19	0.686	0.475	0.331	0.232	0.164	0.116	0.083	0.06	0.043	0.031
20	0.673	0.456	0.312	0.215	0.149	0.104	0.073	0.051	0.037	0.026

$$= \sum_{t=1}^{n} \frac{At}{(1+r)^t}$$

and the net present value (*NPV*) is

$$NPV = \sum_{t=1}^{n} \frac{At}{(1+r)^t} - Io$$

If the net present value of the project is positive, the firm can achieve a higher return by investing in the project than by investing at the opportunity cost of capital.

A variant of discounting involves calculating the Internal Rate of Return (*IRR*) on a project, where the *IRR* is defined as the discount rate that sets the net present value of the project to zero.

Then for the above project, the internal rate of return (*d*) is such that

$$\sum_{t=1}^{n} \frac{At}{(1+d)^t} - Io = 0$$

Thus calculating the internal rate of return finds the discount rate which would set the net present value of the project equal to zero. The internal rate of return can then be compared to the opportunity cost of capital to determine whether investment in the project is more profitable than investing at the discount rate. In terms of economic meaning, the net present value of a project is the value of the surplus the investor makes by investing in the project over and above what could be made by investing at the discount rate. The internal rate of return on a project is the rate of return on invested capital after allowing for the recoupment of the initial outlay. Both methods assume that returns in the future can be reinvested at the discount rate, and that projected returns will actually be realised.

Problem

You win first prize in the 'Monthly Digest' prize draw. The draw organisers offer you the choice of £100 000 as a cash sum, or £10 000 per year for the rest of your life. Which do you choose?

Since you are young, fit and healthy and like most people in these circumstances expect to live forever, the income stream can be evaluated as if continuing indefinitely. The market rate of interest is 8 per cent, at which you'd invest the majority of the £100 000 if you took the cash sum. Then the immediate sum of £100 000 must be compared to the present value of £10 000 every year from now until eternity.[2]

The present value of that income stream is:

$$\sum_{t=1}^{\infty} \frac{10\,000}{(1+0.08)^t}$$

$$= 10\,000\left(\frac{1}{1.08} + \frac{1}{(1.08)^2} + \frac{1}{(1.08)^3} + \cdots\right)$$

The bracketed value is a geometric progression, with a sum to infinity found by dividing the first term by one minus the common ratio, i.e.

$$\left(\frac{1}{1.08} + \frac{1}{(1.08)^2} + \frac{1}{(1.08)^3} + \cdots\right) = \frac{1/1.08}{1 - (1/1.08)} = \frac{1}{0.08} = 12.5$$

Thus £10 000 per year from next year to eternity has a present value of:

$$10\,000 \times 12.5 = £125\,000.$$

Then the income stream has a higher present value than the lump sums. Alternatively, if you could borrow £125 000 now for an infinite period, £10 000 per year would meet the interest payments.[3]

Physical and financial investment: a general model[4]

Consider a firm with a budgeted lump sum for investment. This sum can either be invested in physical assets, such as plant and equipment, to give a return equal to the internal rate of return on these assets, or in financial assets to give a return equal to the current rate of interest. Assuming that the investments are equally risky, the firm will clearly invest in physical assets as long as the internal rate of return exceeds the rate of interest.

For simplicity, assume there are just two time periods. Then investment in period 1 will yield a return in period 2. Since the firm will invest in the most profitable productive assets first, as total physical investment increases, total return will increase at a decreasing rate. The investing firm faces a productive opportunities curve (*P*) as drawn in Figure 13.1.

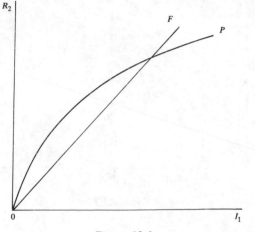

Figure 13.1

The slope of *P* is equal to one plus the internal rate of return, and shows that as total physical investment increases, the internal rate of return on the last £1 invested falls.

Alternatively, if the firm invests in financial assets, the total return is equal to the initial investment times one plus the rate of interest. If the rate of interest is constant, the firm faces a financial opportunities curve *F*, which is a straight line from the origin with slope equal to $1 + i$, where i is the rate of interest (Figure 13.1).

Consider a firm facing the opportunities shown in Figure 13.2 with *Id* to invest. If the firm invests *Id*, completely in financial or physical assets, it will receive the same total return (*R2*). Hence at *Id*, the average internal rate of return must equal the rate of interest.

However, the total return can be increased beyond $R2$, if the firm divides its investment between F and P. The discounting rule encountered earlier was to invest as long as the internal rate of return exceeded the opportunity cost of capital (in this case the rate of interest). Then the firm should invest in P as long as the tangent slope of P exceeds the slope of F. Then the optimal distribution of investment occurs when Ia is invested in physical assets, yielding return ORa, with $Id - Ia$ invested in financial assets yielding $(Id - Ia)(1 + i) = Rb - Ra$, giving a total return of ORb, exceeding the return from investing exclusively in productive or financial assets.

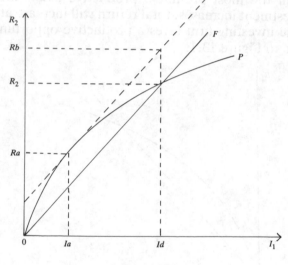

Figure 13.2

The point is that beyond Ia, the rate of interest exceeds the internal rate of return on the marginal £1 invested physically, so that beyond Ia the firm can achieve a higher return on the marginal £1 invested financially. At point Ia, the internal rate of return on the marginal project is exactly equal to the rate of interest. Investment beyond Ia will be in financial assets, moving along the financial opportunities curve F^1 in order to maximise return.

The model outlined can now be used to examine the effect of parameter changes. For example, a fall in the rate of interest (reduction in the slope of F) will move the tangency position between F^1 and P to the right, increasing the optimal investment in productive assets and reducing investment in financial assets (Figure 13.3).

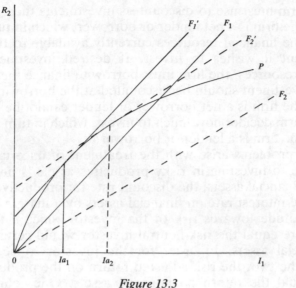

Figure 13.3

A fall in the rate of interest increases the amount of physical investment.

Problems with discounting

The discounting procedure, whilst logically sound, is subject to a number of practical and theoretical limitations. First and foremost is the problem of determining the discount rate, to be used either to calculate net present value or to be compared to the internal rate of return. Defining this as the opportunity cost of capital gives some insight but is of limited practical value, since the opportunity cost is essentially subjective, depending both on the circumstances of the investor and the investor's view of these circumstances. For the personal investor, facing a limited range of alternatives, this may be a minor problem, but for the large commercial organisation the difficulties of defining an opportunity cost of capital can be considerable. The major problems arise because the opportunity cost of capital used for investment is dependent on both the method of financing that investment and the degree of risk associated with that investment.

Consider the simple situation of an imperfect capital market, so that the interest rate the firm gets from lending out money (l) is less than the interest rate the firm must pay to borrow money (b). The rate the firm must use to discount its investments then depends on whether the firm is a net lender or borrower, which in turn depends on both the financial resources currently available to the firm and the amount it wishes to invest. If desired investment exceeds available resources, the firm must borrow to finance the difference, so that investment should be discounted at the borrowing rate. Yet whether the firm is a net borrower or lender cannot be determined until the firm decides how much to invest, which in turn depends on whether the firm is a lender or borrower.

Similar problems arise with the treatment of uncertainty. If the alternative to investing in risky productive assets is investment in risk-free financial assets, the discount rate for productive assets will exceed the interest rate on financial assets by a margin determined by the attitude towards risk of the investor, since if the rates of return were equal the risk-neutral investor would certainly choose the financial assets. In order for the investor to be indifferent between the two, the risk-adjusted return on the productive assets would equal the return on financial assets. One solution to the problem of risk-adjustment is to add a subjective margin to the risk-free rate of return (called a risk premium), which increases according to the perceived riskiness of the physical investment.

Alongside these theoretical problems are the practical problems of computing an internal rate of return. Suppose that an investment of £Io now yields returns $A1$ and $A2$ (net of operating costs) in subsequent years.

Then the internal rate of return is r so that:

$$\frac{A1}{(1+r)} + \frac{A2}{(1+r)^2} - Io = 0$$

or $-Io(1+r)^2 + A1(1+r) + A2 = 0$

This is then a quadratic equation in r, so that two values of r exist which set this equation to zero. In general, an n period problem may have as many as $(n-1)$ solutions for r. The difficulty then is in choosing which internal rate of return is appropriate for discounting. In the above quadratic equation, one solution for r is negative, so that the internal rate of return will be the positive r. The *change-of-sign rule* specifies that there will be as many positive values for r as there are changes in the sign of the cash flow. Thus if a project starts with an initial cost, and yields positive cash flows in future, there is only one change of sign and thus only one positive internal rate of return. However, many projects need future cash outlays to be viable, leading to several changes of sign.

Even with just one change of sign, there may be computational problems in finding an internal rate of return. For an n period project, the internal rate of return r is defined by the equation

$$\sum_{i=1}^{n} \frac{Ai}{(1+r)^i} - Io = 0$$

Given Ai, n and Io, r can only be found by trial and error. Suppose that a firm can invest £100 now, to return positive cash flows of £60, £50 and £12 over the next three years. The internal rate of return is then r, where

$$\frac{60}{1+r} + \frac{50}{(1+r)^2} + \frac{12}{(1+r)^3} - 100 = 0$$

This is a cubic equation, and much too difficult to solve directly. Since the internal rate of return sets the net present value equal to zero, to find the internal rate first find discount rates that result in a just positive and just negative net present value. The calculation is set out in Table 13.2, using discount factors from Table 13.1

Table 13.2 Calculating internal rates of return

Year	Cash flow		df 12%	df 14%
0	−100			
1	60		0.893	0.877
2	50		0.797	0.769
3	12		0.712	0.675
		GPV	101.974	99.17
		NPV	1.974	−0.83

At a discount rate of 12 per cent, the project has a positive net present value of 1.974, whilst if the discount rate is 14 per cent the net present value falls to −0.83. The internal rate of return is estimated by interpolating between these two figures,

i.e. $IRR = 12\% + \dfrac{1.974}{1.974 + 0.83} \times (14-12)\%$

$\qquad = 12 + 0.704 \times 2$

$\qquad = 13.408\%$

Hence the internal rate of return on the project is 13.4 per cent.

Financing investment

Closely related to the investment decision is the decision of how to finance that investment. The profitable firm can finance investment by retaining some profits as an alternative to distributing those profits as dividends to shareholders. Such a decision is, in effect, borrowing from shareholders, who will expect a return on this implicit borrowing, either from increased future dividends or from increases in the value of their shares. The alternative to this implicit equity financing is debt financing, i.e. borrowing money from financial markets at a rate of interest. External finance can be profitably sought as long as the rate of return on investment exceeds the interest to be repaid, but brings with it extra risk (defined earlier as financial risk) because of the possibility of returns being insufficient to repay the debt with interest.

From the manager's point of view, financing investment from retained profits (i.e. retained dividends) is usually cheaper[5] than external financing, although the ability to retain dividends is not unlimited. Dividend retention requires that shareholders share the management expectation of future profit, or else excessive retention may threaten managerial job security (see Application 3).

In a world of perfect information and perfect foresight, shareholders will be indifferent between receiving income in the form of dividends or in the form of capital gains (from increased share prices) and increased future dividends. In the absence of these conditions, investors may well prefer to make their own investment decisions, which they can only do if current profits are distributed as dividends. Then it is clearly in the management interest to persuade shareholders that retained profits for investment will add more to the wealth of shareholders than distributing those profits as dividends.

The sum of these arguments is that the firm's cost of capital will depend on the proportion of investment financed by debt and by equity, and the relative cost of each. Financing by debt involves the payment of interest, although reduced by the fact that debt interest is an allowable expense against tax liability. For example, suppose that the firm borrows at an interest rate of 10 per cent, whilst the corporation tax rate is 30 per cent. Then the after tax cost of debt (d) is

$$d = \text{interest rate } (1 - \text{tax rate})$$

i.e. $d = 0.10(1 - 0.30) = 0.07$

$$\text{or } 7\%$$

The cost of equity capital is more difficult to estimate. In general, the cost of financing investment through retained dividends will be the minimum rate of return required to maintain the share price. If this minimum return is not achieved, the share price will fall as some shareholders sell their holdings, reducing the ability to raise future equity capital and reducing job security (because of dissatisfaction amongst current shareholders and the increased risk of takeover).

The required rate of return on equity capital cannot be observed, and must be estimated. Since shareholders' wealth increases with both dividend income and share price increases, one simple approach is to examine past dividend and share price performance. Then the estimated cost of equity capital is e where

$$e = \frac{\text{dividend}}{\text{share price}} + \text{share price growth rate.}$$

For example, if the share price is £3, the current dividend is 15 pence, and the estimated growth in share price is 6 per cent, then the estimated cost of equity capital is

$$e = \frac{0.15}{3.00} + 0.06 = 0.11 \text{ or } 11\%$$

Given the costs of debt and equity capital, the firm's overall cost of capital will depend on the proportions of debt to equity finance. Suppose that the firm, considered above, finances its new investment through a combination of debt and equity financing in the ratio 25/75 per cent. Then the weighted average cost of capital is

$$0.25d + 0.75e$$
$$= 0.25(7) + 0.75(11)$$
$$= 10\%$$

The question arises why, given that debt finance is cheaper than equity finance, doesn't the firm use wholly debt finance. The answer is that as the amount of debt finance increases, so does the financial risk of the firm, i.e. the risk of bankruptcy or liquidation because of the inability to meet interest payments. Consequently, the firm will choose a *gearing ratio* of external debt to total capital employed that is low enough to convince shareholders that the management is not taking undue financial risks. Excessive external borrowing will raise the gearing ratio to high levels which may adversely affect the share price. Consequently, management must trade off the lower cost of debt finance against the extra risk involved, usually resulting in a gearing ratio of around 1/3. Strong companies with a good profits records may be able to exceed this, whilst companies involved in more risky areas may have to settle for gearing ratios well below 1/3.

Risk and uncertainty

Since the future is unknown, business investment is always an exercise in decision-making under uncertainty. The uncertainty over future returns or business risk is compounded by the financial risk corresponding to the financing decision.

If the probability distribution of future project returns can be estimated, the maximisation of net present value criteria can be replaced by the maximisation of expected net present value. However, as we saw in Chapter 4, expected value is simply a measure of central tendency, and takes no account of the dispersion of possible returns. For example, consider projects A and B, with the relative frequencies of possible net present values shown in Figure 13.4.

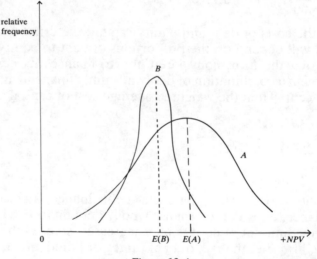

Figure 13.4

Project A has both a greater expected net present and a greater dispersion of possible present values. The choice between A and B is then a matter of how risk is viewed. A risk-averse firm may well choose project B, despite its lower expected value, because of the lower dispersion of possible present values.

One way to reduce the riskiness of investment is to adopt the principle of *hedging*. In practice investment decisions are not taken in isolation: rather the firm faces a series of investment decisions with outcomes that are not independent of each other (as in the decision-trees in Chapter 4). Then the firm will be concerned with the riskiness of its overall investment portfolio, rather than with the riskiness of an individual project. The risk structure of the firm will depend on the degree of correlation between projects as well as the degree of risk associated with each project.

Markowitz[6] demonstrated two important results when considering the adoption of new projects:

(a) If the new project has the same degree of risk as existing projects, then the lower the degree of correlation between the new and existing projects the more the new project reduces the overall risk structure of the firm.

(b) If the new project is more risky than existing projects, positively correlated projects will increase overall risk, whilst negatively correlated projects may reduce overall risk.

Then even if a new project is itself very risky, taking it on may reduce overall risk if that project will perform well when existing projects perform badly. The classic British example is Walls (producer of sausages and meat products) reducing the seasonality of sales by entering the market for ice cream products.

We saw earlier that one solution to the problem of uncertainty is to add a risk premium to the discount rate according to the anticipated variability of the project returns. This may be estimated subjectively, or on the basis of the historically estimated difference between the firm's average yield on long-term debt and the rate of return on some riskless security (such as government bonds), on the basis that an efficient capital market will have allocated funds to the firm according to the riskiness of return. This premium may even be increased according to the difference between the average yield on the firm's shares (dividend plus share price growth) and the average yield on long-term debt, to find the risk premium on share ownership over debt ownership.

A related approach to estimating the risk premium involves the use of the Capital Asset Pricing Model (CAPM).[7] According to this model, shareholders in a particular firm will endure both absolute and relative risk, according to how well that firm performs *per se*, and how well it performs relative to shares on average. Then the required rate of return for any share r_i is equal to the risk free rate of return r_f plus a premium according to the average rate of return on all shares r_s and the riskiness of that firm compared to others, determined by the formula

$$r_i = r_f + \beta(r_s - r_f)$$

Where β is an index of the riskiness of that firm's shares relative to the average on all shares. The *beta coefficient* measures the variability of return on that share compared to the average of all shares, and is estimated by regressing the returns on that share against the average return on all shares. A beta coefficient of 1.0 shows that the share is of average risk, whilst $\beta > 1$ suggests that share is of above average risk.[8] For example, suppose that the rate of return on government bonds is 6 per cent, the average return on shares is 10 per cent and the firm has a beta coefficient of 1.5 (showing that the firm's shares are more risky than the average).

Then the required rate of return on equity capital is:

$$r_i = 0.06 + 1.5(0.10 - 0.06) = 0.12$$

$$= 12\%,$$

and the firm faces a risk premium of 6 per cent (or 1.5 times the average risk premium). If the company's shares had been less risky than average (e.g. $\beta = 0.5$),

$$r_i = 0.06 + 0.5(0.10 - 0.06) = 0.08$$

$$= 8\%$$

According to the Capital Asset Pricing Model, shareholders require a risk premium for holding shares, and an extra premium to hold shares that are more risky than average. Moreover, despite the unique risk associated with each share, shareholders can reduce overall risk by holding a balanced portfolio of shares. Various empirical studies have shown that adding randomly selected shares to a portfolio reduces risk, and that as the variety of shares held approaches fifteen to twenty, virtually all unique risk is eliminated. Figure 13.5 demonstrates the situation and is derived from Koutsoyiannis.[9]

Systematic risk is endemic in shareholding, and cannot be eliminated (hence the average rate of return on shares exceeds the risk-free rate of return). However, as the variety of shares in a portfolio increases, the unique risk associated with that portfolio falls at a decreasing rate.

Note, however, that use of the CAPM model is predicated by the assumption that the past volatility of share returns are an indicator of both future return and the volatility of that return.

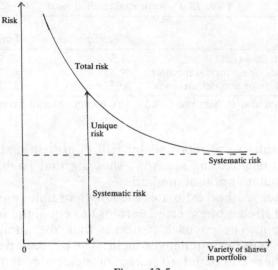

Figure 13.5

Investment in practice

In 1985, gross investment by industrial and commercial companies in the United Kingdom reached £23 473 million (see Table 13.3). Despite the enormous magnitude of company investment, and the elegance and sophistication of investment theory, there is little evidence that firms make investment decisions on the basis of anything other than crude and elementary calculations.

Table 13.3 Gross domestic fixed capital formation: industrial and commercial companies, UK

Year	£m
1981	14 993
1982	15 559
1983	15 810
1984	19 474
1985	23 473

Source: CSO, *Financial Statistics*, no. 293, September 1986, p. 92.

For example, in a survey of 249 manufacturing companies in the United Kingdom, Alam and Stafford[10] found that less than one-third used discounted cash flow techniques in the appraisal of investment projects. Their survey results are reported in Table 13.4, showing that discounting, although a minority approach, was used most by larger companies (defined as 2000+ employees).

Table 13.4   Appraisal method used

	% All companies	Large companies
Discounted cash flow (dcf)	28.5	42.9
Payback, flat rate or no formal method	39.8	18.1
Some combination of non dcf methods	30.5	38.1

Source: K. Alam and L. Stafford (1985) 'Tax Incentives and Investment Policy', p. 32.

Similar results were reported by Hill *et al.*[11] in a survey of the South Wales engineering industry, showing that payback remains the most popular appraisal method.

The payback method estimates the length of time required for the accumulated stream of expected earnings to equal the initial cost of the investment. The payback period is then the number of years needed to recoup the initial investment. The payback period for any project is then compared to some predetermined maximum to determine whether the project is acceptable. Note that payback completely ignores the magnitude and timing of returns beyond the payback period, the timing of returns within that period or the opportunity cost of capital invested. The payback period chosen is usually short (three or four years) and leads to underinvestment.

On the positive side payback is simple to use, well understood and may reflect the true objectives of management. The choice of a short payback period implicitly values early returns very highly, and avoids the difficulties of forecasting returns over a long period. However, the most serious weakness of payback remains its ignorance of the cost of capital, the total earnings from the project and the failure to take explicit account of the timing of returns.

The average or flat rate of return on a project is just the excess of total return over project cost, expressed as an annual rate of return on the initial investment. Table 13.5 calculates the payback period and average rate of return on two projects A and B.

Project A has a payback period of three years, whilst B only repays the initial investment in year four. The average rate of return on project A is 8 per cent, compared to the average return of 10 per cent on project B. Note that if the opportunity cost of capital is 14 per cent, project A has a positive net present value, whilst project B has a negative net present value.

One reason for the prevalence of non-discounting investment appraisal methods is the absence of information, both present and future. As we have seen, estimating the firm's true cost of capital is a difficult and complex process, requiring information about present and past performance, the gearing ratio and some estimation of

Table 13.5 Payback and average rate of return

Project	A	B	df14%
Initial investment	−100	−100	
Return in year 1	50	20	0.877
2	30	30	0.769
3	30	40	0.675
4	20	30	0.592
5	10	30	0.519
Total return	140	150	
Payback period	3 years	4 years	
Average rate of return	40/5 = 8%	50/5 = 10%	
NPV 14%	4.20	−4.25	

average returns. Estimating future costs and revenues is yet more problematic. Miller[12] shows that ranking alternatives by their estimated measure of merit and then choosing the highest ranked alternative may give the wrong answer, even where estimates are unbiased.

Miller gives the following example. Suppose the firm faces three alternative proposals, where the actual benefits of each are unknown and must be estimated. The (unknown) good proposal yields $200 benefits, the medium one $100 benefit and the bad one no benefits. All proposals have an initial cost of $160, and each is considered to have an equal probability of being the proposal with highest benefit. Benefits are received immediately after choosing, so that no discounting is involved.

The decision-maker must estimate the benefit from each proposal. In one-third of cases, benefits are estimated correctly, whilst there is an equal probability (also equal to one-third) of benefits being over or underestimated by $100.

Figure 13.6 is a decision-tree illustrating the situation. Only in one-third of cases are the estimated benefits correct. An estimated benefit of $200 could be from a true benefit of $200, or from a true benefit of $100 plus an overestimate of $100.

An estimated benefit of $100 is equally likely to be from a true benefit of $200 (plus underestimation), from a true benefit of $100 or from a true benefit of $0 (plus overestimation). Prior to making the choice, the decision-maker has no way of knowing which.

Since the cost of each project is $160, one decision criteria may be to accept all proposals with an estimated benefit greater than this. Then any proposal with an estimated benefit of $200 would be accepted. However, from the decision-tree, half the proposals with an estimated benefit of $200 truly have this benefit, whilst half have true benefit of $100. Then the expected benefit of projects with an estimated benefit of $200 is:

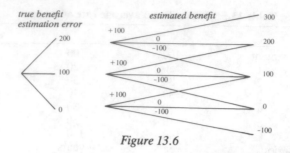

Figure 13.6

Source: Miller (1985) 'Decision-making Under Uncertainty for Capital Budgeting and Hiring', p. 12.

$$200 \times 0.5 + 100 \times 0.5 = \$150.$$

Therefore, proposals with estimated benefits of $200 should not be accepted.

The basic problem is that estimated benefits are the sum of true benefits plus an error term (positive or negative). If proposals with higher estimates are selected, the chance of being selected is higher if the error term is positive. Then the expected value of error must be some positive amount. In choosing between alternatives, some positive allowance for error must be made. Translating into discounting terms, the required rate of return must exceed the opportunity cost of capital by some allowance for estimation error.

Miller goes on to argue that this result explains the observed phenomenon that decision-makers typically require rates of return considerably in excess of the opportunity cost of capital before making investments. 'The wisdom used by firms in providing a high cut-off rate suggests that their actual procedures (perhaps a short pay-off period) probably out performs the more theoretically correct procedures taught in managerial economics.'[13]

Expansion and diversification

We noted earlier that investment decisions are part of a process of strategic decision-making, involving identifying objectives, generating alternatives, evaluating each alternative and then implementing the chosen alternative. The investment decision is then part of an ongoing process of corporate planning, which may involve investing in plant and equipment, moving into new products and/or new markets, or even growth by acquisition or merger.

Diversification is the process of expanding into new products *and* new markets, and may be undertaken for a number of reasons including profitability, the need to use previously generated funds, reducing dependence on declining products, etc. Adherence to a single product or market brings with it the possibility of a decline in demand over time. The product may be rendered obsolete because of changing tastes, new technology or the entry of new products. However, the risks associated with the firm's previous product must be balanced against the risks involved in producing new products or entering new markets. Diversification may be into products with related production technology as when the TV manufacturer produces computer monitors, or unrelated technology (TV manufacturer producing TV cabinets), and into related markets (TV manufacturer producing video recorders), or unrelated markets (TV manufacturer producing tractors). The degree of uncertainty related to the diversification decision depends on the amount of prior information the firm has about demand and cost conditions. The TV manufacturer producing TV cabinets may know a great deal about the potential market but little about potential costs. Alternatively, the TV manufacturer producing computer monitors may know a great deal about potential costs but little about the potential market.

One solution to the problem of uncertainty surrounding entry into new products and markets is to expand by merger and acquisition. Table 13.6 shows company expenditure on mergers in the UK, and when read with Table 13.3 illustrates the extent of the merger boom in Britain in the mid 1980s.

Table 13.6 Company expenditure on acquisition by merger

Year	Expenditure £m
1981	1144
1982	2206
1983	2344
1984	5475
1985	7090

Source: CSO, *Financial Statistics*, no. 293, September 1986.

Merger may be motivated by desires other than that of reducing risks. The acquiring firm may consider that it can increase the profitability of acquired assets by improving the management of these assets. Alternatively, the acquiring firm may make a capital gain when the share price is less than the actual (or potential) value of the acquired assets. However, the weight of empirical evidence suggests that merged firms perform typically less well in profitability terms than either firms that do not merge or the weighted average profitability of acquirer plus victim prior to merger, suggesting that the desire for merger is motivated by reasons other than profitability.[14]

Summary and conclusions

The investment decision is concerned with the acquisition of long-term capital assets in anticipation of a future return on those assets. Consideration of a longer term time perspective brings with it the attendant problems of taking account of the time value of money and the treatment of uncertainty. Present money is more valuable than the equivalent sum in the future because present money can be invested. Discounting is the process of deflating future sums to their present value by taking account of investment opportunities. Thus a future stream of money can be converted into a present value which is comparable to current sums of money.

A variation of the discounting procedure is the estimation of an internal rate of return on a project which is the rate of discount that sets the net present value of that project equal to zero. Many decision-makers are more comfortable with the concept of an internal rate of return than with the present value concept, although the internal rate of return has conceptual and computational deficiencies.

Company investment can be financed by borrowing or by the appropriation of equity capital (dividend retention). Each has its own set of costs and benefits and each presents some difficulty in the estimation of the cost of capital. The adoption of a particular gearing ratio (debt to capital employed) is the product of consideration of the costs of each capital source and the financial risk involved.

Uncertainty over future returns is a recurrent investment problem. One approach to uncertainty is to estimate the probability of various present values and then seek to maximise the net present value of the firm. However, this is equivalent to assuming risk neutrality. An alternative approach is to add a risk premium to the cost of capital, either subjectively estimated on the basis of the anticipated variability of returns, or subjectively estimated via the Capital Asset Pricing Model on the basis of the previous riskiness of returns compared to some average riskiness of investment.

Empirical evidence suggests that many firms are reluctant to use discounting techniques, because of a lack of information or the prediction error implicit in return estimation. Finally, the investment opportunities open to the firm are wider than the simple acquisition of physical and financial assets, and may be motivated by the desire for growth or security as well as profits. Diversification is the process of investing in new products and/or new markets, and brings extra uncertainty which may be mitigated through investment by merger or acquisition.

Application 13

The social return on investment

Introduction

Much of Chapter 13 has been concerned with evaluating the return on investment from the managers' and shareholders' points of view, in order that decisions about the use of funds can be made. It is, however, plausible to examine the firm's activities from a completely different perspective, i.e. to see the firm as a coalition of different interest groups, each devoting resources to the firm in anticipation of a future return. This application reports the results of one investigation which attempted to measure the return on investment to different interest groups, with some surprising results.[15]

Background

Luffman *et al.* defined four interest groups – shareholders, consumers, the community, and the employees – each of which invests in a firm's activities. The return on investment (r) is defined by the equation.

$$r = \frac{B - C}{I}$$

where B, C and I measure benefits, costs and resources invested. This simple framework hides a multitude of conceptual and measurement difficulties, and some ingenuity is necessary in applying this formula to investment by different groups.

The study focused on the activities of a UK subsidiary of a US multinational company supplying non-durable consumer products. This company provided data enabling returns to be estimated.

Measuring the return on investment

(i) SHAREHOLDERS

The return to shareholder investment is defined in Chapter 13 as the sum of dividends plus share price capital gains, adjusted for taxation. However, as the firm was a subsidiary company, it was impossible to separate this information from group figures. Consequently, the return measured was UK profits, adjusted for taxation, as a proportion of capital employed.

(ii) CONSUMERS

Consumer investment in the company is simply the price paid for the firm's products. Hence total consumer investment is equal to total company sales.

The return on this investment was estimated using the economic concept of *consumer surplus*. This is defined as the maximum amount consumers *would* be prepared to pay for the firm's product minus the amount *actually* paid. Consider the demand curve in Figure A13.1.

With the given demand curve, consumers would be prepared to pay 0B for the first unit of the good, a slightly lower price for the second unit, etc., all the way down to 0A for the Qth unit (ignoring

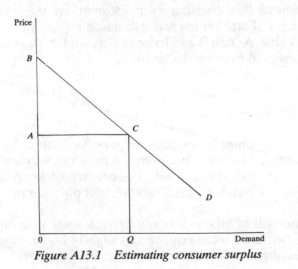

Figure A13.1   Estimating consumer surplus

income effects). If the firm sells $0Q$ units at price $0A$, the first consumer has gained net benefit BA (maximum price prepared to pay minus actual price paid), the second consumer slightly less, etc. The total benefit to consumers is then the area under the demand curve $0BCQ$, for which consumers have paid $0ACQ$, leaving triangle ABC as consumer surplus.

To estimate consumer surplus then requires the complete demand curve to be estimated. Luffman *et al.* were able to achieve this via access to market research data, and consequently to estimate returns to consumers.

(iii)   THE COMMUNITY

The community invests in company activity by providing roads, sewers, education, defence, etc. The resources devoted to this investment can be measured by government expenditure. Measuring the expenditure attributable to each company is, of course, impossible.

As an approximation, it was assumed that government expenditure benefits each UK employee equally, so that government expenditure in the company can be approximated by the formula:

$$\frac{Ef}{E_{UK}} \times G$$

where Ef is the number of employees in the firm, E_{UK} is the total UK workforce and G is total government expenditure.

The returns on this 'community investment' are the taxes received by government. Total return was estimated as the sum of Corporation Tax, Value Added Tax, Income Tax and National Insurance contributions paid over by the firm.

(iv)   EMPLOYEES

Investment by company employees was estimated by using the concept of *economic rent*. Economic rent is the surplus paid to an employee over and above what is necessary to keep him in that employment. Consider the labour supply curve drawn in Figure A13.2.

If just one unit of labour was required, a wage rate of $W1$ would be paid. If two units were required, a slightly higher wage must be paid, conferring an economic rent on the first employee. If the firm

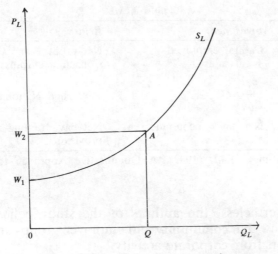

Figure A13.2   Estimating economic rent

employs $0Q$ workers at a wage of $0W_2$, the first employee gains $W_2 - W_1$ in economic rent, the second slightly less, etc. Then at employment $0Q$, total economic rent is area W_1AW_2.

To estimate economic rent it is first necessary to determine the supply curve for labour. In the absence of this information, Luffman *et al.* assumed that the alternative to working was unemployment benefit, and that the intercept W_1 in Figure A13.2 could be approximated by the level of unemployment benefit. The supply curve was then estimated as the straight line between W_1 and A (the number employed at the current wage rate). Note that even if the estimate of W_1 is reasonably accurate, economic rent estimated via the supply curve W_1A is liable to be an underestimation.

Total employee investment was found by subtracting economic rent from net pay, whilst the return on employee investment was the sum of net pay, fringe benefits, training and pension provision.

A summary of the model estimated is given in Table A13.1.

Results

The estimated returns on investment for the different interest groups are shown in Table A13.2. Note that 'it is unreasonable to put too much emphasis on the absolute values for the Return on Investment figures',[16] in view of the theoretical and measurement difficulties outlined above. In particular, estimated investment by consumers (total sales) dwarfs considerably investment by other

Table A13.1

Group	Investment	Return
Shareholders	Capital employed	Net profit
Customers	Total sales	Consumer surplus
Community	$\dfrac{Ef}{E_{UK}} \times G$	Taxes and National Insurance
Employees	Net pay – economic rent	Net pay, training and pension provision

Source: G. Luffman *et al.* (1982) 'A Quantitative Approach to Stakeholder Interests'.

groups. Nevertheless, the authors of the study believe that the results do show that community and employee groups are by far the largest gainers from corporate activity.

Table A13.2   Return on investment: summary %

Group	1975	1976	1977	1978
Shareholders	24	23	37	33
Consumers	8.1	8.2	8.2	9.4
Community	80	88	132	169
Employees	93	102	105	106

Source: Luffman *et al.* (1982) 'A Quantitative Approach to Stakeholder Interests'.

Finally the authors note that, 'the results of such research have far-reaching effects for governments and others with a stake in the firm. At present answers to questions such as how much each stakeholder puts into and gets out of the firm are largely unquantified.'[17]

CHAPTER 14

Concluding remarks and neglected decisions

Contents

Introduction

The necessary conclusion to any book on decision-making must be that the theory of decisions needs to be combined with practical experience before it can become operationally useful. This may seem a meagre reward for the effort involved in reaching this far – but any higher expectations are the result of a false illusion. This book is not a do-it-yourself guide to company chairmanship, but the embodiment of a belief that a logical and structured approach to decision problems, taking proper cognisance of the realistic constraints imposed by the decision environment, will ultimately lead to better decisions.

Potential criticisms

Having assembled the various components of this book into a text, there are two basic criticisms of it that stand out:

(i)   vast business decision areas are neglected;
(ii) the methodological approach adopted is essentially marginalism.

For example, important business decisions such as location and distribution are entirely absent from this book. The text neglects the

329

entire area of public sector decisions such as those made by public utilities or local government. Moreover, each chapter adopts a marginalist approach to the decisions covered.

Both criticisms are essentially valid. My response must be largely practical. Although some decisions are not treated explicitly, the systematic framework developed in the book can be sensibly applied to all business decisions, whether private or publicly motivated. Indeed, in the business world of the late 1980s there seems little difference in behaviour between public and private institutions. Much of the present text is relevant to the decisions made by non-profit seeking organisations. Whatever the nature of the organisation, better decisions can be made by explicitly defining objectives and then organising resources in the most efficient way – i.e. the way that best achieves stated objectives.

A similar defence applies to the methodology adopted. Marginalism is the dominant technique, simply because of the overwhelming logic of that approach. Whenever a decision is made, extra benefits *must* be compared to extra costs. Failure to do so breaks the basic requirement for logically structured decision processes. This is not to claim that application of this principle is always straightforward. In fact one recurring theme has been the difficulties encountered in the search for relevant decision information.

Finally, the text fails to integrate recent developments in systems and systems technology. Most of the decisions encountered in this book are highly amenable to sophisticated modelling using computers. Within the next decade both the practice and teaching of management will be transformed by the advent of inexpensive and powerful microcomputers. However, this merely increases the importance of a fundamental understanding of the principles of decision-making, so that decision models used are an accurate reflection of the realities of the decision situation.

Areas for further study

The classic conclusion to any academic work is to point to areas of future development. In keeping with this tradition, the following can be identified:

(i) The application of decision theory lags considerably behind the development of theory. There seems little point in building ever more sophisticated decision models, when even simple present models (such as net present value) are widely ignored by decision-makers. Why?

(ii)   The economist brings just one perspective to decision problems. Other disciplines such as accountancy, sociology, psychology and management science have valid contributions to make to the study of decision processes. Moreover, many of the most exciting recent developments are in the gaps between disciplines which can only be filled by a multidisciplinary approach.

Examination questions and answer notes

Introduction

The examination questions that follow are actual finals papers from the Economics course within the B.Sc.Econ. honours degree. Each paper represents assessment for a one-year course in Managerial Economics which builds upon a previous course in Microeconomics. Students are required to answer four questions in three hours.

I am grateful to the University of Wales for permission to reproduce these papers. They have been included in an attempt to overcome the artificiality of study questions tacked on to the end of chapters. The questions are followed by some notes on answers to guide the student. Remember that in economics examinations there are no right (or wrong) answers – just answers that gets lots of marks and those that don't!

Within Cardiff Business School, Managerial Economics is taught in three courses, two undergraduate as part of the B.Sc.Econ degree (according to specialism), and one postgraduate (within the M.B.A. degree). Papers are taken from the Economics course for convenience only.

ECONOMICS III 1985

Time allowed – 3 hours

Answer FOUR questions

1. 'The most we can say about the Demand Curve is that it slopes down unless it slopes up.' Discuss.

2. Explain the determination of the optimal price and output combination in a situation of monopolistic competition. Use the resulting equilibrium to illustrate the statement that 'production inefficiency is a necessary price to pay for product variety'. Comment on this statement.

3. Assess the contribution of business games to the study of decision-making processes, illustrating your answer by reference to one business game with which you are familiar.

4. 'Given that the future is unknown, the best we can do is to estimate the likelihood of future events and then use expected profit as the decision criterion.' Discuss.

5. The senior partner in a local accountancy firm is concerned about the error rate amongst assessments issued by her office. A careful check over the past few years enables her to estimate that the error rate has the following probability distribution:

Error rate	Probability
0.05	0.25
0.10	0.35
0.15	0.25
0.20	0.15

Each error costs £40 because of the labour time involved in reassessment. Her firm is just entering the assessment 'season', and is expected to perform 500 assessments over the next few months.

One way to reduce the error rate is to send all staff to a one-day training course at the local university – 'Precision in Assessment'. The university claims this would ensure an error rate of 0.05, but she considers that an error rate of 0.10 would be equally likely.

The course fee is £700 for all her staff, whilst lost profit from one day's work missed would be £500. Advise her on whether to send staff on the course or not.

A careful check of that day's output shows that in ten assessments, two contained errors. Use this information to update the error rate probability distribution and hence determine whether your advice needs amendment.

6. 'The fitting of mathematical trend curves is by far the easiest and cheapest method of forecasting long-run changes in product demand, and is likely to be just as reliable as any alternative method.' Discuss.

7. An engineering firm has applied for patents on two new products and has just learned that only one application has been successful. Compare and contrast the optimal pricing and promotional strategies for each of these new products.

8. Critically examine the view that advertising can be seen as the

provision of information valuable to the consumer, for which the consumer will be prepared to pay extra.

9. (a) Briefly analyse the effect of an increase in interest rates on the investment portfolio of a profit maximising holding company.

(b) The University is contemplating building a new squash court, adjacent to its new hall of residence. To secure local support for its planning application, the University has offered to open the court to local players at student rates for the first five years. After five years, the University can charge what it likes for the courts. Consequently, the University estimates that net revenue from the court will be £1000 for each of the first five years, rising by 10% (compounded) in each of the sixth to tenth years. In the eleventh and twelfth years rising maintenance costs will completely offset rising fees so that net revenue stays at tenth year level. At the end of the twelfth year, the site is due for redevelopment.

The cost of building the squash court is estimated to be £6000. To finance the court, the University must draw from its reserves, currently earning 12% in Local Authority Bonds. Selling sufficient bonds would involve legal and administrative costs of £320. Advise the University on the viability of the project. What other factors should the University take into account?

10. A firm has an annual demand of S units for a good whose purchase cost is £c per unit. Each order costs £a to place, and the cost of holding stock is b% of the average value of stock per annum. Determine the optimal order quantity.

A local firm uses 2000 units of a particular component each year. The component has a purchase price of £4/unit, while the cost of holding stock is estimated at 20% of the average stock value. If the cost of placing each order is £12.50, find the optimal number of orders placed each year. Suppose the component supplier offers a discount of 2% on the purchase price if orders are placed in units of 1000. Is the discount worth accepting?

Suppose that instead of a single figure you had been given a probability distribution for the number of units used each year. Indicate the effect on stock policy.

ECONOMICS 1986

Time allowed – 3 hours

Answer FOUR questions

1. Critically assess the view that an understanding of the principles of 'scientific' decision-making is fundamental to the success of a modern economy.

2.   (i)   Explain the concept of opportunity loss, and show that the minimum opportunity loss is equal to the Expected Value of Perfect Information.

(ii)   The failure rate in a particular examination is estimated to be 40%. Construct a table showing the probabilities of 0, 1, 2 . . . 5 students failing in a sample of five.

(iii)   150 graduate entrants are due to take their first professional accounting exam at the Institute of Certifiable Accountants. The probability distribution for the failure rate is estimated in the following table:

Failure rate	Probability
0.1	0.1
0.2	0.2
0.3	0.3
0.4	0.3
0.5	0.1

Each failing student is entitled to a £10 refund on professional fees. The Institute's senior tutor is confident that she could ensure a failure rate of 0.1 by holding an intensive revision course, at a cost to the Institute of £300. Advise the Institute on whether the revision course should take place.

A tutorial test of five students resulted in no failures. Use this information to revise the failure rate probability distribution, and hence reassess the revision course.

3.   'Despite being a small local shopkeeper I can always beat the price that Woolworths charge for the same product. Woolworths must pay rent on its store while I own my shop and have no rent to pay.' Discuss.

4.   A firm keeps a record of sales and prices over the past seven months, resulting in the following table:

	Price (£/ton)	Sales (tons)
Nov. 1985	7.5	84.5
Dec.	8.0	82.0
Jan. 1986	8.0	84.0
Feb.	7.2	92.0
March	7.0	95.0
April	8.0	92.0
May	8.5	91.5

Use these observations to estimate demand as a linear function of both price and time. Utilise this function to estimate demand for the following month, on the assumption that:

(a)   price remains unchanged,

(b)   price increases to £9/ton.

Hence estimate the price elasticity of demand between these prices and find the price which would maximise sales revenue.

Given the nature of the observations, comment on any difficulties in interpreting your results for decision-making purposes.

5. Critically assess the methods used to generate empirical estimates of both short- and long-run cost functions. Do the empirical difficulties encountered rob the resulting estimates of any general operational utility?

6. 'About half of all advertising expenditure is wasted. The problem lies in knowing which half.' Discuss this statement and assess the usefulness of managerial models of advertising allocation decisions.

7. Analyse the effects of an increase in interest rates on the investment activity of a profit maximising firm. Does it matter if inflation increases in proportion to the increase in interest rates?

8. (a) Show that an increase in the unit value of stock will lead to a less than proportionate fall in the optimum amount of stock held. What assumptions underlie your answer?

   (b) A firm faces a uniform annual demand of 100 000 units. The purchase cost of stock is £10 per unit, whilst the cost of ordering stock is £20, and the cost of holding stock is 14% of the average stock value. Find the Economic Order Quantity and the Minimum Acquisition Cost.

   How are your answers affected by:

   (i) the fact it takes two weeks between placing an order and stock arriving;
   (ii) the offer of a 1% discount off the purchase cost if stock is ordered in lorry loads of 17 000 units.

9. 'The market allocates resources to the firms that best meet the needs of consumers.' Discuss.

10. 'The force of competition, the desires of managers and the needs of shareholders combine to ensure that firms maximise profit.' Discuss.

ECONOMICS 1987

Time allowed – 3 hours

Answer FOUR questions

1. 'Statistically we expect that good decisions will lead to favourable outcomes more often than will either poor decisions, or decisions reached by default. In a sense, this is a statement of faith on which all

rational approaches to human affairs are based' (Amara and Lipinski). Discuss this statement, and assess the value of the analytical decision approach as an operational tool of management decision-making.

2. Critically examine the theoretical and empirical validity of the profit maximisation hypothesis.

3. The Hot-Bake shop sells only bread made that day. Each loaf produced has a variable cost of 30p and sells for 50p. Any bread unsold at the end of each day is thrown away.

At the start of each day, the manager must decide how many loaves to produce. The table below records sales over the past month:

Daily sales	Frequency
1000	6
1200	10
1400	10
1600	4

(a) Fixed costs are estimated at £X per day. Find the breakeven number of loaves produced and sold, and the number if expected daily profit was £50.

(b) Find the number of loaves produced to minimise expected opportunity loss.

(c) Bread is produced by a fully automated machine which mixes the dough, divides it into 1 lb units, fills each baking tin and passes them through an oven. Out of each batch, some are rejected for being underweight or burnt.

The proportion rejected has the probability distribution given below:

Proportion rejected	Probability
0.05	0.25
0.10	0.60
0.15	0.15

   (i) Find the number of loaves produced if the expected number of saleable loaves equals your answer to question (b).

   (ii) The services of a maintenance engineer would set the rejection rate equal to 0.05, but would cost £11 per day. Advise the manager on whether to engage the engineer or not, if the desired daily production is 1300.

(d) Comment on the assumptions underlying your answers, and discuss the relevance of other decision criteria.

4. 'Profit is the maximum value a company can distribute during the year and still expect to be worth as much at the end of the year as it was at the beginning.' Discuss this statement, and comment on its value in measuring profit for decision-making.

5. Cambrian Railways runs a daily container freight train between Cardiff and Birmingham. Its two major customers are British Steel and the Welsh Farming Co-operative. The demand for containers by each customer is given by the equations:

$$P_1 = 500 - 8Q_1 \text{ for British Steel}$$

$$P_2 = 400 - 5Q_2 \text{ for Welsh farming.}$$

P_i is the price charged by Cambrian per container, and Q_i is the number of containers used by each customer.

Cambrian's total cost function is given by the equation:

$$TC = 10\,000 + 20Q$$

where Q is the number of containers per trip.

   (a) What are the necessary conditions for profitable price discrimination by Cambrian?

   (b) What profit-maximising rule will Cambrian use if setting prices as a discriminator? Determine the profit-maximising quantity of freight service Cambrian will supply, show how this will be divided between steel and agriculture and find the prices charged in each market. Calculate Cambrian's total profit.

   (c) Assume that Cambrian is prevented by law from price discrimination. Determine Cambrian's price and output combination to maximise profit, and hence estimate the opportunity cost to Cambrian of the Anti-Price Discrimination law.

6. Define an optimal inventory policy, and assess the impact on that optimal inventory policy of:

   (i)   uncertain demand
   (ii) uncertain lead times
   (iii) customer reactions to product shortages
   (iv) an oligopolistic product market.

7. (a) Compare and contrast the explanatory and extrapolatory approaches to demand estimation. Illustrate your answer with reference to the problem of estimating demand for a new luxury food processor.

   (b) The Welsh Kitchen Design Company sells its deluxe food processor for £150/unit. Company experience suggests that both price and consumer incomes affect sales, with an estimated price elasticity of demand of -3.0, whilst income elasticity is estimated at 4.0. In 1986 the company sold one million units, whilst total consumer disposable income was £600 billion. Estimated consumer disposable income for 1987 is £650 billion.

      (i) Assuming price remains the same in 1987, estimate total sales revenue.

     (ii)   If 1988 consumer income is expected to remain constant at £650 billion, whilst price is expected to fall by £25, estimate sales revenue in 1988.

     (iii) Estimate sales revenue in 1988 if consumer income rises by 10% between 1987/88, whilst price falls by 15%.

     (iv) Use the information above to estimate demand as a linear function of price and income.

8.   'Despite the theoretical advantages of the discounting procedure, capital investment was either justified in terms of some "need to have" case presented by lower management or on the basis of some elementary payback period calculations.' Discuss this conclusion from an empirical survey of investment decision-making.

9.   Explain the inability of economic theory to find satisfactory solutions to the theoretical problem of price and output decision-making in oligopolistic markets.

10.   'Advertising in the modern economy has entered the state of persuasion as distinct from proclamation or iteration' (Turner). Discuss this view of advertising in relation to its role in the modern firm, and explain the determination of an optimal advertising budget.

11.   Analyse the effects of an increase in both wage rates and labour productivity on the costs of the firm.

ECONOMICS 1988

Time allowed – 3 hours

Answer FOUR questions

1.   'Neither empirical evidence nor theoretical logic offers any justification for the persistence of the dominant position of the kinked demand curve as a model of oligopolistic behaviour.' Discuss this statement, and consider whether alternative models of oligopoly represent any advance on the kinked demand model.

2.   Assess the view that privatisation can have little impact on the behaviour of previously nationalised industries, since a state monopoly is simply replaced by a private one.

3.   'Attempting to learn how to make decisions is an exercise in futility. All the most important decisions are made by people with little time and even less information, acting on instinct.' Discuss.

4.   Critically assess the relevance of the 'as if' principle used to justify the reliance on profit maximisation as the working objective of the modern business corporation.

5. (a) Evaluate the operational utility of demand elasticity estimates, and outline any interpretational difficulties in the use of such estimates.

   (b) The annual demand function for a particular motor car is estimated as:

   $$D = 16000 - 10P/3 + Y^2/1000$$

   where D = annual demand, P = price in £'s and Y = average disposable income.

   (i)   Given that the retail price next year will be £12 000, whilst average disposable income is expected to be £8000, estimate next year's annual demand. If the manufacturer receives 80% of the retail price for each car sold, estimate the manufacturer's revenue next year.

   (ii) Find the retail price to maximise manufacturer's revenue next year.

   (iii) If the marginal cost per car is estimated to be £6000, find the price to maximise profit next year.

   (iv) In the subsequent year the retail price is expected to rise to £13 000, whilst incomes should increase by 5%. Estimate demand and manufacturer's revenue for that year, and use this information to estimate the price and income demand elasticities.

6. 'There is a simple relationship between advertising and profitability: the most profitable firms are the ones that advertise most. Therefore advertising must increase profitability.' Discuss.

7. Critically examine the proposition that as the contemplated future volume of output increases, the expected unit cost of output declines.

8. Recommend a price and marketing strategy for the established automobile manufacturer seeking to enter the market for specialist competition motorcycles. Compare your recommendations to those for the automobile firm seeking to enter the volume small car market.

9. An engineering firm about to undertake a production run of 2000 items must decide whether to overhaul the production machinery. Because the machinery is quite old, the cost of an overhaul is uncertain. However, after the overhaul the failure rate for the machinery is certain to be 0.01. Without the overhaul, the machinery has a failure rate with the probability distribution given below. Each defective item costs the firm £6 in hand finishing.

Failure rate	Probability
0.01	0.5
0.02	0.2
0.03	0.1
0.04	0.1
0.05	0.1

(a) Find the expected cost of overhaul that would make the risk-neutral decision-maker indifferent between overhauling or not.

(b) The decision-maker decides to seek further information. Contact with the machinery supplier suggests an overhaul is equally likely to cost either £175 or £225, depending on the problems encountered. Moreover a sample run of 10 items is produced, resulting in 2 defectives. Use this new information to re-assess the overhauling decision.

(c) How would the decision be influenced by:

   (i)   the firm's precarious financial position;
   (ii) the knowledge that the machinery is to be scrapped after the next production run.

10. 'Opportunity cost is both subjective and speculative. As such the concept of opportunity cost has no place in the scientific decision-making process.' Discuss.

11. (a) Briefly explain the significance of the firm's cost of capital. What are the factors determining that cost of capital, and how can that cost be estimated?

(b) Given that debt finance is generally cheaper than equity finance, explain why the firm is unlikely to use solely debt finance to fund expansion.

(c) A commodity broker is contemplating the acquisition of a new computer-driven management information system (MIS). The hardware for this would cost an initial £4 million, whilst software and staff training would cost £1 million for each of the first two years operation, and £200 000 per year thereafter. After six years, the system would be due for replacement. However scrapping the current (manual) system would save staff costs of £1.5 million each year.

To finance the new investment the broker would use a combination of debt and equity capital in the ratio 1:3. The broker can borrow at an interest rate of 10%, whilst interest paid can be set against the corporation tax liability (currently taxed at 30%). The broker is a listed company with a current share price of £3.00, and current dividend of 15 pence. Over the period the share price is expected to grow at an annual rate of 6%.

Use the above information to evaluate investment in the new MIS, finding the net present value and internal rate of return on that investment.

What other factors should the decision-maker take into account?

Answer notes

The answer notes that follow are a brief guide to the relevant question, and in no sense represent full or adequate answers to these questions.

The key to examination success is a series of carefully planned and executed answers that provide the examiner with the information required. It is essential that the student preparing for examinations *practises* answering questions within the defined time limits. It is a sad experience for an examiner to meet a paper where the student has only answered three questions because of time, matched only by the experience of a paper where five questions have been answered. *Please* read the preamble to the questions, and understand what is required.

Economics 1985

1. Questions 1 and 2 are a 'spillover' from the previous year's course, and should only be answered when all else fails.

2. Without attending the course, and participating in a business game, it would be most unwise to answer this question.

4. This question requires a careful definition of uncertainty and explanation of the techniques used to make decisions under uncertainty. It is difficult to argue against the need to make probability estimates in the face of uncertainty, but caution needs to be expressed about the methods available. Expected profit requires definition and consideration as a decision objective, pointing out the circumstances in which it is appropriate (small sums of money or linear utility functions *and* repetitive decisions) and evaluating alternative criteria. Refer to Chapter 4.

5. Explain the criteria of minimising expected cost, and apply it to this problem. Calculate the expected cost with and without the revision course. Note that 'equally likely' implies a probability of 0.5 to each, so that the expected failure rate after the course is $(0.05 \times 0.5) + (0.10 \times 0.5) = 0.075$.

   Then calculate the likelihood of two fails in a sample of 10 using the Binomial distribution and combine with the prior probabilities using Bayes Theorem to find posterior probabilities. Use these posterior probabilities to determine whether the course should run, using expected cost or opportunity loss as the decision criteria.

   List the assumptions made to answer the question, and assess their relevance in these circumstances. Refer to Chapter 4.

6. Examine the methods available for demand estimation, comparing and contrasting the explanatory and extrapolatory approaches. Discuss the decision about resources to be devoted to demand estimation, primarily determined by the use to which forecasts are to be put. Explain what is meant by forecast reliability, and how this can be

estimated prior to forecast use. Refer to Chapter 5 and especially Application 5.

7.   Explain what is meant by a new product, carefully defining the concept of 'newness', and examine the cost and demand estimation problems surrounding new product pricing. Analyse the importance of the competitive environment, and explain the factors determining whether a 'skimming' or 'penetration' policy should be used, using the example given in the question, and its implicit emphasis on the importance of entry conditions. Refer to Chapters 8 and 9.

8.   Examine the role and consequences of advertising, contrasting the market expansion and redistributional implications of advertising. Outline the model of advertising as information, and consider the circumstances in which advertising information reduces the cost of search to the consumer. Refer to Chapter 10.

9.   (a)   The model outlined in Chapter 13 can be used to analyse the effects of an increase in interest rates, but note the qualifications to the model when compared to the evaluation methods encountered in practice.

9.   (b)   First explain the DCF and/or internal rate of return methods of investment appraisal, and then use discounting to evaluate the cash flow generated by the squash court. Note the other considerations the University is likely to take into account. (N.B. The Net Present Value of the project at 12% is £852.59, whilst the IRR is 14.6%.) What is assumed about inflation and the attitude towards risk?

10.   The first part of the question requires a simple determination of the economic order quantity, either by equating the rise in holding costs to the fall in order costs, or by defining a total cost function and then minimising it. Note the assumptions made.

The second part of the question requires application of that model, and the fact that if $K \times E.O.Q.$ is ordered, inventory costs rise by

$$\frac{(K-1)^2}{2K} \times M.A.C.$$

Hence compare the rise in inventory costs to the value of the discount.

A probability distribution of demand requires that inventory be adjusted according to the costs of running out of stock. The analysis used will depend on the information available and the cost of making mistakes (sensitivity analysis). Refer to Chapter 11.

Economics 1986

1. A question to be avoided if at all possible! If you must answer it, explain what is meant by scientific decision-making, by expanding the framework for decisions encountered in Chapter 1, and then providing a critique of this, noting the apparent ability of many decision-makers to 'manage' outside this framework. Refer to Chapters 1 and 4.

2. (a) Define opportunity loss (not opportunity cost!) and *EVPI*. If opportunity loss is defined as the benefit forgone by not making the best possible decision, and *EVPI* is the difference between the best possible decision and the performance best achieved without perfect information, it should be easy to show min $EOL = EVPI$.

   Note a simple example would help.

   (b) this is a simple application of the Binomial distribution, with

   $$P(X = x) = {}^5C_x(0.4)^x(0.6)^{5-x}$$

   (c) refer to Chapter 4, pages 85–9. Note the similarity!

3. This question involves the careful definition of implicit and explicit costs, and is best answered by defining profit as the surplus over opportunity cost. From an economic view there is little difference between owning and renting the store, since opportunity costs are likely to be similar. See Chapter 3.

4. The question involves estimating the parameters of the equation

   $$D_t = a + bP + ct$$

   Given lots of time and some computational ability, a, b and c can be estimated by linear regression. In the absence of either, substitution is an acceptable method *if* the relevant assumptions are made explicit. Note that if November is assigned a time value of 1, December 2, etc., then in April $t = 8$.

   Then estimate elasticity using the arc formula:

   $$\varepsilon p = \frac{\Delta D}{\Delta P} \cdot \frac{P_1 + P_2}{D_1 + D_2}$$

   Sales revenue can be maximised either by finding the total revenue function (when $t = 8$) and then differentiating and setting $=0$, or by finding the price at which point elasticity $= -1$.

   Note that the method used combines both explanatory and extrapolatory approaches and is liable to the problems inherent in each. See Chapter 5.

5. Explain the short- and long-run cost function $C = f(Q)$, and note the limitations of each (e.g. dimensions of output). Consider the com-

putational and data problems associated with each, referring to examples. For what decisions are cost functions necessary? Finally, note that 'it is better to be vaguely right than precisely wrong'. Refer to Chapter 7.

6. Note that the quotation is reproduced in Chapter 10. Consider the methods available for determining the advertising budget, ranging from marginalism through the informational approach to the Dorfman–Steiner model. Contrast these with the more pragmatic approaches encountered in practice. See Chapter 10.

7. Refer to Q9, 1985 and answer notes. Analyse the effects of an increase in interest rates via the allocation of funds model and the discounting approach. Explain the effects of inflation on the discounting approach, noting the consistency required.

8. (a) First derive the economic order quantity, and then illustrate the appropriate sensitivity results, if necessary reproducing the relevant diagram from Chapter 11. Outline the assumptions made, and consider their relevance.

   (b) Apply the model generated in part (a), and then

   (i) show that an order would simply be placed when stock falls to two weeks worth (since demand is uniform). Briefly outline the consequences if 'two weeks' is an uncertain parameter.

   (ii) compare the savings from the discount with the increase in inventory costs as a consequence of ordering beyond the E.O.Q.

9. ⎱ Refers to the first year of the course, and should be avoided, although
10. ⎰ Chapter 3 may provide a basis for answering Q.10.

Economics 1987

1. A question about the basic philosophy of scientific decision-making, to be answered only as a last resort! If you must answer the question, do so analytically, by expounding a scientific framework for decisions, and then examining the circumstances in which that framework may (or may not) improve the decision process. See Chapters 1 and 4.

2. Explain the profit maximisation hypothesis, and briefly outline the price/output decision model with profit as the objective. List the theoretical arguments against this, including informational difficulties, the weakening of competition and the divorce of ownership and control. Finally explain the empirical evidence: do firms maximise profits, either by accident (as if) or by design? This question is *not* an opportunity to parade a summary of alternative models.

3. This question is a relatively simple application of the 'Newsboy

Problem', with one or two little twists. Part (a) is answered by using the formula:

$$\text{Breakeven} = \frac{\text{Fixed costs}}{\text{Price} - \text{Marginal cost}}$$

To answer part (b), find the opportunity loss corresponding to each combination of act and event (production or demand equal to 1000, 1200, etc.). Then convert the frequency to a probability distribution, and find the action to minimise opportunity loss.

The answer to part (c) requires the use of the failure rate probability distribution so that the expected number of saleable loaves is 1200. The expected failure rate is 0.095, so 1326 must be produced to give an expected 1200 saleable loaves ($1326 \times 0.905 = 1200$).

Then the expected cost of producing 1300 (saleable) loaves must be calculated with or without the overhaul, to see if the expected savings from overhaul exceed the £11 per day the engineer would cost. Finally, marks would be wasted by omitting part (d).

4. This is a straightforward question, looking at the Hicksian definition of profit and its relevance for decision-making purposes. Is this definition useful in practice? See Chapter 3.

5. Profitable price discrimination requires that markets be separable and have differing price elasticities of demand. Answers to parts (b) and (c) can be found either graphically or mathematically. Personally I prefer to use the mathematical approach, since graphs need to be drawn with considerable precision. In either case, find aggregate demand and therefore marginal revenue, and set equal to aggregate marginal cost to find total output (and price in the absence of price discrimination). Then set individual marginal revenue equal to marginal cost to find price in each market. The opportunity cost (to the firm) of the law is just the difference in profits with and without price discrimination.

6. An optimal inventory policy is one that minimises the sum of stock purchase and acquisition (holding, ordering and stock-out) costs. It is easy to show that under carefully defined circumstances this occurs when the marginal increase in holding costs equals the marginal fall in order costs. However each of the specified conditions deviates from these circumstances, and has implications for an optimal stock policy. For example uncertain demand introduces the possibility of profitable sales forgone, and thus increases the average stock level.

7. Outline the explanatory and extrapolatory methods, listing the benefits/disadvantages of each, and show how each could be used to estimate demand for the new food processor. Note that past experience may not be much of a guide if the new processor has special characteristics.

Answering part (b) requires that differing price and income values be used with the elasticity estimates to estimate sales revenue under different conditions.

The answers (i) to (iii) generate enough information to set up simultaneous equations that can be used to answer (iv).

8. Explain what is meant by the discounting approach to investment appraisal, and contrast this to more *ad hoc* methods such as payback. Show that there may be circumstances where information is inadequate for discounting, and where other methods more adequately reflect the firm's objectives. Finally discuss the empirical evidence (which seems to point to the use of other methods in smaller companies, but that discounting is increasingly used by large corporations).

9. This question is a spillover from the previous course, although Chapter 8 might help towards an answer.

10. A difficult question that asks you to judge the effects of advertising in shifting the demand curve. Whether adverts are persuasive or informative is a matter of psychological judgement: whether advertising shifts the demand curve is a matter of empirical observation. The determination of an optimal advertising budget requires a comparison of the costs and benefits of advertising that may proceed in a number of ways, from marginalism through the Dorfman–Steiner theorem to an informational approach.

11. Another spillover from microeconomics, although Chapter 7 may help. Basically the answer involves the factors that determine costs, and the relation of these particular circumstances to the general theory. The net effects depend on whether the increase in labour productivity outweighs the increase in wages, together with any substitution effects.

Economics 1988

1,2. Both of these questions reflect the earlier (microeconomics) course, and should only be answered when all else proves impossible.

3. The evidence that very good decisions are made by some people with no reference to any decision model is not a refutation of that model. Bad decisions are also made by not using any decision model, or by using a model badly. The issue is really whether using a relevant decision model in a consistent and sensible way leads to decisions that are, on average, better than the alternatives. In the absence of reliable data, this remains a matter of belief rather than fact, although it is interesting that talking through the decision process with managers often reveals a process that is consistent with the decision model i.e. objectives are stated, alternatives considered, etc., even though this process is more implicit than explicit.

4. The question is really whether firms behave as if they maximised profit, even though this may not be an explicit process. Arguments in favour include the efficient markets hypothesis, the force of competition, and the self-interest of managers. Unfortunately the same arguments can be used against 'as if', i.e. that efficient markets requires unreal assumptions, that competition is weak enough to allow managers discretion, and that it is in the managers' interests to exercise such discretion. Related arguments include whether actual objectives are a compliment or substitute for profit. A full answer would include an outline of the profit maximisation model together with a summary of alternatives.

5. How useful are elasticity estimates, and how easy are they to make? Clearly price, output and advertising decisions each require some assessment of the impact of relevant variables upon demand, which is precisely what we mean by elasticity.

   The numerical parts of the question are the straightforward matter of substituting numbers into the demand equation, and using the resulting answers. Note that revenue is maximised either when marginal revenue equals zero, or when price elasticity equals minus one.

6. The relationship between advertising and profitability is a complex matter of sorting out causation. It is equally possible that increasing profitability leads to increased advertising. Basically a good answer would look at why advertising may increase profits (by shifting the demand curve), and note that advertising may be carried on beyond this point (so that the marginal cost of the last advert exceeds marginal revenue). Note also that other objectives may be important, for e.g. the sales maximiser advertises more than the profit maximiser. Finally the empirical evidence is less than clear, but should be outlined.

7. This question relates to Alchian's definition of the dimensions of output and the impact of each upon costs. A greater contemplated volume of output may be associated with different technologies, methods of production, etc., although not without limit. A full discussion of economies of scale is only tangentially relevant to this question.

8. These market-entry situations differ in the amount of production and market knowledge available, and the likely extent of economies of scale, differing elasticities, etc. Basically the market situation is such that a skimming price policy is likely in the competition motorcycle market, whilst a penetration price policy is more likely in the volume small car market. See Chapter 9.

9. This is a simple 'newboy problem', and is readily answered using the techniques of Chapter 4. Note that the expected cost of overhaul is £200. Part (c) is concerned with the attitude towards risk, and its impact on the decision.

10. This is an awful question, where sustained 'waffling' produced few marks. Clearly opportunity cost *is* both speculative and subjective, *and* occupies a fundamental position in rational decision-making. Basically the question confuses scientific with precise. A scientific decision approach requires that the likely consequences of any action be compared to the next best alternative. Knowing that this calculation cannot be precise doesn't detract from its validity.

11. The firm's cost of capital is the opportunity cost of investment, and depends upon the source of funds (equity or debt). Each has implicit and explicit costs that must be estimated before an investment can be evaluated.

   The numerical part of the question requires the cash flows to be estimated and then discounted using the estimated cost of capital obtained by the combined weighting of debt and equity. Note that the costs of the manual system must be subtracted from the MIS costs to find net savings to be discounted.

   Other factors include attitudes towards risk, the differing attributes of the two systems and any non-pecuniary considerations.

Notes and References

Chapter 1

1. S. Hill and P. Blyton (1985) 'The Practice of Decision-making – Some Evidence', *Managerial and Decision Economics*, December.
2. The same approach appears in the literature in a variety of guises. One interesting (and often humorous) introduction is J. D. Bransford and B. S. Stein (1984) *The Ideal Problem Solver* (New York: W. H. Freeman).

Chapter 2

1. This is actually a necessary but not sufficient condition for maximum profit. Certain conditions about the nature of the cost and revenue functions must also be satisfied.
2. For the mathematically initiated,
   $$AC = \frac{TC}{Q} \text{ so that } TC = AC \times Q$$
   $$MC = dTC/dQ$$
   Therefore
   $$MC = AC \cdot dQ/dQ + Q \cdot dAC/dQ$$
   $$MC = AC + Q \cdot dAC/dQ$$
   Now dAC/dQ is just the rate of change of average cost. If AC is falling, $Q \cdot dAC/dQ$ is negative, and $MC < AC$.
3. A linear equation is of the form $y = ax + b$, and a and b are constants. This equation describes a straight line when plotted, with intercept b and slope a.
4. Unless the slope of the constraint coincides with the slope of the objective function, in which case the appropriate corner solution must be as profitable as any point along the constraint.
5. Readers with a burning desire to follow the Simplex method can find it explained in chapter 12 of J. Gough and S. Hill (1979) *Fundamentals of Managerial Economics* (London: Macmillan).

350

6. In the expression for y, a is called the co-efficient and b the exponent. The derivative of y is then the exponent times the co-efficient times x to the power of the exponent minus 1. This is the golden rule for differentiation, and needs engraving on your heart.
7. One of the assumptions of classical optimisation is that the relevant function is differentiable and therefore continuous. The number of engineers is discrete rather than continuous – it is difficult to envisage 5.85 engineers, for example. Once again, calculus can only be used with considerable caution!
8. Appendix 2C uses the second order conditions to show that $K = 4/3$, $L = 5/3$ is indeed a maximum for Q.
9. This is generally, but not universally, true. However, this assumption is necessary to make the constraint an equality condition.

Chapter 3

1. Joel Dean (1951) *Managerial Economics* (Englewood Cliffs, NJ: Prentice-Hall), p. 3.
2. Ibid., p. 260.
3. The economist usually denotes profit by π (Greek pi). This is used in preference to the more obvious notation P, because P is reserved for price.
4. The process of discounting is extended in Chapter 13.
5. The symbol Σ (capital Greek sigma) is used to denote the sum of an expression. Thus $\sum_{i=1}^{n} x_i$ is the sum of all the x values from x_1 to x_n.
6. J. R. Hicks (1946) *Value and Capital*, 2nd edn (Oxford: OUP), p. 172.
7. The situation is analogous to student assignments. Students often claim that their objective is to maximise marks. But maximum marks would require continuous and concentrated effort over the assignment period. Hence, a trade-off is made between marks and effort that is unlikely to result in maximum possible marks.
8. The shape of these functions is examined in later chapters.
9. The profit maximising output was derived in Chapter 2 as the point where $MC = MR$. Note that MC/MR are the slopes of TC/TR respectively, and that output Q satisfied this condition.
10. W. J. Baumol (1967) *Business Behaviour, Value and Growth*, revised edn (New York: Harcourt, Brace and Wold).
11. See A. Koutsoyiannis (1979) *Modern Microeconomics*, 2nd ed. (London: Macmillan), chapter 15.
12. R. L. Marriss (1963) 'A Model of the Managerial Enterprise', *Quarterly Journal of Economics*, vol. 77, pp. 185–209.
13. O. Williamson (1963) 'Managerial Discretion and Business Behaviour', *American Economic Review*, December; reprinted in M. Gilbert (ed.) (1973) *The Modern Business Enterprise* (London: Penguin).

14. See, for example, G. H. Rice (1980) 'But How Do Managers Make Decisions?', *Management Decisions*, vol. 18, part 4.
15. The progenitor of this approach was Herbert Simon. See especially H. A. Simon (1955) 'A Behaviour Model of Rational Choice', *Quarterly Journal of Economics*, February.
16. R. Cyert and J. March (1963) *A Behavioural Theory of the Firm* (Englewood Cliffs, NJ: Prentice-Hall).
17. This application is derived from S. P. Neun and R. E. Santerre (1986) 'Dominant Stockownership and Profitability', *Managerial and Decision Economics*, vol. 7 (3), pp. 207–10.

Chapter 4

1. The source of Figure 4.1 is S. Hill (1986) 'Decision Making Under Uncertainty – The Divergence Between Theory and Practice', in S. Jones (ed), *Modelling Uncertainty* (Fulmer, Hilger).
2. This also assumes that previous stock was always sufficient to meet demand. The sensible decision-maker would, in addition, use his experience of any particular circumstances (such as a TV advertising campaign) to adjust this probability estimate.
3. Given perfect predictive powers, if the probability estimates are correct, 25 per cent of the time demand of 20 would be predicted, 50 per cent of the time demand of 30 would be predicted, etc.
4. Ira Horowitz (1972) *An Introduction to Quantitative Business Analysis* (Tokyo: McGraw Hill), pp. 57–8.
5. Note also that for individual *B*, the marginal utility of money ($\delta u/\delta £$) is decreasing.
6. Derived from D. Bunn and H. Thomas (1977) 'J. Sainsbury and the Haul of Contraband Butter', reprinted in G. Kaufman and H. Thomas (eds) *Modern Decision Analysis* (Harmondsworth: Penguin), pp. 260–8.
7. A *Poisson* distribution is described by the formula
$p(X = x) = a^x e^{-x}/x!$ where *a* is the mean and *e* the natural exponent (= 2.718), and is discussed more fully in Chapter 11.
8. Bunn and Thomas, 'J. Sainsbury and the Haul of Contraband Butter', p. 267.

Chapter 5

1. For a more comprehensive explanation, see D. Salvatore (1986) *Microeconomics: Theory and Applications* (New York: Macmillan), pp. 108–23.

2. H. S. Houthaker and L. D. Taylor (1970) *Consumer Demand in the United States* (Cambridge, Mass.: Harvard University Press).
3. Ibid.
4. See, for example, S. C. Wheelwright and D. G. Clarke (1976) 'Corporate Forecasting: Promise and Reality', Harvard Business Review, vol. 54, December.
5. The classic reference is E. J. Working (1927) 'What Do Statistical Demand Curves Show?', *Quarterly Journal of Economics*, vol. 41, February, pp. 212–35.
6. T. H. Naylor (1981) 'Experience with Corporate Econometric Models: A Survey', *Business Economics*, vol. 16, January, pp. 79–83.
7. Fujii, E. T. (1980) 'The Demand for Cigarettes: Further Empirical Evidence and Its Implications for Public Policy', *Applied Economics*, vol. 12, pp. 479–89.
8. It is assumed that the dummy variables each have a value of 1 for 1974.
9. Data were obtained from the CSO *Monthly Digest of Statistics*, published by HMSO.

Chapter 6

1. N. Chacholiades (1986) *Microeconomics* (New York: Macmillan), p. 173.
2. A curve is convex to the origin if the straight line between any two points on the curve lie above that curve.
3. It is possible that the slope of the isocost may coincide with the slope of the isoquant. However, even in this case, production at the corner point will be at least as inexpensive as production anywhere along that segment of the isoquant.
4. D. J. Pearl and J. L. Enos (1975) 'Engineering Production Functions and Technological Progress', *Journal of Industrial Economics*, vol. 24, September, pp. 55–72.

Chapter 7

1. J. Dean (1951) *Managerial Economics* (Englewood Cliffs, NJ: Prentice-Hall), p. 271.
2. A. A. Alchian (1973) 'Costs and Outputs', in M. Abramovitz (ed.) *The Allocation of Economic Resources* (Stanford: Stanford University Press, 1959), reprinted in H. Townsend (ed.) *Price Theory* (Harmondsworth: Penguin, 1973), pp. 228–49.
3. J. Dean (1951) *Managerial Economics*, p. 253.
4. U. E. Reinhart (1973) 'Break-Even Analysis for Lockheeds Tri Star: An Application of Financial Theory', *Journal of Finance*, vol. 28, September, pp. 821–38.

5. J. Dean (1951) *Managerial Economics*.
6. J. Johnson (1960) *Statistical Cost Curves* (New York: McGraw-Hill).
7. A. A. Walters (1963) 'Production and Cost Functions: An Econometric Survey', *Econometrica*, vol. 31, January, pp. 42–50.
8. V. Gupta (1968) 'Cost Functions, Concentration and Barriers to Entry in Twenty-Nine Manufacturing Industries of India', *Journal of Industrial Economics*, vol. 17, November, pp. 57–72.
9. C. F. Pratten (1971) *Economies of Scale in Manufacturing Industries* (Cambridge: Cambridge University Press).
10. Derived from: S. Hill and J. Gough (1980) *Concentration and Efficiency in the Building Society Industry*, UWIST Discussion Papers in Economics, February.

Chapter 8

1. E. A. Robinson, quoted in J. Dean (1951) *Managerial Economics* (Englewood Cliffs, NJ: Prentice-Hall), p. 67.
2. G. Stigler (1978) 'The Literature of Economics: The Case of the Kinked Demand Curve', *Economic Inquiry,* vol. 16, part 2, April, pp. 185–204.
3. D. Needham (1970) *Economic Analysis and Industrial Structure* (London: Holt), p. 19.
4. Ibid., p. 25.
5. J. S. Bain (1956) *Barriers to New Competition* (Cambridge, Mass.: Harvard University Press).
6. Ibid.
7. A. Singh (1975) 'Takeovers, Economic Natural Selection and the Theory of the Firm: Evidence from UK Post-war Experience', *Economic Journal*, vol. 85.
8. This application is based on R. W. Shaw and S. A. Shaw (1984) 'Late Entry, Market Shares and Competitive Survival: The Case of Synthetic Fibres', *Managerial and Decision Economics*, vol. 15, no. 2, June, pp. 72–9.

Chapter 9

1. See F. M. Scherer (1970) *Industrial Pricing: Theory and Evidence* (Chicago: Rand McNally), chapter 4.
2. F. Modigliani (1958) 'New Developments on the Oligopoly Front', *Journal of Political Economy*, vol. 66, pp. 215–32.
3. See S. Hill (1982) 'The Multi-product Firm: Demand Relationships and Decision-making', *Managerial and Decision Economics*, vol. 3, no. 2.
4. See, for example, J. L. Pappas, E. F. Brigham and B. Shipley (1983) *Managerial Economics*, UK edition (London: Holt, Rinehart & Winston), chapter 12:

5. See A. Silberston (1970) 'The Price Behaviour of Firms', *Economic Journal*, September.
6. R. L. Hall and C. J. Hitch (1939) *Price Theory and Business Behaviour*, Oxford Economic Papers, pp. 12–45.
7. One managing director interviewed by the author had developed a complex microcomputer simulation model to determine precisely the average cost of each of the firm's products. A variable profit margin was then added, according to what the director thought the market could bear. See S. Hill *et al.* (1984) *Decision Making in the S. Wales Engineering industry*, UWIST Discussion Papers, September.
8. R. P. Manes, F. Shoumaker and P. A. Silhan (1984) 'Demand Relationships and Pricing Decisions for Related Products', *MDE*, vol. 5, no. 2, June.

Chapter 10

1. Quoted in N. Piercy (1986) *Marketing Budgeting* (London: Croom-Helm), p. 2.
2. Quoted by W. Duncan Reekie (1975) *Managerial Economics* (Oxford: Philip Allan), p. 208.
3. See, for example, A. Koutsoyiannis (1982) *Non-Price Decisions* (London: Macmillan), pp. 84–6.
4. N. Piercy (1986) *Marketing Budgeting*, p. 39.
5. This section, loosely based on Blair and Kenny, may be omitted without loss of continuity. However, perseverence with the concepts involved may yield a high return. See R. Blair and L. Kenny (1982) *Microeconomics for Managerial Decision Making* (Tokyo: McGraw-Hill), pp. 347–59.
6. The sum of an infinite series is the first term divided by one minus the common ratio. In this case, the first term is fN, and the common ratio is $(1-f)(1-b)$.
7. See, for example, S. Schoeffler *et al.* (1974) 'The Impact of Strategic Planning on Profit Performance', *Harvard Business Review*, March.
8. N. Piercy (1986) *Marketing Budgeting*.
9. A. Koutsoyiannis (1982) *Non-Price Decisions* (London: Macmillan) provides an excellent survey of advertising evidence.
10. H. M. Mann *et al.* (1967) 'Advertising and Concentration', *Journal of Industrial Economics*, vol. 15, pp. 81–4.
11. D. F. Greer (1971) 'Advertising and Market Concentration', *Southern Economic Journal*, vol. 38, pp. 17–32.
12. This case history is based on actual companies, but their names and the figures given have been altered to protect commercial confidentiality.

Chapter 11

1. H. A. Taha (1982) *Operations Research*, 3rd edn (New York: Macmillan), p. 495.
2. F. Lowenthal (1982) 'Cost of Prediction Error in the Economic Order Quantity Formula', *Managerial and Decision Economics*, vol. 3, no. 2, June.
3. Recall that a rectangular hyperbola describes a downwards sloping curve of constant area. In this case, the area under the curve (TOC×q) is always constant at rD.
4. It is evident that the expression on the right-hand side has two roots, and equally evident that only one makes economic sense.
5. This may be an opportune moment to review pages 73–5.
6. $P(D \geqslant n)$ reads as the probability demand is greater than or equal to n.
7. A Poisson distribution is described by the formula
   $P(X = x) = a^x e^{-x}/x!$ where a is the mean and e the natural exponent (=2.718). The Poisson distribution is a useful approximation for random arrival times.
8. For example, J. E. Freund (1972) *Mathematical Statistics*, 2nd edn (Englewood Cliffs, NJ: Prentice-Hall), p. 434.
9. $P(D \leqslant 16) = P(D < 17) = 0.899$. Then stocking 16 gives a 90 per cent service level.
10. Since $\sqrt{2rDhc} = 2 \cdot \sqrt{\dfrac{rDhc}{2}}$.
11. $\dfrac{\delta^2 TRC}{\delta q^2} = \dfrac{2DS}{q^3} > 0$, so q^* is a minimum.
12. The idea for this application came from R. Martin and B. Moores (1935) *Management Structures and Techniques* (Oxford: Philadelphia) p. 150, and subsequent conversations with Brian Moores.

Chapter 12

1. In Chapter 7, the marginal cost of output was related to the wage rate and labour productivity by the equation $MC = W/MPL$, for a fixed wage rate. To maximise profit, $MC = MR$. Substituting, $MR = W/MPL$ or $MPL \times MR = W$, so that $MRPL = W$.
2. Generally, $MFC = W + \Delta W \times N$, where W is the new wage rate, ΔW is the increase in wages necessary to employ an extra worker, and N is the number previously employed. In the above case, $MPC = 1 = 5 + (5 \times 10) = 155$.

3. F. Brechling (1965) 'The Relationship Between Output and Employment in British Manufacturing Industries', *Review of Economic Studies*, vol. 32, pp. 187–216.
4. See S. Hill (1984) *Worksharing: Some Cost and Other Implications* (London: Unemployment Unit).
5. See Chapter 13 for a full explanation of present value.
6. For a full discussion see Thomason, G. (1981) *A Textbook of Personnel Management*, 4th edn (London: IPM).
7. See, for example, C. Handy (1985) *The Future of Work* (Oxford: Blackwell).
8. See S. Hill *et al.* (1984) *Decision-making in the South Wales Engineering Industry: A Survey*, UWIST Discussion Paper, December. See also P. Blyton and S. Hill (1985) 'Output and Employment', *Industrial Relations Journal*, Summer.

Chapter 13

1. See S. Hill and J. Gough (1981) 'Discounting Inflation', *Managerial and Decision Economics*, vol. 2 (2), pp. 121–3.
2. Alternatively, a cursory glance at Table 13.1 reveals that £10 000 in fifty years time (your life expectancy from now) will have a present value approaching zero, especially when inflation is also taken into account.
3. Generalising, the present value of a perpetuity offering a uniform £A per year is A/r, where r is the interest rate expressed as a decimal.
4. This section is loosely based on J. Gough and S. Hill (1979) *Fundamentals of Managerial Economics* (London: Macmillan), pp. 210–14.
5. Although the implicit cost may be higher; see p. 316.
6. H. M. Markowitz (1952) 'Portfolio Selection', *Journal of Finance*, vol. vii (1), March, pp. 72–91.
7. For a full explanation of CAPM, see A. Koutsoyiannis (1982) *Non Price Decisions* (London, Macmillan), pp. 609–30.
8. See Koutsoyiannis (1982) *Non Price Decisions*, pp. 626–30 and Rosenberg, B. and Guy, J. (1976) 'Prediction of Beta Co-efficients from Investment Fundamentals', *Financial Analysts Journal*, 32, July.
9. Koutsoyiannis, *Non Price Decisions*, p. 621.
10. K. Alam and L. Stafford (1985) 'Tax Incentives and Investment Policy', *Managerial and Decision Economics*, vol. 6 (1), March, pp. 27–32.
11. S. Hill *et al.* (1984) *Decision-making in the South Wales Engineering Industry: A Survey*, UWIST, Cardiff, December.
12. E. Miller (1985) 'Decision-making Under Uncertainty for Capital Budgeting and Hiring', *Managerial and Decision Economics*, vol. 6 (1), March, pp. 11–18.

13. Ibid., p. 14.
14. For a review of evidence, see Koutsoyiannis, *Non Price Decisions*, pp. 256–62.
15. This application is based on G. Luffman, S. Witt and S. Lister (1982) 'A Quantitative Approach to Stakeholder Interests', *Managerial and Decision Economics*, vol. 3, no. 2, June, pp. 70–8.
16. Ibid., p. 76.
17. Ibid., p. 78.

Further reading

Chapter 1

Baumol, W. J. (1961) 'What Can Economic Theory Contribute to Managerial Economics', *American Economic Review*, 51, pp. 142–6.
Bransford, J. D. and Stein, B. S. (1984) *The Ideal Problem Solver* (New York: W. H. Freeman).
Call, S. T. and Holahan, W. L. (1984) *Managerial Economics* (Belmont, CA: Wadsworth) chapter 1, 'Studying Managerial Economics', pp. 1–16.

Chapter 2

Chiang, A. C. (1974) *Fundamental Methods of Mathematical Economics*, 2nd edn (Tokyo: McGraw Hill), chapters 2, 6, 9 and 18.
Gough, J. and Hill, S. (1979) *Fundamentals of Managerial Economics* (London: Macmillan), chapters 2 and 12 ('Marginal Analysis' and 'Linear Programming').
Pappas, J. L., Brigham, E. F. and Shipley, B. (1983) *Managerial Economics*, UK edn (London: Holt Rhinehart & Winston), chapters 3 and 8.

Chapter 3

Dean, J. (1951) *Managerial Economics* (Englewood Cliffs, NJ: Prentice-Hall), chapter 1.
Kay, J. A. (1977) 'Inflation Accounting – A Review Article', *Economic Journal*, 87, 346, pp. 300–11.
Koutsoyiannis, A. (1979) *Modern microeconomics* (London: Macmillan), chapters 15–18.
Lee, T. A. (1980) *Income and Value Measurement*, 2nd edn (Walton-on-Thames: Nelson), chapters 1 to 3.

Rice, G. H. (1986) 'But How Do Managers Make Decisions?', *Management Decisions*, 18, 4.

Silberston, A. (1970) 'Price Behaviour of Firms', *Economic Journal*, 80, 319, pp. 511–82.

Chapter 4

Call, S. T. and Holahan, W. L. (1984) *Managerial Economics* (Belmont, CA: Wadsworth), chapter 8.

Gough, T. J. and Hill, S. (1979) *Fundamentals of Managerial Economics* (London: Macmillan), chapter 3.

Horowitz, I. (1972) *An Introduction to Quantitative Business Analysis*, 2nd edn (Tokyo: McGraw Hill), chapters 1 to 4.

Raiffa, H. (1968) *Decision Theory* (Reading, Mass: Addison Wesley).

Chapter 5

Davies, J. R. and Chang, S. (1986) *Principles of Managerial Economics* (Englewood Cliffs, NJ: Prentice-Hall), chapters 4 to 7.

Heineke, J. M. (1976) *Microeconomics for Business Decisions* (Englewood Cliffs, NJ: Prentice-Hall).

Salvatore, D. (1986) *Microeconomics: Theory and Application* (New York: Macmillan), chapters 3 to 6.

Chapter 6

Baird, C. W. (1982) *Prices and Markets*, 2nd edn (St Paul: West), chapter 4.

Davies, J. R. and Chang, S. (1986) *Principles of Managerial Economics* (Englewood Cliffs, NJ: Prentice-Hall), chapter 8.

Heineke, J. M. (1976) *Microeconomics for Business Decisions* (Englewood Cliffs, NJ: Prentice-Hall), chapters 3, 4 and 5.

Salvatore, D. (1986) *Microeconomics: Theory and Applications* (New York: Macmillan), chapter 9.

Chapter 7

Dean, J. (1951) *Managerial Economics* (Englewood Cliffs, NJ: Prentice-Hall), chapter 5.

Salvatore, D. (1986) *Microeconomics: Theory and Applications* (New York: Macmillan), chapter 8.
Wagner, L. (1981) *Readings in Applied Microeconomics*, 2nd edn (Oxford: Oxford University Press), Reading 9.

There are a number of case studies in cost estimation. One of the most interesting is: L. Cookenboo (1971) 'Cost of Operation of Crude Oil Trunk Lines', reprinted in H. Townsend (ed.) *Price Theory* (Harmondsworth: Penguin).

Chapter 8

Dean, J. (1951) *Managerial Economics* (Englewood Cliffs, NJ: Prentice-Hall), chapter 2.
Griffiths, A. and Wall, S. (1984) *Applied Economics* (London: Longman), chapters 5 and 6.
Monopolies Commission (1981) *Competition in the Wholesale Supply of Petrol*, reprinted as Reading 3 in L. Wagner (ed.) *Readings in Applied Microeconomics* (Oxford: Oxford University Press).
Needham, D. (1978). *Economic Analysis and Industrial Structure*, 2nd edn (New York: Holt), chapter 3.
Pappas, J. L., Brigham, E. F. and Shipley, B. (1983) *Managerial Economics*, UK edn (London: Holt, Rhinehart & Winston).

Chapter 9

Dean, J. (1951) *Managerial Economics* (Englewood Cliffs, NJ: Prentice-Hall), chapters 7, 8 and 9.
Kotler, P. (1986) *Principles of Marketing*, 3rd edn (Englewood Cliffs, NJ: Prentice-Hall), chapters 13 and 14.
Pappas, J. L., Brigham, E. F. and Shipley, B. (1983) *Managerial Economics*, UK edn (London: Holt, Rhinehart & Winston), chapters 11 and 12.
Silberston, A. (1970) 'The Price Behaviour of Firms', *Economic Journal*, September.

Chapter 10

Kotler, P. (1986) *Principles of Marketing*, 3rd edn (Englewood Cliffs, NJ: Prentice-Hall), chapters 17 to 19.

Koutsoyiannis, A. (1982) *Non-Price Decisions* (London: Macmillan), chapter 2.
Piercy, N. (1986) *Marketing Budgeting* (London: Croom Helm), chapters 2 and 3.

Chapter 11

Horowitz, I. (1972) *An Introduction to Quantitative Business Analysis* (Tokyo: McGraw-Hill), chapter 11.
Martin, R. and Moores, B. (1985) *Management Structures and Techniques* (Oxford: Philip Alan), chapter 8.
Taha, H. A. (1982) *Operations Research*, 3rd edn (New York: Macmillan), chapter 13.

Chapter 12

Blair, R. D. and Kenny, L. W. (1982) *Microeconomics for Managerial Decision Making* (Tokyo: McGraw-Hill).
DeSerpa, A. C. (1981) *Microeconomic Theory: Issues and Applications* (Boston: Allyn & Bacon).
Thomason, G. (1981) *A Textbook of Personnel Management*, 4th edn (London: IPM).

Chapter 13

Pappas, J. L., Brigham, E. F. and Shipley, B. (1983) *Managerial Economics*, UK edn (London: Holt, Rhinehart & Winston), chapter 14.
Koutsoyiannis, A. (1982) *Non-Price Decisions* (London: Macmillan).

Chapter 14

Bodily, S. E. (1985) *Modern Decision Making* (New York: McGraw-Hill).
Dennis, L. B. and Dennis, T. L. (1986) *Microcomputer Models for Management Decision Making* (New York: West).

Index

Index